The Foundations of the National Welfare State

This book provides the first detailed account of the 'heroic period' in the history of Australia's welfare state — that network of social policies which is now under attack.

Four decades ago, federal governments, conservative and Labor, laid the foundations of the welfare state. In this original study of a crucial decade, Rob Watts draws on a rich, hitherto-unused collection of archives to analyse the real reasons why governments implement welfare legislation.

This major new study of the political and economic factors behind 'welfare reforms' will challenge anyone interested in the course of Australian history. It will be of special interest to students of welfare, politics and history.

Rob Watts teaches at Phillip Institute of Technology. An editor of Thesis Eleven, his long-standing interests include the history of social policy, and contemporary social theory. He is a born-again cyclist.

For Jamie, Alastair and David

The Foundations of the National Welfare State

Rob Watts

ALLEN & UNWIN
Sydney London Boston

First published in 1987
Allen & Unwin Australia Pty Ltd
8 Napier Street, North Sydney, NSW 2060 Australia

Allen & Unwin New Zealand Limited
60 Cambridge Terrace, Wellington, New Zealand

George Allen & Unwin (Publishers) Ltd
18 Park Lane, Hemel Hempstead, Herts HP2 4TE England

Allen & Unwin Inc.
8 Winchester Place, Winchester, Mass 01890 USA

National Library of Australia
Cataloguing-in-Publication

Watts, Rob.
 The foundations of the national welfare state.

 Bibliography.
 Includes index.
 ISBN 0 04 994012 0.

 1. Social security—Australia—History—20th
 century. 2. Social security—Australia. 3. Welfare
 state. I. Title.

361'.994

Set in Hong Kong by Asco Trade Typesetting Ltd.
Produced in Malaysia by SRM Production Services Sdn Bhd

Contents

Acknowledgements

I wish to record my gratitude to the many people and organisations who have assisted in the production of this book, both in its initial form as a thesis and in this form.

The book is heavily dependent upon material contained in the Commonwealth Archives, Canberra, and I would like to acknowledge the great courtesy and consideration shown me by all the staff. Likewise, to the staff of the Australian National Library (Canberra), the Australian War Memorial Archives (Canberra), the Victorian State Library (Melbourne), the Baillieu Library (Melbourne University), go my thanks for expert assistance. Special thanks are due to Professor J.C. Neild, Director of the Commonwealth Archives, for intercessions on my behalf to secure the release of certain materials.

I was also the beneficiary of advice and comments given by a number of people who replied to queries or letters. In particular, I must thank Mrs Jean Downing for assisting me to gain access to her late husband's papers, which I examined at the University of Melbourne Archives. Dr R. Mendelsohn, Dr H.C. Coombs, Sir Frederick Wheeler, Professor H.G. Burton, Professor W. Prest and Mrs Marjory Harper, all were kind enough to reply to questions addressed to them.

My friends in the Department of Sociology and Politics at Phillip Institute of Technology have provided support and intellectual stimulus in ways too numerous to count; to Kerreen Reiger, Peter Beilharz, Peter Christoff, Mark Considine, Patricia Moynihan, and Elaine Weisel, go my thanks for intellectual comradeship. Likewise to colleagues like Cynthia Turner, Laurie O'Brien, Geoff Sharp and Kent Middleton at Melbourne University.

The supervisor of the thesis on which this book is based, John Hirst, secured me from slipping into the abyss of sloppy argument and dogmatism; I owe much to his integrity and acumen. John Iremonger, Stuart McIntyre and Roy Hay provided helpful comments which have been incorporated here. I would also like to acknowledge the editorial help provided by Catherine Baker.

To the typists, especially Grace Colosimo, Ann Volkanis, Meg Barr and Livia Helou, go my deepest thanks.

To my wife, Ruth Louise Barr, this book is offered in gratitude for the support and love which came unceasingly.

Abbreviations

ACTU   Australian Council of Trade Unions
AIPS   Australian Institute of Political Science
ALP   Australian Labor Party
ARU   Australian Railways Union
AWU   Australian Workers Union
BMA   British Medical Association
CP   Country Party
CPA   Communist Party of Australia
CPD   Commonwealth Parliamentary Debates
CPP   Commonwealth Parliamentary Papers
ILO   International Labour Organisation
MLA   Member of Legislative Assembly
MHR   Member of House of Representatives
NIC   National Insurance Commission
UAP   United Australia Party

Note on footnote references to Australian archival material: To reduce the bulk of those footnotes referring to Commonwealth archival material, I refer to the author(s), the name of the report (or indicate correspondence), date if available, and the general Australian Archives reference, thus:

L.F. Giblin, 'Inflation 1940', 20 June 1941, in CP 7/1.

The bibliography can be consulted to establish the Department of origin.

Introduction

In the 1940s, successive Commonwealth governments consolidated the framework of Australia's 'welfare state'. To the invalid and old-age pensions scheme of 1910, child endowment, unemployment and sickness benefits, funeral allowances, widows' pensions and special benefits were added between 1941 and 1945, programmes brought together by the 1947 Social Services Consolidation Act. Forty years on, however, this 'welfare state', along with many other western 'welfare states', is in crisis.

On 17 December 1985, the Australian Minister for Social Security, Brian Howe, announced that his department would carry out the first major review of Australia's social security system in 40 years, explaining:

> The review will examine the three key areas of social security policy.
>
> These are, help for families with young children, programs for people of working age and help for the aged. That (earlier) review under the Curtin Government established the basis for the post-war welfare state. Now is the time for a fundamental re-examination of existing programs and priorities.[1]

Howe pointed out the major social and economic changes of the previous decade, including growth of long-term unemployment, increasing numbers of single parents in poverty and the rise in child poverty, as factors necessitating such a review.

Due to be completed by the end of 1987, the review is one more symptom of the crisis of the 'welfare state'. The economic and social problems of which this crisis is a consequence are apparent in many other capitalist societies. Since 1974 Australia has experienced historically high inflation levels and mass unemployment has become an enduring problem. With the official rate of unemployment put at 8 percent of the workforce in 1986, it has become a major burden on government, which is expected to maintain the unemployed on a minimum income. (In 1986 the married rate of unemployment benefits is around $163 per week.)

Australian and other capitalist economies face what James O'Connor has called 'the fiscal crisis of the state', a no-win situation in which governments are called on to reduce their levels of taxation to promote private sector recovery, while simultaneously increasing expenditure to meet the special needs of this or that group.[2] Since the mid-1970s, Australian governments have had, most years, to deal with substantial deficits. For 1985–86 the deficit is likely to be around $6 billion; interest payments on loans raised to meet earlier deficits will exceed $6.7 billion. Hence the welfare budgets of Australian governments have come under increasing scrutiny, both financial and political.

There can be no doubt that welfare states are expensive and appear likely to become more so. In Australia, expenditure on welfare and social security is now the biggest item of Commonwealth government expenditure. From the 1970s to the present, spending has risen from around 25 percent to 30 percent of the Commonwealth budget. (Even so, Australian expenditure on welfare is lower than for comparable societies; the OECD average is 19 percent of gross national product compared with the Australian figure of 12 percent.) As expenditures have risen, so political debate and criticism have mounted, producing restraints on the rate of expansion and something that looks like a crisis of confidence—or legitimacy—in the welfare state itself. Sporadic cuts in welfare spending have been made, a process begun during the Fraser years (1975–1983). During this period the 'social wage' (i.e., the value per capita of federal social services) was cut from $5 867 (1975–76) to $5 069 (1982–83) in 1986 dollar terms. Under the Hawke Government in 1985–86 the social security budget rose by only 6.6 percent, well short of the overall budget increase of 8.4 percent and less than the inflation rate.

More significant than these financial restraints is the way in which once dominant views about the welfare state have been undermined. As Ramesh Mishra puts it:

> The techniques of state intervention in the market economy. . . conveniently labelled as Keynesianism—seem to work no longer. . . The effectiveness of state action and therefore its scope of action is in question. In short, both the practice and the rationale of the welfare state is in jeopardy.[3]

The welfare state is now a subject of ideological contest.

From the 'new right', represented by the lucid and acidic pen of

Milton Friedman, comes an indictment of the welfare state as one of the major causes of economic recession.[4] Left to itself, suggests Friedman, a capitalist market economy will be vastly more productive and more just than the present mix of government regulation and private enterprise. 'Big Government', Friedman says, has robbed the people of the incentives to work hard and to invest, while the pursuit of social and economic equality by welfare states has eroded freedom. What is more, Friedman says, the increasing costs of welfare do not seem to improve the lives of the poor. Insensitive bureaucracy and increased incomes for public servants and professionals are the chief effects of the welfare state, while poverty remains untouched.

These are serious charges, if only because they frequently appear in revised form from the pens of the left. Marxist writers like Jeffrey Galper and Ian Gough suggest the welfare state has not undone the pernicious consequences of capitalism, such as poverty, homelessness, social inequality and unemployment. Yet to the extent that it offers minimal income support it has bought off or co-opted criticism from the working class. The social status quo is thereby maintained by the welfare state by virtue of its maintainence of the ideological justifications for an unequal society and in terms of its circulation of money.[5]

Between these extremes of left and right the welfare state is seen as a benevolent, pragmatically necessary solution to the problems of a modern industrial society. This view is sustained by an ever-increasing army of community service workers, employed by governments to provide health, welfare or educational services. In Australia they now form the second biggest occupational group, bigger even than secondary industry. For these workers, and for the makers and analysts of social policy, the history of welfare states is usually understood as inevitable linear progress. If there is anything wrong with todays welfare state, say the proponents of what has been called the 'social conscience model' of social policy, it is that there is not enough of it.[6]

In Australia this optimistic picture of a morally responsive welfare state, the history of which is a history of reform, is closely allied to the view of labor parties and labor governments as agents of social change and progress. Within the labour movement there is a widespread belief that labor parties are especially well equipped to act as midwives at the historical birth of welfare states. It is a view given typical expression by Brian Dickey when he writes:

> Consideration of social welfare developments in Australia in the 1940s must inevitably be dominated by the initiatives of the Curtin and Chifley Labor governments. . .
> . . . the labor governments positively welcomed this access of power and set about not only winning the war, but winning the peace too. Here at last was the opportunity to set right the social inequalities the labor movement had endured and observed so closely during the 1930s.[7]

   The long-running dichotomy between the 'party of change' and the
'parties of resistance' has been made apparent since the 1983 Wages
and Prices Accord, with the factions of the ALP and the broad left
being asked to rally around the labor movement. As Brian Howe, the
leader of the socialist left faction in federal caucus, has put it, '. . . we
need a broad alliance of labour's constituency. This alliance has to
use a thoughtful economic strategy and engage with, rather than
detach itself from the political process'.[8]
   Central to this modern program is a memory of the 'successful governments of the forties' which are held up to labour supporters in the
1980s as the very model of successful socialism based on thoughtful
economics and a commitment to social reform. For Howe, as for
many within the labour movement, it has long been *de rigeur* to
believe that then, as now, only the 'labour movement has the commitment and the energy to attack the inequalities that lie behind
poverty'.[9] For Laborists, the 'welfare state' stands as a triumphant
vindication of the ALP's special role in the 1940s, as in the 1980s, as
the party of progress.
   This book begins with no presumptions about the merits of any of
the arguments about the welfare state provided by the new right,
Marxists or by laborists. What it does is to explore the origins of a
number of major welfare policy initiatives between 1935 and 1945 by
successive non-Labor and Labor governments, with a view to establishing whether any of the current propositions about the welfare
state have any points of connection with its 'heroic age'. It addresses
two questions in particular. First, are Labor governments to be
understood as unequivocally reformist and progressive agents of
change? Second, are the welfare measures that established the
Australian welfare state after 1941 best described in terms of 'state-
sponsored benevolence' oriented to equality? The book's focus is on
the context of government action and on the roles and motives of the
key actors involved in the introduction of welfare measures. It has
relied on traditional historical investigation of documentary records
in an attempt to recover the interplay of interests and intentions,
while also taking into account the proposition first identified with
Marx, that if people make their own history, they do so in contexts
not always of their own making.
   Detailed consideration of government records held in the Commonwealth Archives suggest that long-standing views of the Curtin
government's achievements, and of the social character of welfare
state legislation may need to be revised. A comparison of the welfare
policy of the much-abused Lyons government after 1935, and the
Menzies government after 1939, with the much-admired Curtin government after 1941 suggest that labor's welfare state arose out of political and fiscal considerations of these governments. A comparison of
the national insurance legislation of 1938 with child endowment
(1941) and the welfare fund proposals of 1943 underlines the extent

to which welfare reforms can be as much about solutions to pressing political and fiscal problems as they are expressions of benevolence or a commitment to social reform. Indeed, government advisers acknowledged, especially between 1939 and 1945, that welfare policy was necessarily subordinated to the higher demands of macro-economic and fiscal policy.

Particular stress is given to the development of liberal ideology in the inter-war years, and to the role of liberal collectivists, intellectuals and social technicians, especially after 1939, when a small but influential number of economists were recruited into the public service. Committed to a moderate degree of social change, these men were placed after 1939 to pursue their vision of a reconstructed and refurbished capitalism. Central to that vision was the goal of 'high' or 'full' employment. The subsequent codification of this goal as official Commonwealth Government policy after 1945 was to ensure that welfare policy remained secondary and subordinate to the Keynesian-inspired measures designed to secure full employment.

With the benefit of hindsight, we who are the children of the post-war compact may well see the convergence between liberalism and the Labor Government after 1941 as a striking testament to the strength of inter-war liberalism and to its resolve to transcend the damage done by years of mass employment. Yet the unwillingness of the liberal reconstructionists to deal with the problem of state power in relation to the prerogatives of capital meant that the wartime planners bequeathed an ambiguous legacy to the post-war world. The health of capitalism was accorded a primacy which the social values of equity, equality and human welfare could never match. In that respect the problems of unemployment, poverty and social inequality in the 1970s can be traced in part to the ambiguities built into the welfare state of the 1940s.

1

The origins and strange death of national insurance, 1935–39

Between 1937 and 1939 the United Australia Party (UAP) Government of J.A. Lyons struggled to bring a comprehensive and sophisticated programme of social insurance into being. The National Health and Pensions Insurance Act (1938) was, however, not destined to last. Its demise accompanied major upheavals in the UAP Government and preparations for war in distant Europe. Yet the efforts made by this Government and the substance of the national insurance scheme provoke some interesting questions.

The years bridging the two immensely diverting and destructive world-wars were dominated by a great economic and social crisis. These years are best described as a kind of *intermezzo*, in which the second war completed business put on international and domestic agendas by the first war and the great Depression. The inter-war years have frequently been described by historians as a period of 'marking time', and a period in which Australia fell from grace in terms of its reputation as a 'social laboratory'.[1] These later judgements echoed the views of at least one contemporary commentator, Meredith Atkinson, who suggested in 1919 that, 'once famed as pioneer workers in the social laboratory, we have fallen behind, smugly satisfied with our achievements'.[2] There is also a tendency to see the inter-war years as a period of largely unrelieved rule by 'the parties of resistance', as the non-Labor parties are frequently characterised.

By contrast, Labor's years of ascendancy are often seen as years of heroic leadership, social reform, the humanising of capitalism and the construction of a welfare state. In short, there is a tendency to make a radical distinction between the inter-war years, portrayed as a period

1

of inactivity and conservative ascendency, and the years after 1941, which are allegedly dominated by an activist and reforming Labor Government. This chapter seeks to establish a basis for revising this uncomplicated view. While its focus is on the Lyons Government and its attempt to bring in a scheme of social insurance, it incorporates something of the broader context for better understanding the achievements of the highly-regarded Labor governments of the 1940s.

The politics of legitimation and social policy in the inter-war years

We should perhaps begin with the tendency to see the inter-war years as years of a conservative ascendancy, characterised by an absence of reforming Labor Governments, and the triumph of *laissez-faire* economics. This picture attributes novelty and an abrupt redefinition of policy directions to the wartime Labor Government. Such a temptation must be strong for those historians who work from a model of Australian party politics dichotomised between a 'party of progress' and the 'parties of reaction or resistance'.

In 1915 the ALP formed Governments at Commonwealth level and in five of the six State Parliaments. Not until 1942 would Labor again be so strongly represented in Australian Governments. Labor's political suicides in 1916–1917 over conscription, and again in 1931–1932 over economic and fiscal policy, are the most dramatic indication of the political eclipse of Labor in the inter-war years. However, there are other issues which require consideration before the significance of the 'conservative ascendancy' becomes clear.

Joan Rydon, accepting that the demise of Labor is self-evident, nonetheless suggests that the dominance of non-labor forces is neither as compelling nor unambiguous as it is usually assumed to be. As Rydon points out, '. . . the dramatic schisms within the ALP have tended to obscure the fact that the period was one of splits, divisions and realignments on all sides'.[3] She goes on to suggest that 'it was not the ascendancy of a single party—the conservatives built no steady organisation, no continuous electoral machines'. The non-Labor governments of this period 'were a changing mixture of Conservatives, ex-Labor and Country-Party men'. J.A. Macallum, anticipating Rydon in 1935, observed of the UAP that it is '. . . the latest of a number of coalitions or fusions, formed round a conservative core, but comprising men, professing all political creeds, compatible with constitutional government'.[4]

Both the Nationalist Party and the United Australia Party were such fusions. From 1917 until 1923 the ex-Labor Prime Minister, W.M. Hughes, headed a Nationalist Government which included four ex-Labor Ministers. In 1931 an ex-Labor Treasurer, J.A. Lyons, became Prime Minister of a UAP Government which included three ex-Labor Ministers. Only between 1923 and 1929 perhaps, was there a clear non-labor cast to the Nationalist Government of S.M. Bruce and Earle Page. Even so, internal debates between 'radical' and conservative elements within the Country Party added some diversity and tension to the Coalition Government.

All of this throws into doubt the precise character of the 'conservative ascendancy'. In particular, it raises larger questions about the nature of Australian 'conservatism' in its party-political forms, and about the relation of 'conservative' parties to labor parties in Australia's political culture.[5]

Identifying the precise nature of non-labor parties' conservatism may well be an impossible task. Contemporaries and later commentators alike have identified 'anti-laborism' as the only useful characteristic of the non-labor parties. For Duncan-Hughes, the Nationalist Party 'has been that which has shown the strongest opposition to socialism'.[6] For F.W. Eggleston, National Development was the most significant component of 'liberalism' in the non-labor parties.[7] Later writers have also emphasised the absence of anything but a desire to resist the ALP. As Overacker puts it, '. . . the parties of resistance have frequently changed names, and their organisation, but until the emergence of the Liberal Party in 1945 at least, opposition to Labour was the source of unity and continuity'.[8]

On such an account, Australian conservatism becomes a rather colourless and reactive matter, taking its cues from the activity of 'socialist' or radical themes being worked out within the ALP. Hazlehurst suggests that Australian conservatives are those who are 'contented with society as it is, or as less government would make it'.[9]

Yet this is not itself sufficient to permit a clear-cut distinction between non-labor and ALP views in the inter-war years. The participation of the Australian state in economic and social matters had been so well established by the end of the nineteenth century that a commitment to reducing it was not on the agenda. More to the point perhaps, were differences about the interests to be served by particular kinds of state interventions. If the state attempts to seek the consent of all classes and interests, there are more likely to be arguments about both more *and* less government intervention with respect to different interests at any one time. Equally Hazlehurst's suggestion fails to take into account the possibility that ALP members may be as happy with the *status quo* as non-Labor Party affiliates may be concerned to seek change.

The Lyons UAP Government between 1931 and 1939 has received faint praise.

Hasluck, for example, summarised the political and ideological character of the Lyons' Government as 'an emergency government that outlasted the emergency'.[10] This judgement partly relies on a traditional view of the ALP as a stable ideological entity while non-labor parties are purely pragmatic. The corollary view is one of Lyons as a nice but ineffectual man, who provided Australians with a calming image of ordinariness and domesticity, which they craved after the high drama of 1930–1931. In this account Lyons becomes a kind of Australian Baldwin. Yet this very comparison should suggest that Lyons, like Baldwin, possessed the talents and even the ruthlessness which enabled Lyons to stay on the top of the greasy pole for a decade.[11]

In many ways, the political and ideological predispositions of the Lyons Government were those of a cautiously reforming liberalism which envisaged a refurbished capitalism partnered by an interventionist state. Lyons' personal popularity in 1931, his seduction by Melbourne Nationalist politicians and his electoral victory as leader of a new conservative government cannot conceal the underlying continuities in his own Laborist redaction of 'new Liberalism'. He saw the new United Australia Party as a truly national party above sectional interests; in September 1934 he urged that the UAP 'be not Tory, sectional or conservative'.[12] He personally supported a progressive range of social and economic policies around the theme of 'equal opportunity'. Hart describes the UAP formula for state-economy relations as one which provided for government interference in an otherwise untrammelled private enterprise framework.[13] Specifically, this meant strict financial orthodoxy including balanced budgets and restrictions on government extravagance, coupled with assistance for capital through tariff protection and a 'sympathetic' taxation system.

All of these predispositions could well have inclined Lyons himself to press for the kind of programme which became national insurance. Yet the record suggests that he played a relatively insignificant role in this case. Why then did the Government take on national insurance?

It is important to note that by the 1930s a commitment to social insurance had become a feature of Australian political and social commonsense. It was widely regarded as an irreducible minimum component of a 'modern' society, even if divergent values and interests sustained this consensus. Differences between social commentators like F.A. Bland and E.R. Walker could not conceal a common-sense view that social insurance was an emblem of modernity and rationality.[14] All the major political leaders of the thirties, including Lyons, Page, Scullin and Curtin, saw in it the principle of progress.

Yet such general commitments do not of themselves explain why the National Insurance Bill of 1938 emerged when it did, or why it took the particular form it did. Recourse to structural explanations, couched in terms of 'function', ideology, or class, do not go far in explaining either the timing or the character of the policy commitment. However, when viewed in the light of the politics of legitimation, it becomes clear that certain common political characteristics underpin the existence of adversary political parties, and that for parties in government, the search for legitimacy does much to diminish the apparent differences between parties.

Claus Offe has argued that the reproduction of capitalist economic and social relationships has retained its singular compatibility with liberal democratic processes and institutions through the twentieth century because of the emergence of mass political parties.[15] In particular, Offe has suggested that such parties with their machine apparatuses, fund raising organisations and publicity processes evolved at about the time when the market place began to be politicised by state interventionism.

In Australia there is such a coincidence at the turn of the century. The organisation of politics as a marketing problem, i.e., how to win 'consumer' support, required the kinds of organisation of parties that we have seen develop in the twentieth century. Such a relationship, Offe suggests, is one of the mechanisms which rises up to deal with the fundamental problems of managing and resolving class conflict. John Rickard made a parallel observation when he wrote, 'In place of the fragmented politics of 1890, in both Commonwealth and State spheres a comparatively rigid two party system now operated. These polar entities, labor and anti-labor, irrevocably bound to each other as all opposites are, had arrived'.[16]

Parties are essentially means to routinise and organise political perceptions and aspirations. Their own internal bureaucratic structures may be seen as reflecting a larger attempt to routinise the consciousness, loyalties, and interests of their supporters. Equally liberal-democratic institutions and processes like parliaments, opposition parties and elections are attempts to routinise the exercise of power and the practice of dissent. Political parties and parliamentary governments are frequently connected both to the existence of classes and their opposed interests, and to the attempts to regularise, if not harmonise these class relations. That is to say that if political parties on occasion articulate ideological and social differences, these differences are also bounded by clear restraints and by the need to solve a common problem, the problem of legitimacy.

Legitimacy has not received the attention it deserves from Australian scholars, thought it occupies a central place in European social and political theory.[17] The concept of legitimacy is used throughout this book in two distinct senses, each referring to a different level of analysis. In the first sense, the state is involved in the problem of legitimacy as a social structural problem. With respect to the general social order, I share with German social theory the presumption that there is a central problem within a capitalist social formation which requires a process of justification for the status quo. That status quo is contradictory, caught between the social organisation of economic use values, and the continued private appropriation of surplus value.[18] At this level, legitimacy is defined as a systemic or structural goal, in which the social order is widely presented as just, normal, inevitable or even desirable. It is in this sense that one of the roles ascribed to social policy is defined, namely that of managing social dissent. At this level, the problem of legitimacy involves many social institutions other than the state, and the analysis focuses more on institutions and less on individual motives.

In a second, and lower-order sense, legitimacy will here be used to identify the mundane and daily preoccupations of party governments with winning electoral support. In this less exalted sense, governments in the political market place in the twentieth century have come to see welfare reforms as part of the currency of legitimacy. Generally the context of my discussion will identify the meaning of legitimacy I am relying on.

The notion of legitimacy thereby raises the possibility of rethinking the traditional distinctions drawn in Australia between the 'party of initiative' and the 'parties of resistance'. All political parties seeking government are possibly bound by similar structural constraints. There is, for instance, abundant evidence of how non-labor governments seek to secure working class support, or complicity, through the adoption of welfare and industrial legislation.[19]

The appeal of 'social reform' was rarely experienced just as an appeal to maintain the facade of an unjust social order. A corollary in my distinction between the two levels of legitimacy is the difference between what belongs to the social structure and what belongs to individual consciousness. Men and women of good will and a refined morality who were genuinely concerned to promote justice have played key roles in shaping welfare policy. It is not my intention to suggest that they were really hypocrites intent on justifying a socially unjust order. Of particular interest are the links between individual intentions and the social and political consequences, intended and unintended, of public policy, as well as the failures of public policy. Welfare policy in particular reveals the tension between human intention and structural constraint.

Winning an election is only the first step to winning support from the people for policy, which the practice of opposition parties and the media in particular seeks to criticise. For governments in the twentieth century the problem is complicated by continuously discovered 'new needs', and the demand that governments meet those 'needs' in ways which are acceptable to their electorates. Social legislation conferring economic and social benefits on increasing numbers of people represents both an answer to the problem of legitimacy and an open invitation to undermine that legitimacy.

This, it can be suggested, was the problem confronting the Lyons Government in the 1930s, a government which had to deal with the unintended consequences of social reform undertaken at the beginning of the century. By world standards Australia's old-age and invalid pensions, provided by the Commonwealth Government after 1908, were unusual, if not anomalous in that they were non-contributory with the costs being borne by consolidated revenue. This was long a bone of contention among fiscal conservatives, and numerous Governments after 1908 considered revising their financial foundations. But many of these proposed revisions encountered political difficulties, preventing any easy rectification of the 'mistake of 1908'. Recognition of these difficulties confronted the Lyons Government through the 1930s, but any solution to the problem had to be one which would not bring electoral disaster.

The origins of National Insurance

R.G. Casey, as *de facto* Treasurer and a self-confessed 'reformer', played a key role in the story of national insurance.[20] War hero, sometime dandy, engineer and confidante of important men, he was also one of the most talented of Lyons' Ministers. Casey had demonstrated loyalty, tact and diplomacy as Bruce's London agent in the 1920s.[21] As assistant Treasurer to Lyons from 1933 to 1935 and thereafter as Treasurer, he demonstrated the capacity to work hard and to master a tremendous range of administrative and technical detail.

Like several of his colleagues, his background and his values predisposed him to liberal reformism, albeit with a strong commitment to the values of established institutions and hierarchy. He provided his own exegesis on the inter-war conception of an organic community welded together by a harmony of interests. For Casey, a *noblesse oblige* indicated a duty to remedy the lot of the unfortunate; social insurance would ensure that the class most likely to benefit from this reform would also be paying for it. For Casey, social reform was 'an instance of a practical, instead of a visionary, socialism'. Like many of his class, more 'applied rationality' seemed to him the only answer to the social problems of his time. He seems never to have doubted the fundamental rightness of capitalism even if he allowed that in the Depression it had failed to deliver the goods. As he put it in 1935, 'Generally speaking, the system of private enterprise remains essentially intact. Private enterprise still provides the driving force of modern civilisation'.[22]

Even so, Casey insisted that capitalism would stand or fall on its capacity to 'achieve the greatest good for the greatest number'. The means to this end entailed what Casey called, 'a more kindly state in the background to succour those whose lot in life, for various reasons, requires amelioration'. A 'kindly state' was in Casey's view the best means to ensure a 'healthy individualism'; specific admixtures of state intervention would ensure that the social machinery worked better.

Casey shared with some of his colleagues the view that the non-contributory basis of the pensions programme was a mistake. Casey, as Minister assisting the Treasurer, sought Cabinet approval in May 1934 to investigate the costs of a limited National Insurance scheme providing sickness and disability benefits. Treasury, however, reported that such a scheme was 'impracticable'; the continued levels of unemployment, reduced wages, and the likelihood that contributions to such a scheme would be 'an added burden to industry' were the reasons advanced by Treasury.[23]

More to the point, any revision of the 'mistake' of 1908 would have to deal with old-age pensions. There was much support for putting the old-age pensions scheme on a contributory basis. In public, this intention was justified in terms of 'progress', 'reform' and 'compassion'. In private, the Treasury Secretary expressed 'deep concern' about the mounting cost of pensions. He was a 'strong supporter of any scheme' which would 'relieve the burden', preferably by means of an increase in revenue which would *not* be gained 'through an increase in direct Commonwealth taxation'.[24]

In this respect Sheehan and other Treasury officials were merely restating their enduring interest in reforming the basis of old-age pensions. However, attempts at such reform made during the fiscal crisis of the Depression revealed that reform could be as much a problem as a solution.

The fiscal crisis which confronted Australian governments after 1920 obsessed contemporary political observers and fuelled some of the most heated political debates of the twentieth century. Consensus was arrived at early that a deflationary policy and cutbacks to government expenditures were essential. The extent of expenditures on pensions was one of the first items of state expenditure to be scrutinised.[25]

The first review came from the Auditor-General's Department in 1930. Then, as now, this powerful and often feared independent statutory authority was charged with examining and often constraining government 'extravagances'. With the onset of depression it was not slow to argue for reductions in areas like social services. The incumbent Auditor-General, C.J. Cerutty, had long espoused a traditional Treasury view that the non-contributory character of the pensions scheme was morally irresponsible and fiscally unsound.[26] In 1930 Cerutty argued that the increase in pensions expenditure was the result of higher benefits attracting more applicants. He castigated those pensioners who qualified for their benefits 'through drink, gambling, laziness, extravagance and waste'.[27] In terms redolent of nineteenth century poor law discourse, Cerutty advised the Scullin Government to impose tougher conditions on pension payments.

The mounting fiscal crisis confronting the Scullin Government would soon compromise the ALP. As unemployment rose in 1930, the Scullin Government was urged by the right to deflate and by the left to inflate. It took the fatal road of compromise. By now the pensions vote was double that of the 1923 expenditure. As Cerutty and Treasury pointed out, the pensions bill for 1930–31 of £11 million was only a little less than the total Commonwealth revenue derived from direct taxes of £1 100 000 for that year. To the Treasury officials this ratio of social service expenditure to revenue was likely only to worsen.

In May 1931 the 'experts committee', including L.F. Giblin and D.B. Copland, drew up the outlines of the so-called Premiers' Plan, designed to reduce all Government expenditures in Australia by 20 percent and to reduce the level of all Government deficits from £41 million to £14 600 000 in 1931–32.[28] In Parliament Scullin tried to head off suspicious Labor queries about how these reductions would be effected. At the Premiers' Conference of 25 May 1931, the worst suspicions of Scullin's vociferous critics, now led by J.A. Beasley, were confirmed. Pensions, along with other government expenditures, were to be cut by 20 percent on the grounds of 'equality of sacrifice'. If adoption by the seven governments of 'the Plan' gave Australia the semblance of a Depression policy, it administered to the Scullin Government a terminal shock.[29]

The Premiers' Plan split the Labor movement almost as decisively as had the conscription crisis of 1916–17. Ministerial resignations were followed by the spectacle of the Opposition voting with the Government to save it from defeat at the hands of Labor backbenchers. On 26 June 1931, almost half of the Federal Labor Party voted against the Premiers' Plan legislation. The pension cuts generated the greatest anger. As a desperate concession the pensions were cut by only 12½ percent, but it was too late. The complex internecine warfare between NSW Lang Labor men and the Federal ALP led to the final debacle of 25 November 1931, when the Beasley Lang group defeated the Scullin Government on the floor of the House. The 'unforgiveable' assault on the social services by a Labor Government taught a lesson which the Lyons UAP government remembered well throughout the 1930s.

The imperatives to secure a fiscally responsible programme remained a powerful component of UAP policy after 1931. It had been elected to office on the basis of its advocacy of 'sound finance'. Lyons, unlike Scullin, could also count on a united Cabinet and party. Yet even Lyons would soon experience resentment directed at his attempts to 'reform' the pensions scheme.

In his first Budget speech of 1 September 1932, Lyons, as Treasurer, indicated his own accord with the sentiments of the Auditor-General in 1930.[30] Australia, Lyons declared, could not afford the ever-increasing costs of pensions 'on their present basis'. A contributory scheme was 'the only answer'. Lyons approached the Auditor-General, and on 31 October 1932 Cerutty produced a proposal which he argued would remove pensions from the realm of 'vicious politics' and encourage work and thrift by putting all pensions on a contributory basis.[31] His proposal called for compulsory contributions from all employees (who would pay half of the total contribution) and from employers and the Commonwealth (who would each pay a quarter of the contribution). He calculated that if sixpence a week came in from 2 800 000 employees and threepence a week from Government and employers, then a pension of 15 shillings a week for invalids and old people would be possible. (This benefit compared with the current maximum rate of 20 shillings per week.)

However, other Treasury officials were not so convinced. L.F. Giblin, then Acting Commonwealth Statistician, and H.C. Green, who had been secretary to the 1925 Royal Commission on National Insurance, were asked by Treasury's Secretary for comments. Giblin condemned Cerutty's proposal out of hand. In his view, '. . . it contributed nothing useful to the solution of the difficulties of a contributory system of pensions. . . Moreover both the statistical data and the actuarial estimates. . . are open to serious criticism'.[32]

Green and Giblin's comments appear to have ensured that no further consideration was given to Cerutty's proposals. They had also defined the terms of Treasury's position on old-age pensions. Treasury clearly wanted a contributory scheme, but it had to be done in such a way as to ensure either immediate or long-term savings to the Commonwealth. However, how to do this without raising a political furore remained a key problem.

Even before this internal review was completed, the Lyons Government had exerienced the problems involved in meddling with pensions. Lyons had proposed in September 1932 to reduce pensions by a further two shillings and sixpence a week. Public and political opposition was so strong and immediate that this proposal was dropped. Another suggestion that near relatives of pensioners be compelled to support them was condemned as 'unduly harsh'. It was nonetheless given legislative effect before its repeal in June 1934. Lyons, if he needed any reminder, had been cautioned by this attempt to revise the pensions programme.

In the coming years the Lyons Government, careful to maintain its image as a sound and cautious economic manager, kept alive its interest in revising the pensions scheme. Between 1933 and 1935 key individuals remained alert to the possibility of some measure of social insurance which might achieve this goal, though the strategy of using a larger scheme of social insurance to camouflage alterations to old age pensions did not emerge until later. Treasury took the view that any social insurance scheme could only be introduced when unemployment was much reduced, and when it could be shown that the Commonwealth would benefit. It would have nothing to do with any 'rash proposals', as the new Secretary to Treasury, H.J. Sheehan, made clear to Lyons in May 1933.[33]

By 1935 a number of factors combined to set the Lyons government on the road to national insurance. Casey for one remained convinced of the need to reform the Commonwealth's finances. As he pointed out in 1935, the total Commonwealth budget for 1934–35 amounted to £62 900 000 as against the total of £55 700 000 for 1933–34. To meet these expenditures a total of £11 500 000 came from income and other direct taxes. (The balance of Commonwealth revenues came from excise and customs duties.) As Casey indicated, by this time the Commonwealth was paying out more on pensions than it received in direct tax revenues. In 1934–35 the pensions bill was £19 100 000.[34] Worse, the long-term trend, as projected by Treasury seemed to involve income tax revenues continuing to decline relative to pension costs. Using J.B. Sutcliffe's early attempts to compute Australia's 'national income', Casey suggested that the pensions bill would also consume more and more of the Government's revenue.[35]

Due for retirement as Auditor-General in 1935, Cerutty in his last annual report again emphasised the need to relieve the intolerable financial burden of the pensions system.[36] Cerutty's report seems to have achieved a larger impact than might have been expected, largely because of apparently minor changes to the political environment.

Throughout 1935 Casey acted as *de facto* Treasurer, easing Lyon's burden of responsibilities, before officially becoming Treasurer on 2 October. Casey's own views about the 'pensions burden' were well known; he was predisposed to listen to Cerutty. Cerutty's report was also well received by Sir Frederick Stewart, who had resigned as Minister for Commerce in 1934 and accepted a post as Under-Secretary for Unemployment. In this largely honorary post the controversial Stewart was able to indulge his penchant for social reform.

Sir Frederick Stewart had been elected MHR for Parramatta in the UAP landslide of 1931, bringing to Parliament an unusual independence and a variety of talents and interests. An aviation entrepreneur in the heroic age of Kingsford-Smith and Charles Ulm, Stewart was a land developer and a founding director of the Metropolitan Omnibus Company, designed to run buses to the Sydney suburb of Chullora, which he had developed. He was a devoted Christian who embraced teetotalism and philanthropic works. As a parliamentary 'new chum' after 1931 he was confident and powerful enough within the NSW UAP network to be indiscreet, unusual for new MHRs. In early 1935 he was hampered neither by Cabinet accountability nor by a Department, and he had a strong personal commitment to the principles of social insurance. As he explained to a church breakfast group in 1936, he would push for social insurance until it was achieved. 'I want to see', he said, 'the present social schemes on which there was some stigma of charity, displaced by something to which every member of the community would contribute and everyone be entitled to its benefits'.[37] His commitment to principle rarely wavered. In 1935 he paid for his overseas fact-finding trip out of his own pocket; even in 1935 this was a somewhat eccentric gesture.

Cerutty's draft report seems to have inspired Stewart to suggest to Casey that a mission to Great Britain to investigate its social insurance schemes was in order. Approval was received from Cabinet for Stewart to travel to Britain.[38] He returned late in October 1935, and presented a 32-page report to Lyons on 14 November.

Stewart's report epitomised the consensus about social insurance. He maintained that a comprehensive scheme embracing health, pensions and unemployment benefits was appropriate—a view which the Lyons Government disavowed. Beginning with a clear statement of the fiscal *motif*, Stewart said:

> My knowledge of the extraordinary burden imposed on Australian governmental budgets in the care of, and provision for the sick and the unemployed, and also of the serious concern regarding our growing old age pension account impelled me to make a very close study of . . . the British scheme. . .[39]

If Australia adopted a comprehensive plan after the British model, Stewart reckoned the annual cost would be about £7 million. He argued that most of the benefit of the reform would be felt by the state governments but that the Commonwealth would benefit in the long term from a reduced old age pension bill.

Lyon's initial response was unethusiastic. He chastised Stewart for failing to specify a 'revised financial balance between States and Commonwealth'. Stewart apologised for this lapse and added that he did appreciate the difficulties of 'constitutional interference'. Lyons remained cool.[40] Even so, two actuaries were asked to prepare a memo on the financial aspects of Stewart's report and Cabinet agreed, at Casey's request, to form a sub-committee on National Insurance. Casey was to chair the committee comprising R.A. Parkhill, R.G. Menzies and H.V. Thorby. Its brief was to review Stewart's and the actuaries' reports. Treasury meantime was trying to avoid undue public debate about Stewart's report. Sheehan sought to prevent the Report being published,[41] but Stewart was determined to subvert these efforts.

Since his arrival back in Australia, Stewart had conducted an able campaign on behalf of social insurance. His lengthy articles in the Melbourne *Argus* and the *Sydney Morning Herald*[42] sparked off the required response. The Victorian Premier, Sir Stanley Argyle, said, '. . . the time is ripe for a consideration of the need to relieve the charitable burden and to protect workers from unemployment, sickness and accident'.[43]

Casey, however, was concerned about the need for more technical expertise to make clear judgments—apparently lacking in Stewart's report—and the need for more time. He favoured the plan which was eventually adopted: '. . . I wish we could get out to Australia a British official who is well acquainted with social insurance in Britain in its social *and* financial aspects'.[44]

Meanwhile the Cabinet sub-committee had not received the actuaries' report. In desultory fashion it had considered Stewart's proposals, decided that more committees would need to be set up, and that some letters to the State Premiers be written. The stage was set for an endless series of delays.

Sir Frederick Stewart, however, was a determined opponent. In February 1936 he again submitted articles to the Melbourne and Sydney press, in which he called for a firm Government commitment. And then, on 20 March 1936, without prior notice, he resigned his position as Under Secretary for Unemployment. He accused the Government of deliberately delaying action on his report. A minor storm of newspaper and Opposition reaction roundly condemned the Lyons Government, and Casey was given permission to discuss the matter further with his advisers.

Following consultation between Casey and Sheehan, Cabinet agreed in March 1936 to request the British government to second a 'senior officer' to the Commonwealth Government to prepare a report on National Insurance. The outcome was the arrival in August 1936 of two senior British advisers, Sir Walter Kinnear and G.H. Ince. Ince was to produce a Report on Unemployment Insurance which had no practical consequences whatsoever.[45] Kinnear's Report on Health and Pensions Insurance, however, provided the basis for much of the policy development which lead to the legislation of 1938.[46] It drew heavily on English experience and examples and as such attracted criticism from some economists who saw it as a theoretical approach to what was an essentially 'practical problem'.[47]

In his Report, Kinnear outlined a clear policy option for the Commonwealth Government and one which coincided with the expectations already held about the kind of scheme which was needed. Kinnear had no doubt that a 'national insurance scheme should be on a contributory and compulsory basis'. Commonsense reasons were advanced: 'apart from financial considerations, it increases self-respect amongst insured persons and encourages thrift'.

Furthermore, Kinnear linked health insurance to the pensions insurance scheme, as Britain had done in 1925. He pointed out, 'The contributory pensions scheme is closely interlocked with the health insurance scheme and applies to practically the same people'.

This linkage was probably one of the more attractive features of Kinnear's report, at least in the eyes of the Treasury. It must remain a matter of conjecture as to how much Treasury officials linked health insurance to changes in the pensions scheme with a view to disguising their intentions. There is no extant evidence to suggest that this political strategy was consciously formulated. Equally, Casey was concerned that this interpretation should *not* be made. Yet there is little doubt that the linkage reveals a strategic conception which Kinnear's report seems to have articulated.

Kinnear likewise provided support for Treasury concerns about the fiscal implications of continuing with the present pensions scheme. Kinnear agreed that financial disaster seemed imminent if the number of old people increased. He estimated that by 1977 the cost of pensions on a tax-basis would exceed £30 million. His own recommendations envisaged a situation whereby the Commonwealth would only be paying £15 million in 1977, a saving of £15 million. As Kinnear argued, 'The central problem which must be faced in any attempt to frame a general scheme of old-age pensions. . . is necessarily one of finance. The cost of any scheme on any reasonably acceptable lines must be heavy. . .'

This restated conclusions already familiar to Treasury. He also indicated, 'Any attempt to meet the whole cost of a general scheme from Commonwealth funds must fail. If a scheme is to be feasible there is no option but to adopt the contributory principle'.

The structure of his report also clearly underlined the priorities given by Treasury to the pensions problem. The first eight pages of Kinnear's report were given over to the health scheme; the last thirteen pages to his pensions proposals. Likewise his recommendations of a cost of £900 000 per annum for his health insurance scheme suggested that this scheme would play a subordinate role in the costs of the total proposal. It is not too difficult to envisage Treasury seeing the health insurance scheme as a useful diversion with respect to the proposed changes in the pensions scheme.

The real thrust of Kinnear's report lay in its costing proposals for a revision of the pensions programme. In addition to its ordinary pensions scheme for those already eligible for old-age pensions, Kinnear suggested that the Commonwealth would need to allocate £1 million per annum for five years, with incremental increases of £500 000 per annum thereafter until 1960. (These funds would be put into an Insurance Investment fund into which contributions from the other parties would also be put.)

Yet it was not these proposals which provoked the subsequent controversy. Kinnear, in his discussion of health insurance, provided not only for sickness and disability benefits, but also for a form of medical insurance in which insured persons would be eligible for medical treatment by approved doctors as well as free medicines from registered chemists. Kinnear may have felt confident about this novel provision, granted that he had discussed it with representatives from the BMA while in Australia. It was these proposals which became the focus for a public campaign which would eventually destroy the national insurance legislation of 1938.

Treasury saw an advance draft copy of the report in April 1937 and Sheehan prepared an appraisal of the report on at the end of the month, focusing on the financial aspects of Kinnear's proposals. Sheehan did not expect any miracle cures. He began his appraisal with a criticism:

> A criticism might be offered in regard to the proposals, in that they do not afford the relief to the Commonwealth Budget which might have been expected from a contributory scheme as opposed to the present non-contributory scheme.[48]

Even so, Sheehan was able to find some comfort, if only that 'In no one year will the Commonwealth be faced with a greater burden that it will in any case have to bear in respect of the existing Invalid and Old Age Pensions payments if no contributory scheme is introduced'.

Prospects for relief improved with time, a point noted with growing warmth by Sheehan. A long-term saving of £4 million a year would occur if a contributory scheme were introduced using Kinnear's projected costing, with savings beginning in the 1960s. On this basis Sheehan recommended that here was a reasonable demonstration of the long-term savings which could be made with a contributory scheme. Sheehan's approval was crucial. With Treasury approval it now became a matter of political judgement as to how to implement the proposals.

Sometime after June 1937 a commitment was made to proceed with legislation.[49] A bleak response at the Premiers' Conference of 13 August made it seem that unemployment insurance would not be included in the legislative package. Yet Lyons and Casey could not ignore the looming federal election, and they may have believed that a proposal to initiate a large social reform measure could revive the fortunes of a tiring government. Kinnear's proposal, with its reiteration of fiscally orthodox principles added significant weight to the case for introducing legislation. Sir Frederick Stewart also influenced the decision. He let it be known that he would stand as an Independent candidate in the federal elections unless the Lyons government made a principled commitment to national insurance.[50] Stewart's prestige within the NSW UAP establishment made this no insignificant gesture. As a colleague in the 'Social Betterment' faction of the UAP, Albert Lane said in late June, 'Stewart has set a cracker in the pace'.[51] Menzies and Page were sufficiently concerned about their errant colleague to cable Lyons about this 'delicate political situation'.[52] There is no extant reply from Lyons, but there can be little doubt that Stewart's action added to the momentum.

The decision to go ahead with national insurance was reflected in the work of a small Cabinet sub-committee of Lyons, Page, Menzies and Casey. Their task was to prepare a draft policy speech, which was to include reference to a national insurance bill should the Government be re-elected at the federal elections scheduled for 23 October

1937. In his policy speech delivered in Deloraine, Tasmania, on 28 September, Lyons referred to the scheme, saying:

> . . . it is utterly impossible to establish an enduring system of National Insurance paid for solely out of the funds available to the Commonwealth Government. Do not be led astray by those who are not above promising something for nothing.[53]

On 23 October 1937 Australians went to the polls to return the UAP-CP Government of J.A. Lyons, albeit with a reduced majority. Work which had begun in September on a legislative proposal to enact national insurance was now speeded up. On 22 November 1937, R.G. Casey announced the Government's intention to introduce a National Insurance Bill into the House in 1938.

Planning for this exercise began in earnest before the end of the year. It was agreed that Kinnear should be asked to return to Australia to advise the government on the technical and administrative aspects of the legislation. Casey was concerned to have the best advice available, although as it eventuated, what killed National Insurance was political, not technical.

Casey was already building up a small group of Australian advisers to assist him in producing memorandum for the Cabinet. The need for such a working party had become apparent by January 1938, when Casey had agreed that Sheehan should leave Treasury to become Governor of the Commonwealth Bank. Stuart McFarlane, Sheehan's deputy, formally became First Secretary of Treasury on 23 March 1938.

McFarlane's tenure of this office provided a degree of continuity in advice for Casey.[54] It was one of the longest and most significant tenures by a First Secretary. He presided over radical changes that affected both the Treasury and the Commonwealth Government before his retirement in 1948.

He was the last Treasury secretary to have risen laboriously through the public service machine. He would also oversee and encourage the recruitment of professional policy-makers, especially economists with experience and an interest in macro-economic policy-making. Known familiarly as 'Misery Mac', and for his 'essentially conservative financial views' and his pragmatic restraint of 'radical reformers', he was nonetheless to preside over the construction of an interventionist state, in the Keynesian sense.[55]

McFarlane was one of a small group of advisors working on national insurance. Cabinet had its own sub-committee made up of Lyons, Page and Casey, and it was agreed that Casey would take the main burden of parliamentary work in piloting the Bill through the House.[56] Cabinet also agreed to set up a national insurance branch within Treasury, until formal legislation established more enduring administrative forms. Both Kinnear and Lindsay were seconded to this branch and were joined by a third British expert, G.S. MacKay. Three Australians were also seconded to this branch; Professor J.B. Brigden, who would become the first Chairman of the National Insurance Commission and play a key role in negotiations with the doctors, and H.C. Green and D. McVey joined the Branch in February and March 1938.[57]

These six men along with McFarlane were to provide a high level of technical and administrative expertise to the Government. They were involved in devising the legislation and negotiating with key interest groups like the BMA and the friendly societies. In the early months of 1938 things seemed to be progressing smoothly. Kinnear, Lindsay and MacKay had arrived in Australia early in February. A steady stream of papers began to flow from Treasury to Cabinet and Brigden prepared the administrative organisation for national insurance.

As early as 7 February, Casey had outlined the general framework of legislation.[58] On 4 March 1938 another major presentation to Cabinet took place, this time with a draft bill for Cabinet discussion.[59] For the first time Cabinet saw the full scope of the intended legislation. The Cabinet papers suggested that the Government would provide old-age pensions, and disablement, medical and sickness benefits on a contributory basis. Widows' and orphans' pensions would also be provided. The paper dealt with the scale of contributions, the eligible beneficiaries (all under an income limit of £365 per annum) and the scope of benefits. Brief mention was also made of the need to include general practitioners in the scheme, though details were not provided. In general there was a lack of detail, largely because Kinnear advised that with a bill so complex, and affecting so many groups, any attempt to meet all the likely objections might mean they would never get a bill through Parliament.[60] He advised passing a basic bill which could be amended later. The wisdom of this was evident to Page, an experienced parliamentarian, who recalled:

> I conferred with Casey and his British advisers, and urged them to avoid the sorts of complications and delays which had confounded my own efforts ten years previously. I believed that if the new measure attempted to cover all the suggestions . . . the Government would be burdened with a child of such size that only a Caesarean section would permit its birth. . .[61]

Heeding this advice, Casey and his colleagues pressed on, negotiating with the key interest groups who were to be involved in the National Insurance scheme, and preparing legislation.[62]

On 4 May 1938 Casey introduced the long-awaited National Insurance Bill into the Parliament. The parliamentary passage was made relatively smooth by the determined use of the Government's numerical superiority. Casey made his Second Reading speech on 4 May after which debate was adjourned. John Curtin, as Opposition Leader, resumed the debate on 24 May. By 30 June it had been passed by both Houses and was given vice-regal assent on 6 July 1938. The following day the National Insurance Commission was established.

Such a summary omits the often stormy debates in Parliament, many of which revealed weaknesses and omissions in the bill which would later cripple the legislation. The Parliamentary response to the bill, in short, presaged something of the slowly mounting storm of extra-parliamentary criticism which gathered in the last half of 1938.

Curtin's elegant speech in the House on 24 May 1938 was a strong statement of principled opposition to the bill:

> The Labor Party [expresses] its utter condemnation of individual con-tributions as a principle in regard to invalidity, old age and widows' pen-sions. These services should be a charge upon the consolidated revenue of the Commonwealth. To impose special levies either on workers or employers is unjust . . . [Such services] should be free to all members of the community.[63]

Curtin's speech was also a catalogue of the omissions and deficiencies of the bill. It contained no provision for unemployment insurance, 'this most deadly cause of anxiety and unrest'. Worse, it made no provision for self-employed workers, farmers or shopkeepers and it failed to deal adequately with the needs of the medical profession. It was a convincing statement of problems with which the bill did not deal. Even so, by 6 July 1938, the bill had received Royal Assent.

With these formalities out of the way, the Government proceeded to gazette the establishment of the National Insurance Commission which was to administer the Act, as well appoint the first Commis-sioners, J.B. Brigden, H.D. Green, and D. McVey. It was thought that the next six months would see the establishment of the complex machinery to implement the legislation.

The Government may now have felt that the most difficult part of the process was over, but in fact its difficulties were only just be-ginning. The rank and file of Australia's medical profession—the general practitioners—fought a long, hard campaign to white-ant the medical component of national insurance. Their opposition, ex-tending from May 1938 into the middle of 1939 drew the Lyons Government into a quagmire of fruitless discussions and an incom-plete Royal Commission.[64] This opposition along with significant 'popular' opposition organised by a motley crew of Communist and anti-socialist 'grass-roots' organisations persuaded the Lyons Gov-ernment that the measure no longer had wide electoral support.

The 'death' of national insurance was neither swift nor uncompli-cated. The Government's commitment to it had always partly de-pended upon a belief that it was a measure commanding general sup-port. Casey had clearly stated that so long as 'members of all parties have united in advocating National Insurance', then the legislation would be pursued.[65] As public opposition mounted, so party political support became increasingly tenuous. Equally, the fiscal commitment to national insurance could remain acceptable only in the absence of alternative competition for funds. The Government was committed to finding £11 million for national insurance, and this became increasingly difficult in the wake of Munich. Defence spending, the fate of national insurance, and the credibility of Lyon's leadership, became intertwined in the last months of 1938.

Casey and Page had, as early as June 1938, promised the Country Party backbench that once the main Bill was passed, additional legislation would be passed to include the self-employed and farming groups. It was on the basis of this pledge that the CP had backed the legislation in June. By late 1938 it was clear this promise was unlikely to be honoured, due to extra costs.

In addition to the restiveness among the Country Party, there were a host of otherwise trifling matters which led to a major crisis in confidence. The Premiers' Conference of 21 October devoted to defence planning was a shambles. Page's proposals for a ten year co-operative plan of development, to be monitored by an Advisory Council, was watered down. Angry debate diverted the Assembly and Lyons, who was both palpably ill and ineffective, rejected the amendments made to Page's memorandum. The Conference ended with no decisions forthcoming.

This debacle must have influenced Menzies who, three days later, delivered a speech at the Constitutional Association in Sydney on the subject of leadership. His speech was read as an attack on Lyons. The *Age* now spoke of 'Government apathy and vacillation' and reminded Lyons 'that the Cabinet had to have the best men available'.[66] There was little option and Lyons duly carried out a Cabinet reconstruction on 8 November 1938 in an attempt to staunch the political haemorrhaging.

One of the victims of the political crisis was national insurance. By early November, Casey had accepted 'that there might be a delay in bringing medical benefits into operation'.[67] Reluctantly Casey agreed with Brigden that the initiation of national insurance would have to be delayed from January till April 1939. On 16 November a small amending bill (National Health and Pensions Insurance Bill No. 2 of 1938) was introduced to accomplish this. In the ensuing debates, Arthur Fadden, one of the more colorful CP mavericks, delivered an effective speech on the issue of the appropriateness of national insurance. He described it as an 'expensive venture' at 'a time of mounting defence costs'.[68] Fadden observed that the scheme would cost £12 million while the defence estimates stood at £20 million. Fadden drove his point home later by asking, with defence needs paramount, if the people could afford both.[69]

Casey, alert to the need to secure coalition support for the scheme, sought Cabinet approval to proceed with an amendment which would satisfy the Country party by preparing a scheme for the self employed and small employers. Cabinet approved this request on 8 December.[70] Casey's move seemed to be the best course of action open to him, as no one could have foreseen what would happen.

In January 1939, Casey's attempt to preserve Cabinet solidarity fell apart. Treasury made an authoritative attempt to veto national insurance expenditures for 1939 on the grounds that the extra costs were unjustified.

Discussions in Cabinet were deferred several times following Treasury's veto. Then on 15 February Casey dropped a bombshell. Casey may well have been working with Brigden, following the Treasury vote, on a fall-back position. Their new proposal envisaged a radical dismantling of much of the 1938 Act and a 'new' start. Casey's paper to Cabinet on 15 February entailed the abolition of the most expensive part of the Act, old-age pensions, the retention of the health and medical benefits component, and the introduction of an unemployment insurance scheme with a view to regaining the support of public opinion.[71]

Implicit in his paper to Cabinet was the problem that could not be named: the coalition was at risk of tearing itself apart. Only by oblique means could Casey circumvent the conventions of cabinet solidarity by referring to the terrible prospect of the Labor Party forming Government. (Such a prospect was possible only in the event of a coalition break-up.) Casey argued that the Government was in 'dire straits', and that the campaign of public resistance would mean that '. . . it will be extremely difficult, if not impossible, to bring National Insurance into existence under the present Act. . . The political dangers of attempting to bring the existing Act into operation are clear'.[72]

The whole problem of restoring the image of the Government was epitomised in his final sentence: 'A bold line would create a good impression'. Casey's judgement seems to have been that the political survival of the Government was now more important than the fiscal policy in forming the drive to place old-age pensions on a contributory basis. Yet other factors intervened to frustrate Casey's intentions.

Menzies appears to have been infuriated by this turn of events. Until a comprehensive biography of Menzies is available, the balance of motives behind his action can only be surmised. He may have seen this decision as one more sign of Lyons' lack of political nerve. He may also have seen it as a basis for a challenge to Lyons' leadership. He was almost certainly angered by Page's part in events and saw the CP as a source of much of the vacillation in Government policy. Whatever the mix of motives, Menzies' resignation on 14 May 1939 had one immediate consequence. It neatly undid the whole force of

Casey's political strategy to retain coalition unity and to provide an image of an effective and united government. The resignation of Menzies, heir-apparent to Lyons, reinforced the picture of a divided and brawling Government unable to initiate an Act it had had on the statute books for nearly a year.

Following Menzies' resignation and his return to the backbench, Lyons 'put out feelers' for a National Government, a move rejected by Curtin. And then Lyons fell ill on 5 April, dying two days later in Sydney from a heart attack. Menzies' path to the Prime Ministership was now clear, although it was accompanied by Page's famous attack on Menzies and the collapse of the coalition, events which delighted the Labor opposition.

Menzies was forced to form a minority UAP Government of 28 MHRs, dependent upon the selective support of some fourteen CP MHRs. What had been foreshadowed in the last months of Lyons' life had come to pass, but with no real increase in effective leadership. Menzies was now the leader of a minority Government, elected narrowly to the leadership of a party where there was considerable doubt about his fitness for the office, and where the coalition partner had rejected Menzies as an appropriate leader of a coalition government. With hindsight it is clear that Menzies' leadership, rather than stopping the rot, was integral to the slow decline of the UAP.

Obituary for a strange death

It is commonly held that the national insurance scheme was abandoned in March 1939.[73] However, discussion of the future of the scheme in fact continued on into August 1939 under the aegis of a new Department of Social Services. Only then did it truly die.

The decision to establish a Department of Social Services seems to have had a number of political motives. In the light of his anticipated victory in the UAP ballot, Menzies conferred with Sir Frederick Stewart on the possibility of Stewart entering the Cabinet in charge of the new department. Such an offer would both consolidate Stewart's support for Menzies and provide an administrative framework in which to locate the National Insurance Commission and so resolve any embarrassment while its fate was decided. On 26 April the new Cabinet was sworn in with Stewart as Minister of Health and as Minister for Social Services in charge of the newly established Department.

The new department's origins testify to the political travails of national insurance. It was responsible for the still extant National Insurance Commission as well as for the old-age and invalid pensions benefits schemes.[74] In theory, the new department was to incorporate the Pensions and Maternity Allowance Office then residing in

Treasury under Commissioner A. Metford. (This transfer did not actually occur until April 1941.) Menzies needed to be seen to be keeping faith with his resignation speech of 13 March and his commitment to national insurance. He may also have felt that rather than rewarding Stewart's loyalty, having him in the Cabinet meant his enthusiasm for social services could be better controlled. Finally the new department resolved, at least for the short term, the embarrassment of Brigden's position. As Chairman of the NIC, the future of which was unclear, Brigden's right to expect some continuity of employment could be resolved. Brigden became the first Permanent Secretary of the new department.

While the establishment of the department might be seen as a considerable novelty, when Jill Roe writes that its creation entailed 'the assumption of separate responsibility for social security, and its bureaucratic expression represents a benchmark in the history of social policy',[75] and that now social policy became distinguished from economic policy, she overstates the case. If anything, this separation occurred only as a propaganda device. As will be demonstrated in later chapters, no such separation was achieved, and the subordination of social policy to economic and fiscal criteria was if anything heightened during the war years. Indeed social policy became in part a legitimator of unpalatable economic and fiscal policy. The subordinate relationship of the new department to Treasury reflects the larger subordination of 'social policy' to dominant fiscal criteria.

The new department in its first years was nominal. It lacked policy and research staffing resouces so that through both the Menzies Government and the period of Labor Government, social policy initiatives continued to be developed either within Treasury or in other departments like Labour and National Service. Its chief function initially was to hide from public scrutiny the subsequent dismantling of the machinery of national insurance. The nominalism of Brigden's appointment as Secretary to the department is shown by his appointments in May 1939 as Economic Consultant, and in December as Permanent Head of the Department of Supply and Development, a position entailing onerous duties.

In another respect, the appointment of Stewart as Minister for Social Services provided for a continuous though ambiguous role in social policy in the emergent war economy after 1939. Indeed Stewart himself is an important source of policy continuities, upon which subsequent chapters will elaborate. Stewart remained a persistent advocate for a 'social insurance' or 'social security' scheme right up to the death knell of the UAP Government in 1941.

National insurance remained above all else an embarrassment for the Government. Rearmament radically altered the policy agenda and would complete the process of attrition affecting the 1938 Act. Menzies himself foreshadowed some of the new elements of the political agenda in his first major broadcast after becoming Prime

Minister, when he identified external security as the first priority of his Government.

Stewart did his best to keep national insurance on the political agenda. In a speech in May 1939 he argued that the establishment of the new department signified

> . . . the intention of the Commonwealth Government of giving greater attention than heretofore to the social, economic and physical needs of the Australian people generally, and in particular, its determination to bring into operation a comprehensive scheme of National Insurance.[76]

Stewart identified his own place in the larger liberal framework when he went on to argue that

> . . . a national stocktaking reveals much that . . . is disturbing and in need of correction. And the extent to which corrective action is taken will very largely determine the future influence and destiny of this and other great democratic powers. A vast amount of work and money is needed to remove social ills, to provide better housing conditions, and security against the nightmare of unemployment, malnutrition and ill-health.

Stewart may not have been the first to adopt the terminology of 'social security', which replaced 'social insurance', and which became so dominant during the war years and after, but he was certainly in the vanguard. Its precise meaning and its agency, a rational state with planning capabilities, would be endlessly elaborated over the coming years. If Stewart can lay partial claim to being the architect of the social security theme, he was also a persistent politician, reminding his audience that he was breathing 'new life into National Insurance by developing . . . a new measure which would more completely provide the social security envisaged by the Commonwealth government'.

But his brave words were still being subverted by the march of events.

On 18 May Menzies made his long-awaited statement on the future of national insurance. He intimated that the revised schedule of 4 September was now unlikely, just as it was clear that the 1938 legislation was now dead. All he could suggest was that 'further delay was unavoidable'. He added that 'as there must be delay, the occasion will be used to review the whole scheme . . . I propose to ask Parliament to set up a committee of members of Parliament . . . to examine the subject'.[77]

It was in the light of these statements that Stewart introduced minor bills on 7 and 14 June which sought to suspend most of the legislation and establish a Select Committee to 'produce an enlarged plan to deal with the health of family life in Australia'. It was to be given until 30 September 1939 to report.[78]

Here was an opportunity too good to miss.

The Country Party voted with the Government to suspend the legislation, but then voted with the ALP against the Government to reject the proposal to establish a Select Committee. Stewart's strategy for seeking co-operation collapsed amidst a welter of attacks and innuendoes. Curtin chided the Government for wanting to set up 'yet another committee',[79] while Page made another bitter attack on Menzies.[80] The Country Party then voted to defeat the proposal to establish a Select Committee. Cabinet records reveal that both Stewart and Spender maintained some interest in the matter of 'national insurance' into August 1939. However this flurry of activity in June 1939 may be understood as signifying the public death of national insurance.

If national insurance became a footnote to the history of the 1930s, it was in its context a brave and important instance of the liberal reforming impulse. In its scope and complexity it far exceeded anything which the Labor Government later introduced by way of social policy, and its reliance on the contributory principle hardly distinguishes it from the Labor Government's fiscal proposals for the national welfare fund of 1943. Indeed the very scale of the intervention intended by national insurance left it vulnerable to attack from interest groups affected by the legislation.

If national insurance was a victim of the crisis of confidence which beleaguered the Lyons' Government after October 1938, its demise had been foreshadowed by the strength of opposition from the medical profession and by a campaign of resistance run by some trade unions and the Communist Party. Equally its place in the political priorities of the Government had been redefined by the gathering European crisis, as questions of defence and national sovereignty came increasingly to the fore.

No single factor led to the death of national insurance. Rather the contingent character of a variety of factors points to the fragile balance upon which political legitimacy frequently depends. The product of concern about the viability of Commonwealth finances, national insurance became the first and most notorious of casualties in the redefinition of fiscal policy as the threat of war mounted.

Social policy did not cease to be on the political agenda after September 1939. If anything, the onset of war increased the political attractions of 'social reforms' as war brought forth major new problems of fiscal and organisational policy and with them the need to find solutions. As successive chapters will illustrate, the development of a 'war economy' provided a new context in which social policy was shaped and developed, even as the structural potential of social policy as legitimation for fiscal policy was given continuous, albeit redefined, emphasis. The onset of war too, provides the basis for a comparison between the ALP (after 1941) and the UAP with respect to social policy.

2

'To tax or not to tax': the war economy
and social policy 1939–40

To tax, or not to tax, that is the question:
Whether 'tis easier in the main to suffer
the slings and arrows of expanding credit,
Or to take arms against uprising prices
And by taxation stay them? To tax: to rule:
No more: and, by a tax to say we ban
Inflation and the thousand consequent shocks
Th' economy is open to, 'tis a consummation
Definitely to be wished. To tax, to try;
To try: perhaps to fail: ay, there's the rub:
For in that tax debate what things may happen—
We may be shuffled off the Treasury bench—
Must give us pause. There's one way out
That makes us compromise to lengthen life,
For who could bear to tax both rich and poor
When he himself might this misfortune lose
By a mere compromise. But see you now
The sad Economist! Sage, in thy murmurings
Be not thy sins remembered.[1]

At 9.15 pm on 3 September 1939, Prime Minister R.G. Menzies informed Australians by radio that they were now at war with Germany. Australia's economy, society and government would all be reshaped profoundly during the following six years of war.[2]

The question of the relationship of war to the formation of social policy and the making of the welfare state is of primary importance. In Australia, this relationship has generally been seen in terms of the accession to Government by the ALP after 1941. As Jill Roe notes, '. . . neither that relationship, nor the social history required

to suggest its dimensions have yet been much explored, probably because it had seemed self-evident that Labor was only doing what it
would have done anyway, war or no war'.[3]

Perhaps too many Australian writers have embraced the self-
evident. Here it is suggested that it is important to distinguish between the onset of war and the advent of a Labor government, just as
it is necessary to remember and to examine the achievements of
the UAP Government between September 1939 and October 1941.
Continuities may be found between these two governments which
illuminate the relationship between war and social policy.

On a broader scale this relationship has tended to elicit high-level
generalisations. For W.J. Mommsen it is very simple: '. . . the second
world war and its impact upon the working classes sparked off the
idea of creating a comprehensive system of social insurance that
would include all citizens'.[4] For Richard Titmuss, arguably the first
great social theorist to deal explicitly with the relation of war to social
policy, the answer lay in the pressure for 'a higher standard of welfare
and a deeper comprehension of social justice'.[5] It was a systemic
pressure, because:

> The reality of military disaster and the threat of invasion in the summer
> of 1940 urged on these tendencies in social policy. The mood of the
> people changed, and in sympathetic response values changed as well. If
> dangers were to be shared then resources should also be shared. Dun-
> kirk and all that the name evokes, was an important event in the war-
> time history of the social services. . . The long, dispiriting years of hard
> work that followed these dramatic events. . . served only to reinforce
> the war-warmed impulse for a more generous society.[6]

Titmuss here skilfully weaves a nexus between Britain's welfare state
and the Dunkirk spirit. It is above all, an optimistic account framed
by Titmuss' functionalism, in which the threat to social solidarity
invokes a new-found generosity.

Whatever their merits as social theory, such accounts have forgot-
ten the interplay between real people and the circumstances they confronted and tried to shape. 'Social policy' is one of the things governments do. It must therefore be seen, not as the product of social
system pressures, but as the creation of administrators, politicians
and policymakers. Nor must social policy be put into a special com-
partment of its own but must be seen as part of a larger spectrum of
political and economic issues. The evolution of 'social policy' under
both the UAP and ALP Governments is best seen as part of novel
taxation and fiscal policies, which formed so crucial a part of Australia's war economy. Yet the war economy was no inevitable response
to the war; it was as much a political exercise as a technical exercise in
economics, calling as it did for the mobilisation of popular and electoral support. Social policy played an integral part in the unfolding
war economy, as much because of its capacity to mobilise support for

unpopular taxation policies as because it was seen by the liberal economists and planners as an integral part of their redefinition of Australia's economy. In this respect, it is important to remember the extent to which the architects of the war economy and of the welfare state were drawing both on their experience of the 1930s, and on significant theoretical and ideological commitments.[7]

The origins of a war economy and the liberal planners

Colin Crouch has written: 'In modern wars of total mobilisation, all capitalist societies are corporatist; the need to win the war created an overwhelming moral unity and defines an external enemy so clearly that internal conflicts pale into insignificance'.[8] However useful such a generalisation may be, it does not allow for the possibility that significant 'internal conflicts' may still be present, nor is it clear how war by itself can bring about the moral or national unity yearned for especially by governments or opinion makers. Witness the experience of the 1914–18 war and the divisiveness which had erupted in 1916–17 over conscription. Equally, the politicians and policy-makers of the 1930s were operating in an intellectual milieu affected deeply by the Depression experience.

War provided an overwhelming reason for governments and their advisors to seek national unity. This objective was informed by memories of war and Depression, and by the experience of a capitalist economy with profound structural and class-interest differences. Even in 1939 it was not entirely clear to liberals that war would inevitably invoke national unity, and to this extent the problem of securing unity was always on the margins of the political agenda.

This point was acknowledged by one of the more perceptive of Keynesian economists and a war-time advisor to Australian governments, E.R. Walker. In discussing wages policy in a war setting he located his discussion in the ongoing context of a capitalist economy. He argued that adjustments to the basic wage might lead

> . . . to a further increase in prices to take account of the rise in costs of production; and this requires a further adjustment of wages and so on . . . with no advantage to the wage earner. This is all the more likely if employers attempt to maintain a constant rate of profit on their costs.[9]

In this respect he envisaged no basic alteration in this normal manifestation of labour and capital relations. Yet the achievement of a satisfactory war effort and of national unity hinged on the complete mobilisation of all available economic and human resources. As he put it, 'The extent to which the Government can obtain the co-operation of all classes is a political question, although its outcome may turn on economic conditions'.[10]

What remained unclear in 1939 was the extent to which total war would require any fundamental alteration to the normal structural relationships of a capital economy. As Walker argued,

> War is never . . . carried on regardless of its effects on the rest of national life. Even if the prosecution of the war becomes an end in itself, its effects upon . . . national life have to be taken into account, because they may determine the possibility of carrying on the war. This is . . . the fundamental point of 'total war'.[11]

What was envisaged, however, was a vastly increased role for Government. It was clear there could be no reliance upon the haphazard exigencies of the market to prepare for war. In Walker's eyes it was unrealistic to assume that the UAP Government would, being so 'strongly representative of business interests . . . impose such control.'[12] It was also recognised that the existing state of the art in public administration would not immediately enable the state to assume its prescribed role. Much of the actual planning and consolidation of a 'war economy' rested ambiguously somewhere between the perceived 'inevitability' of a war economy and a recognition of the difficulties involved in actually building one.

To the extent that Australia's liberal intellectuals had evinced an interest in 'planning' as a mechanism for dealing with an economy and a society in deep distress in the 1930s, the onset of war provided them, especially economists, with significant institutional bases from which they could work.[13] The importance of planning had received official rhetorical support some months before the declaration of war, when economic planning was put on the agenda.

On 20 February 1939 a National Planning Conference chaired by the Minister for Defence took place. The Panel on Industrial Organisation summarised the views of many of the advisers present when it argued that, '. . . the potential economic strength of Australia must be mobilised and co-ordinated with some definite pre-established plan. . .'[14]

One of the direct consequences of this conference was a recommendation that a Department of Supply be created. Duly established, the new department acquired a small committee of economists known as the Financial and Economic Advisory Committee which until then had been located within the Defence Department. Popularly known as F and E, this small committee came to play a central role in fiscal policy making.[15] It also provided much of the detailed policy advice on social policy matters in the years up to 1943. F and E accordingly figures in much of this book as the central source of policy analysis and advice which directly shaped much of the social policy of the time.

Even in April 1939 the broad economic and financial aspects of a national war effort were being considered by F and E, which consisted of a chairman, L.F. Giblin, and two other members, Roland Wilson and L.G. Melville. F and E had begun life in December 1938 within the Defence Department, studying and surveying 'the effects on the national, financial and economic structure of the loss of command at sea, and the closing of the trade routes'.[16] On 12 September, Casey (as Minister for Supply) and Roland Wilson (as Economic Consultant to Treasury and a member of F and E), recommended that it transfer to Treasury. At a stroke, Treasury acquired for the first time a small, authoritative nucleus of economic expertise, and F and E remained a source of influence far in excess of anything its informality and size might have implied. In formally approving this change, Acting Treasurer Spender accepted Wilson's definition of F and E as

> . . . a small central thinking committee to which all sorts of problems could be submitted for general advice. Its functions would be purely advisory, as heretofore, and its services would be available to Cabinet, or to any other Department or Committee calling on it for assistance with general economic problems.[17]

Spender made Giblin the full-time, paid Chairman of F and E, charging it with co-ordinating all relevant departmental and advisory work on economic policy.

The relocation of F and E into Treasury also foreshadowed something of the large-scale redefinition of the role of Treasury which followed the war. Until 1939 Treasury had remained essentially an 'in-house' accounting department to the Government, with a well deserved reputation for fiscal orthodoxy. The inclusion of F and E presaged a fairly rapid reorientation of the role of Treasury as an agent of macro-economic management in which the annual budgets, for example, became an instrument of economic policy. Though this would take some little time, the contiguity of Treasury officials and the members of F and E ensured that any influence exerted by F and E would be felt immediately by S.G. McFarlane, Secretary to Treasury. The academic authority of the members of F and E and their individual involvement in policy making since the 1920s gave them a significant edge over the Treasury officials.

As evidence of the growing scope of its deliberations J.B. Brigden, D.B. Copland, H.C. Coombs, R.C. Mills, Sir Ernest Fisk, S.R. Carver and Sir Harry Brown became members of F and E. It was serviced by a succession of young economists beginning with F.H. Wheeler, R.T. Downing, J.F. Nimmo and H.P. Brown, all of whom would win position and influence in the postwar world.

The onset of war gave the economists an important breakthrough. They had certainly been involved informally in the 1920s in advising governments. Their role in the Depression gave them a new public visibility and possibly an unwarranted reputation. Writing in 1936 W.D. MacLaurin argued that whatever success they had had in forming a fiscal policy in 1930–31 was due to the high level of unaninimity on policy issues, the closeness of their association and the political deftness of men like Giblin and Copland. Yet MacLaurin anticipates Schedvin's later caution about overestimating their role when he notes that in the Depression:

> . . . the economists were used only in a haphazard fashion . . . they were called in only on special tasks and with a particular problem to report on. And if they tried to broaden the base of their inquiries . . . governments not infrequently were resentful.[18]

Yet the persistence of key figures like Giblin, self-promotion through vehicles like *The Economic Record*, and the growing confidence in their worth held by men like Lyons and Casey, ensured that by the end of the thirties they remained well placed to advise governments. Their enlarged responsibilities after 1939 provides a suitable close to what in many respects was a Promethean epoch in Australian economics.

Of all the members of F and E, L.F. Giblin, D.B. Copland and H.C. Coombs were undoubtedly the most influential. Each of these men presupposed the moral superiority of a social consensus, based on popular and widespread respect for institutions embodying a common purpose. Each was concerned that inter-war capitalism had failed and must be reformed if the social order was to survive. They were all liberal reformers, genuinely committed to a vision of a more humane, more efficient economy. They were rationalists in the best Enlightenment tradition. Divisiveness, even class conflict, could be resolved or ameliorated by rational analysis which informed gradual, piecemeal institutional change. They were the epitome of the Webb's conception of 'an elite of unassuming experts who could make no claim to superior social status, but content themselves with exercising the power inherent in superior knowledge and large administrative experience'.[19] That they might later be accused of developing their own class interest might have struck them as a blow below the belt; this kind of theoretical reflexivity was a luxury these busy 'unassuming experts' did not allow themselves.[20]

The success of F and E owed much to its chairman, L.F. Giblin, one of the most fondly remembered of all Australian economists.[21] For Roland Wilson, Giblin was 'that fabulous old man', who almost 'single handedly founded an Australian school of political economy and who did more than most to discover, train, aid and encourage its acolytes and prophets'.[22]

Hasluck conjures an equally glowing portrait of Giblin:

> The wisdom and experience of. . . Giblin and his human qualities as well as his professional standing made the small room at the sunny corner of the top floor of West Block, Canberra, where he crouched over his pipe among a litter of papers, not only a cell of economic thought but a place where many departmental and interdepartmental tangles were unwound by honest and straightforward commonsense.[23]

Giblin was the quintessential liberal professional, the traveller on the middle of the road. A some time ex-miner, apple orchardist, teacher, war hero and ex-Labor politician, he became, after his retirement from the Ritchie Chair of Economics at Melbourne University in 1940, the Government's chief economic adviser and remained so for the whole war period.

His working style and his brand of economics avoided radical postures in preference to moderate and sensible programmes of social reform; he had advocated national insurance as early as 1914. His strength was practical policy-making. He was in many aspects the ideal professional economist in the public service; hard working, politically adept and persistent. He was also a cautious and late convert to Keynes' arguments in the *General Theory* of 1936.[24]

Douglas Berry Copland, Giblin's junior by 22 years, provided Giblin with indispensable assistance through the war years. Copland was very much the powerful and committed academic who came early to economics. Born in New Zealand in 1894, Copland was a lecturer in economics at the University of Tasmania in 1917 and became Professor there at only 26. He was Professor of Commerce at Melbourne University from 1924 to 1945, where he established a powerful nexus between applied economic theory, the world of business and advice to governments.[25] With Giblin, he can be credited with forging the professional identity of economics through the Economics Society and its journal *The Economic Record*. With Giblin too, he entered the public arena on the side of fiscal orthodoxy, as chairman of the Committee of Economists and Under-Treasurers which drew up the so-called Premiers' Plan.

Like Giblin and Coombs, Copland was animated by a liberal view of the state as an agent of harmony. Copland's sympathy for the oppressed and downtrodden was an abstracted business. His natural sympathies lay more with the business class. However, he brought to bear his own collage of enthusiasms for an elite administration of technocratic experts advising and guiding a 'free society'. He was ever disdainful of the limited intellects of modern politicians and had no doubt that 'mediocrity triumphs in modern democratic politics'.[26] He saw social reforms like unemployment insurance as a way of restoring 'discipline and unity' to society and never tired of the theme of a 'half-way house' between capitalism and socialism and communism. His own views on social security echo the impatient reformism of the Webbs. Social security was simply part of a rational and disciplinary mode of economic control which would provide

> economic security and a more rigorous handling of the unemployables and those among the underemployed who are malingering. . . It is no use a democracy bravely talking about disciplinary finance . . . and leaving its morons to propagate their species in comfort. This is what the sloppy exponents of a dying system call defending the rights of the people.[27]

The last and youngest of the trio, H.C. Coombs, was just beginning a career in the public service.[28] Coombs shared with Giblin a temperamental non-conformity, a predisposition not ordinarily equated with the successful civil servant. Born in 1906 in the Darling Ranges in Western Australia, Coombs was the eldest son of the railway stationmaster at Kalamunda. He was a scholarship boy at Perth Modern School and worked as a country school teacher between 1924 and 1926. He returned to Perth to complete university degrees before travelling to London (1931–33) where he submitted a doctorate on central banking. His English experience did not incline him to socialism but rather towards a liberal radicalism. Like his colleagues, he believed rational management promised the solution:

> If good management could help sustain a high level of employment and a just allocation of resources between private and social purposes, we could, I believe, look forward to rising standards of material welfare in which even the poorest could share.[29]

For Coombs, the Depression showed that the real problem was a failure in existing management techniques:

> My interest in central banking dated from a period when management had failed . . . when Australia was torn by political controversy about measures to deal with the growing economic problems . . . which developed into the depression of the early thirties.[30]

Keynes' offer to abolish 'divisiveness' by discovering a magical 'common interest' comforted Coombs and his colleagues:

> It was one of the most attractive features of the Keynesian analysis that it seemed to by-pass the most divisive issues within our society. It seemed in everybody's interest that expenditure should be pitched at levels adequate to sustain business activity reasonably close to capacity and so to maintain high levels of employment.[31]

It was Keynes' greatest achievement that he reaffirmed the liberals' faith in a unified society even as he gave them the technique which apparently would realise that 'common interest'.

If Giblin, Copland and Coombs provided a tangible administrative reality to the themes of liberal planning during the war years, the distant but no less powerful presence of John Maynard Keynes can also be discerned in the making of Australia's war economy. As Coombs recalled:

> Whilst the core of the committee remained unchanged, it operated in a fairly informal fashion, and increasingly younger economists, including myself, became involved in its work. It was the work of this committee which progressively gave to the economic planning of the war an essentially Keynesian character.[32]

Keynes' work of the 1930s revealed new possibilities even as it confirmed old hopes. His theoretical framework provided a general orientation as well as delineating the specific problems of a war economy. The consequences of this for social policy were to be far-reaching—and ambiguous.

It would be inaccurate to characterise the response by Australian economists to Keynes in terms of a Keynesian deluge. There was some selection and discrimination. But agreement about Keynes' achievement and acceptance of his main ideas were general. In 1943 Giblin made it clear that a Keynesian answer to unemployment was at hand.[33] Coombs perhaps best summarised the Keynesian impact when he wrote, 'The publication in 1936 of John Maynard Keynes' *General Theory of Employment, Interest and Money*, was for me, and for many of my generation the most seminal intellectual event of our times'.[34]

The responsiveness of these economists to Keynes' theoretical break with orthodoxy is due to a number of factors. Their tendency to conceptualise the Australian economy as a whole, as shown by the work of Colin Clark, who was involved in methodological and substantive inquiry into National Income Accounts, predisposed them to Keynes'.[35] Also, the small-scale and closeknit character of the Australian economics community may explain the rapidity of the 'Keynesian effect'. The excitement in Melbourne in February 1936 that greeted advance copies of *The General Theory* suggests a lively and responsive intellectual culture.

Keynes' *General Theory* also came at a time when many economists were acknowledging the near-bankruptcy of economic orthodoxy. L.G. Melville said in 1934 that no one knew how to put together an adequate policy: economists must '. . . return to their studies and common rooms until they have thrashed this problem out. . .'[36] Keynes provided convincing answers to those in search of renewed clarity. The younger economists responded well to the intellectual iconoclasm of Keynes' inversion of the traditional elements of theory associated with Pigou and Marshall.

Above all else, Keynes held out the promise of a practical policy to deal with unemployment. His treatment of mass unemployment touched the raw nerves of inter-war liberals everywhere and had a powerful effect on those like Coombs and Walker who had emotionally rejected the necessity for unemployment long before they encountered Keynes. The theoretical elegance and the promised practical efficacy of Keynes' work spoke volumes to the progressive liberals of the 1930s. Keynes had indicated why, left to its own devices, a free enterprise economy might never generate sufficient effective demand. (By effective demand, Keynes meant the level of expenditure on all goods and services which clearly affected the need for labour.) The theory indicated the kind of role which the state could play in maintaining effective demand should the private sector fail to maintain a sufficiently high level of expenditure on goods and services. Provided that Government had relevant information on economic performance, it could always intervene to 'top up' effective demand, if need be, by going into deficit budgetary expenditures. Where Adam Smith had put his faith in the 'invisible hand', Keynes proposed to put it in planned rational action by the state.

Australia's war economy gave Keynesians a chance to implement his theories. They did not hesitate to seize that chance and for the duration of the war economic policy was linked with the Keynesian redefinition of the relations between state and economy.

As important as the general reorientation entailed in Keynes' work was the specific direction he imparted to war-economic policy after 1939, a point clearly demonstrated by F and E's planning.

The war economy and the problem of inflation, 1939

It has already been suggested that the evolution of a war economy was no inevitable or functional response to the exigencies of war. D.E. Moggridge summarised the problems confronting the war economists thus:

> Any policy proposal must satisfy. . . four criteria: it must intensify the war effort of the nation by mobilising domestic resources for war and maintaining that mobilisation; it must increase the resources available by drawing as far as possible on unused resources. . . it must make the burdens resulting from these transfers of resources. . . as tolerable as possible; and it must minimise the complications of the war that spill over into the post-war world.[37]

These problems were comprehended by the members of F and E from the first days of war, but the solutions were not immediately forthcoming.

In formal terms it was intended that F and E would study and report on matters referred to it by the Treasurer—or any other Minister—of general economic and financial interest. In practice, as Giblin noted in 1941, '. . . more often action is taken of its own initiative, or on the suggestion of the Secretary of the Treasury. It is the business of the Committee to look ahead and try to see the implications of a constantly growing war effort'.[38]

The inclusion of so many senior advisers in the public service gave it much of its early authority and influence.[39] Formal meetings were held every one or two months, with circulation of papers amongst its members, and smaller informal meetings also took place. As Butlin notes, other courses of action were open to its members. Copland and Giblin already had access to senior ministers including Menzies and Spender. With direct access to Treasury policy channels it became a formidable source of ideas, rapidly overshadowing the Economic Cabinet (introduced by Menzies in December 1939 and one of the first casualties of 1940).

Following a formal meeting on 21 September 1939, the role of F and E as an architect of 'war economy' was established. Giblin wrote in 1947:

> The Committee understood that its job was to look ahead for the difficulties and dangers that were likely to beset our economy as resources were increasingly diverted to war purposes.
>
> [F and E] found that the general problem of the diversion of resources, physical and financial, to war, extended its field of survey to every aspect of the economy from the balance of payments to incentives, to saving, from the conservation of manpower to cash order activities.[40]

F and E discussed most of the basic elements of a war economy, including the redirection of resources to supply the military forces, the supply of manpower to the armed forces and the civilian workforce, the establishment of controls over financial institutions, and international economic issues such as maintaining viable import and export levels.

Perhaps most central to F and E discussions was the question of how the state could pay for the war. In this regard the Keynesian paradigm was soon taken for granted. Not the least of the war economy problems was the perceived need to impose fiscal measures on a fully employed labour force chasing fewer and fewer civilian goods, invoking the spectre of inflation. F and E soon appreciated the complex interplay between fiscal policy and political implementation of that policy.

At its first meeting F and E discussed the need to divert resources rapidly to the war effort, increase the level of employment, and try to restrain the cash income which increased employment would generate when there were fewer commodities in the civilian sector.[41] Giblin and Copland warned of the potential for inflation if and when full employment was achieved. Taxation was suggested to soak up excess income, making it a political issue of the first importance. Copland said, '. . . the problem of course is to persuade Cabinet to accept taxation. Now is almost the time for increased taxation, because there is some competition for resources, which if allowed to continue, must ensure prices continue to rise'.[42]

In objective terms the threat of inflation did not become real until mid-1943. Yet between 1939 and 1943 the economists were predicting it as a consequence of their policies.

The issue of taxation also arose in the context of paying for the war. The Government in 1939 had basically two choices. It could seek voluntary loans from the public or it could increase its direct and indirect taxation. In these first months, F and E advised Treasury that loans would be a suitable preliminary method, but that some increase in taxation should be foreshadowed for 1940, advice the Menzies Government did not want to hear.

As most twentieth century political experience would suggest, taxation policy, which is by definition coercive, depends for its success on being administratively feasible, enforceable and subject to at least grudging acceptance by its victims. Taxation policy in short always entails political evaluation of its potential for securing consent. Successive non-Labor and Labor governments faced major political problems in taking the policy advice coming from F and E for increased taxation. This became apparent in November 1939 when the advisers began to think about ways of making this taxation pill easier to swallow.

On 30 November 1939 Percy Spender, as Acting Treasurer, introduced a revised war budget, which attempted to spell out the detailed principles on which a war economy might run. It deserves greater recognition that it has perhaps had from historians. It is a recognisably Keynesian budget and arguably the first budget whose architects constructed it as if it were to be an instrument of economic management.

In Percy Spender, the effective Treasurer after April 1939, F and E found an efficient, intelligent minister who was sympathetic to the premises on which his advisers were operating. Especially revealing was Spender's reaction to the way in which Treasury Secretary Mac-Farlane had come to him in September 1939 with the budget papers:

> He presented me with a large foolscap piece of paper. . . on which he had worked out what I can only call his sums. . . There was nothing however to indicate a financial policy geared to war or any statement of principle or planning. . . My view was that the Treasury's function went far beyond what appeared to me to be a hand-to-mouth method of budgeting.[43]

Henceforth Spender relied on the advice of F and E, which permeated his revised war budget.

The new budget envisaged a defence expenditure of £62 million, of which £46 million would have to come from loans. The Keynesian ethos lay in both the stress on credit expansion to absorb unemployment and the foreshadowing of later taxation to soak up the extra income resulting from full employment. Heavy initial reliance on loans would avoid disruption to the economy.

The Keynesian influence is also present in Spender's longer term view:

> When our resources are as fully employed as is practicable, and our 'real' national income at its peak, borrowing should not exceed the savings of the people available at any time. Any additional requirements should be drawn from taxation.[44]

Yet in spite of its aspirations, it would be too much to claim that this budget was an effective Keynesian instrument of economic management. It was too fitful a statement of economic intent for that, and it relied on assumptions then little in evidence. The forecast it contained of a co-ordinated war economy, with full use of economic resources, full employment, and restricted civilian consumption, remained just that until the far different context of 1942 catalysed policy-making.

Crisp has suggested that it was not until the advent of Labor after 1941 that the mark of Keynes was made on Australian budgets. While he is correct in his assessment of Keynes' impact on Treasury, Crisp misstates the case by ascribing too much novelty to the Labor Government.[45] The far-reaching 'planning' functions of budgets were being developed even in 1939. Then too the F and E economists were not only regarding taxation as a traditional way to raise revenue, but as part of a machinery to shift current resources from present income earners and so pre-empt inflation. The November budget of 1939 was far from being a perfect example of such thinking but in tandem with Spender's financial statement of May 1940, such a redefinition is clearly evident. This is apparent in the early attempts to analyse economic problems, rationally forecast the likely impact of certain measures, and measure the impact of fiscal, especially taxation and credit expansion activities, all of these hallmarks of the Keynesian approach.[46]

F and E's December meeting saw an emphasis on the need for a taxation policy which would help redirect resources. Giblin spoke of the need '. . . to compel wage earners with very low incomes to make a worthwhile contribution to war expenditure'.[47] Copland had already argued, 'If the war lasts, taxation will be greatly increased, mainly by income taxation at first on higher income, but spreading later to lower incomes'.[48] He insisted too, on the need to avoid any inflation, by which he meant the use of bank credit. Yet Copland, Giblin and others were only too aware of what the F and E minutes referred to as the 'practical difficulties' associated with taxation increases.[49] Copland had already noted in November that 'The main burden [of policy] will thus fall on taxation and loans from current savings but the success of this plan will depend on the state of political opinion'.[50]

The test would come 'when the whole programme has to be financed from normal borrowings and heavy taxation'.[51]

In the months to come the Menzies' Government would experience the difficulties consequent upon the slow but steady disintegration of its political legitimacy. That Government's path to extinction originated in perceptions of Menzies' leadership and in the state of parliamentary politics.[52]

There is little reason to dispute the general view of Hazlehurst that after 1939, Menzies was 'engulfed by the torrent of events. Neither his talents nor his accumulated experience provided sufficient protection'.[53] The manner of Menzies climb to UAP leadership identified him as ambitious and ruthless even as it alienated many potential supporters. Worse, after 1939 he looked less and less like a winner. In non-labor politics, the greatest handicap a leader can carry is to be perceived as a loser. Lyons' lengthy and perhaps idiosyncratic period of leadership was due largely to his image as a winner. But Menzies was unable to staunch the slow ebb of electoral support away from the UAP. Through 1940 he lost the experience and support of R.G. Casey, who went to Washington as a *de facto* ambassador. Menzies was compelled to end his minority Government status and bring the Country Party back into a Coalition Government in March 1940, which merely added new voices to the chorus of critics within his own government. After a number of by-election losses, the final blow came in August 1940 with the Canberra airport crash which killed three of Menzies' senior ministers.

In other respects too, Menzies was unable to overcome some of the elements of novelty confronting both governments and electors since the advent of war. Many of the problems involved in administering a 'total war' were new to the public service, to its temporary advisers, and to the politicians of the day. It is not surprising that innovations like an Economic Cabinet failed, or that resistance to certain measures, like Industrial Registration or the threat of civilian rationing, should thwart the early plans. Until the Blitzkreig of April 1940 ended the 'phony war', there was little to excite enthusiasm for the measures being raised. 'Public opinion' remained in this first year of war a fickle factor in the politics of a war economy.

The slow electoral decline of the Menzies Government had to be taken into account by F and E when trying to develop economic policy. They acknowledged that the first budget exercise was necessarily half-hearted.

Equally, by the end of 1939 all of the economists on F and E were in agreement that the next budget must embody heavy taxation measures as a counter to inflationary pressures. All were agreed that 'full employment' was just around the corner, and with it the threat of inflation. The problem was simple: 'to persuade Cabinet to accept taxation'.[54] Copland reported that Australia had almost '. . . reached full employment and there is already an acute shortage of certain types of skilled labour. . . Accordingly we must now face a combination of heavier taxation and loans obtained from ordinary savings'.[55] Copland, ever the realist, acknowledged that raising new taxation would be difficult:

> . . . We shall have a real test as to whether it is politically possible for a Government in a democracy to obtain the support of the people for deliberate sacrifices. Signs are not wanting that there is already considerable opposition to such measures as moderate rationing [of petrol]. . . The taxation proposals will doubtless meet with much greater resistance involving as they must a considerable increase in rates on higher incomes

and an extension of the field to lower incomes not hitherto taxed by the Commonwealth.[56]

F and E were already considering how much extra taxation would be required to reduce consumption to the level desired in 1940–41.[57] The answer, in the form of some attractive measure of social reform, was at hand. F and E secretary, Frederick Wheeler, commented, 'The practicality of sweetening the pill of substantial taxation on the low incomes by combining it with a scheme of unemployment insurance is under consideration'.[58]

In November 1939 J.M. Keynes had written two long articles for *The Times* entitled 'How to Pay for the War'. With characteristic lucidity Keynes had outlined the very problems Giblin and others were confronting in Australia:

> In peacetime . . . the size of the cake depends on the amount of work done. But in wartime the size of the cake is fixed. If we work harder we can fight better. But we cannot consume more. . . It means, broadly speaking that the public as a whole cannot increase its consumption by increasing its money savings.[59]

Keynes had in mind the problem of adapting the distributive system of a 'free economy' to the limitations of war.[60]

He outlined the three criteria which he believed would sustain an effective war economy, finance the war, soak up excess income and maintain social coherence:

> The first provision . . . is . . . to determine a proportion of each man's earnings which must be deferred—withdrawn—from immediate consumption and only made available as a right to consume after the war is over. . . The second provision is to provide for this deferred consumption without increasing the [post war] national debt . . . The third provision is to protect from any reduction in current consumption those whose standard of life offers no sufficient margin. This is affected by an exempt minimum, or sharply progressive scale [of taxation] and a system of family allowances.[61]

Keynes' proposal sketched out the total income to be withdrawn by way of taxation and by voluntary savings loans, which still left, in his estimation, £450 million to be 'withdrawn'. His scheme gave to the Inland Revenue or Social Insurance offices the task of extracting this additional income. Known as 'deferred pay', this money would be repaid in the post-war period. His notional rates of 'deferred pay' seemed to go no further down the income scale than those on £5 a week or more.

In a crucial passage, Keynes mooted an alternative approach which would resurface in Australia some years later. He suggested that another way to achieve the same effect was to increase income-tax payments, lower the tax threshold to capture lower-income earners, and provide a form of social security like family allowances. This he suggested was a 'sound alternative' which would achieve the same results as his own deferred pay scheme.[62]

Keynes' argument had considerable attraction for his Australian followers. From February to April 1940, F and E considered it as part of a larger exercise of trying to devise a solution to the political difficulties of imposing higher taxation. But for reasons which are not entirely clear, in April 1940 it rejected the proposals 'as a poor substitute for a simple increase in income tax'.[63] Even so, discussion centred on proposals for taxation schemes which did not look like taxation schemes.

Roland Wilson had proposed a compulsory scheme of public loans which would capture the excess of war-time incomes (as against peace-time incomes). At a meeting on 5 March, Giblin rejected this option, suggesting it had no advantage over a simple excess-income tax scheme. Melville spoke for all the members, it seems, when he affirmed their fear that such a scheme would arouse as much opposition as any simple taxation increases.

Far more weight was attached to a proposal first mooted by Coombs in December when he had suggested the use of an unemployment insurance scheme tied to increased taxation.[64] Both Coombs and Copland had strong arguments in favour of such a scheme.[65] Coombs later wrote:

> . . . there must be a reduction in expenditure from all private incomes including those down to £150 pa. This might be done by taxation, some of which might be debited as contributions to Unemployment Insurance fund at about the rate of £6m. p.a. It would be safe to say that payments out of this fund would be small during the war years and that the remainder would be invested in loans. This would reduce private consumption.[66]

Certainly the proposal to reach down to incomes of £150 per annum (i.e., incomes less than the basic wage) was fraught with political dangers. D.B. Copland, ever the political realist, argued for an unemployment insurance scheme on largely political grounds. He noted that he was making the proposal only 'because of the need to meet a political difficulty'.[67] Beginning with the premise that increased taxation on low incomes would arouse deep opposition, Copland argued for a scheme which 'divided the taxation into income tax and a social insurance tax'.

Here Copland foreshadowed the essential logic of the Labor Governments National Welfare Fund exercise of 1943. It exemplifies continuities in policy advice underpinning the apparent shift in political character following the change of government in 1941. As Copland pointed out, to incorporate an unemployment insurance contribution into the income system would have the added virtue of not only appearing to conform to ALP policy on this matter, but would also:

1 effectively reduce consumption now
2 be capable of stimulating consumption and investment . . . when the economy requires it
3 provide at least rough justice to the wage earner and be acceptable to him[68]

The majority of F and E members thought that this scheme 'would not make it appreciably easier to get the total contributions and all were agreed that any unemployment scheme which was not strictly contributory would raise very difficult [post war] problems'.[69] Even so they agreed that an unemployment insurance scheme had virtues 'as a method of finance under the present circumstances [that] were recognised'. Their review was going on in the context of pre-budget planning in which proposals to tax incomes down to £150 per annum were being drawn up. The connection between increased taxation and an unemployment insurance scheme was obvious, and Giblin argued that '. . . some wage earners would not be slow to interpret . . . that they pay the whole cost of the scheme, whereas under previous schemes they were called on to pay only a third'.[70] Melville and Wilson both strongly argued against tying any unemployment insurance plan to the tax proposals.

The result of these lengthy discussions was a compromise. F and E recommended that unemployment insurance be kept 'separate from taxation [but] should be considered as part of the Government's financial policy'.[71] The Committee agreed that the Coombs-Copland proposal would not help win assistance for increased taxation, which might indeed suffer by association with the failed national insurance plan. Even so, it was agreed that unemployment insurance could be proposed independently of the tax proposals, since it was clear that contributions to an unemployment insurance plan would function as taxation.

Immediately the relatively weak and insignificant Ministry of Social Services intervened. Its Minister, Sir Frederick Stewart, held discussions with Spender and Giblin. On 11 March, at the second round of Economic Cabinet seminars, Stewart presented a paper to the Cabinet calling for an immediate start to a scheme of social services, including unemployment insurance.

Stewart's paper stressed the benefits which might accrue from the social reforms he was proposing, but he was mindful of the political context for a Government facing a general election:

As our Government . . . has now held office for three terms, it would be natural, in the ordinary course of events, for the pendulum to swing against us. I know there is a confident hope that the exigencies of war . . . will help us . . . [but] I feel that we would be very unwise to repose our hopes in that direction. I believe however that it is possible for our Government, by a very strong social policy, to consolidate itself in public favour, whether the election comes in three months or nine. . .[72]

Stewart's paper proposed a broad range of initiatives though the bulk of it concerned unemployment insurance and the link between fiscal policy and the scheme in the way F and E had developed: 'If, as is now being advanced by economic experts, compulsory savings by the workers are essential to war finance, such a policy is more likely to win support when savings are invested in an Insurance fund'.

He was not hesitant in promoting the scheme on the grounds of 'political expediency'. As he noted, 'full employment was just around the corner'. It would cost the Government perhaps £1 million while the revenue—of approximately £6 million—'. . . would be available [because of the absence of unemployment] for investment by the Trustees of the fund, in the Government war effort, reducing to that extent the necessity for direct taxation'. It was a persuasive case.

The Economic Cabinet agreed to refer the matter to full Cabinet. Here on 27 March Spender received permission to explore the matter further. At this meeting Spender's Cabinet paper clearly reflected the advice of F and E. It accepted the need for increased taxation and the political need to justify such an exercise. It also reflected the decision in F and E to split increases in taxation from unemployment insurance 'because of doubts as to whether its introduction would make the taxation proposals more acceptable'. Spender observed that any extension of taxation to lower incomes was risky, adding 'that careful consideration has been given . . . to off-setting that burden to some extent by introducing a system of unemployment benefits'.[73] Spender made the crucial observation that it did not really matter whether the two proposals were linked or not: '. . . financially, whether the funds are collected by taxation or by contributions, the effect would be to reduce expenditure now, particularly in fields of income which it is difficult to approach in other ways'.

He was careful to stress the benefits to the Government: 'Because Unemployment is so low, the greater part of the unemployment fund would be available for defence purposes through investment in Government loans'.

Cabinet agreed. Unemployment insurance was henceforth under active consideration until the end of May 1940, when Coombs was given the job of preparing an analysis of its use in fiscal management. As was frequently the case in investigations of social policy options, the Minister for Social Services and his department were not involved.[74] Invariably it was a matter for Treasury and F and E, and this administrative division speaks volumes about the subordination of social policy to fiscal policy. Following a Cabinet enquiry into the progress being made about unemployment insurance on 10 May,[75] Coombs presented his report to S.G. McFarlane on 21 May 1940.

Whereas in March Coombs had supported the idea, he now effectively damned the utility of an unemployment benefits scheme as part of a larger fiscal programme. He provided a persuasive and detailed case. He examined the alternative bases of a contributory and tax-based scheme and found they would not reduce civilian consumption by significant amounts, perhaps by only £3 200 000 per annum, an amount which 'would be no substitute for other measures if the war effort is to be intensified. Unemployment insurance is not a viable means of enforcing large reductions in consumption'.[76] At the same time he allowed that political factors might counter-balance this: '. . . if the non-contributory scheme was put to the public as a great measure of social amelioration, it would be accepted and would strengthen the position of any government which introduced such a measure'.

Coombs conceded that such a scheme would make increased taxation more agreeable, which 'on the grounds of war necessity, would be infinitely more acceptable to the working class'. In his summary, he revealed the strength of his liberal convictions thus: 'As unemployment insurance cannot greatly affect war finances . . . the reasons for its introduction must be largely political—to consolidate the unity of the nation by genuine reform'.

For Coombs, as for many of his colleagues, social policy measures were an expression of their commitment to social reform. Yet they cannot have been unaware of the political value of such schemes when linked to fiscal policy designed to enhance the war effort, or of their value in promoting social consensus. 'National unity' achieved by 'genuine reform' would become the central motif in the liberal ideology of post-war reconstruction; This would be Coombs' enduring achievement as Director of Post-War Reconstruction. On this occasion, however, considered as part of a fiscal measure, Coombs was not able to recommend its adoption.

Coombs' analysis revealed the relative inefficiency of unemployment insurance as a fiscal measure and spelled its demise. Unemployment insurance was now shuffled off the political stage and into the wings to await its recall in 1943. F and E were left with the task of trying to persuade the Menzies Government to adopt alternative taxation prescriptions, a task which fell before the ruthless imperatives of electoral politics. The best that F and E could achieve were the rhetorical affirmations contained in Spender's Financial Statement of May coupled to an absence of any real mechanism to achieve its aims.

If the economists had hopes for a stronger, more assertive Government, the results of the federal election in September 1940 dashed them. The elections confirmed the erosion of support for the UAP-CP Government without actually evicting it from office. The drift of support was greatest in NSW, and left the Menzies Coalition Government without a majority and dependent for its survival upon the support of two independents, while the ALP emerged stronger after September with the election of J.B. Chifley, Dr. H.V. Evatt and A.A. Calwell, all future leaders of the Party. Another year of intrigue, ambiguity and the ebbing fortunes of the UAP, however, lay between it and government. In that time the frustrations of the advisers would mount.

This detailed account of an abortive policy-making exercise is important for its illustration of themes and motives that would recur through the war years.

Conceived within highly theoretical and political terms, the 'war economy' was the product of discernible intellectual and political processes. In particular, a small but influential group of liberal-Keynesian advisers confronted their political masters with options requiring unpalatable political decisions. Social policy entered the political arena in part as a way of making hard-edged fiscal policy proposals more palatable to politicians and to the electorate alike. For a variety of reasons, the social policy options of 1939–1940 were not destined to be taken up. Yet the historian cannot help but be intrigued that such proposals would be developed by a non-labor government. In terms both of their substance and political rationale, there are important continuities visible between 1939 and 1941 and the years of Labor ascendancy.

3

'Avoiding a kick in the rear': child endowment and the war economy, 1940–41

On 16 January 1941, Prime Minister Menzies indicated his Government's intention to introduce 'some proper scheme of child endowment to deal with the case—which is recognised as possessing difficult features—of the basic wage as it applied to wage earners with substantial family obligations'.[1] In March, his Minister for Labour and National Service, H.E. Holt, described the proposal as 'evidence of the Government's determination to make Australia a better place to live in—a place worth working and fighting for'.[2] Thus was introduced the first real innovation in Australian social policy during the war and the last major instance of non-labor welfare policy until 1949.

Given its intrinsic significance it is surprising that it has not attracted more critical attention. The traditional tendency has been to include it in the linear sequence of reforms which make up the history of Australia's 'welfare state',[3] although there has been some suspicion that political motives may have played a part in its introduction. Claudia Thame wrote that it was 'mainly a political gesture by the United Australia Party government which had a very narrow majority and was attempting to gain Labor's agreement to the formation of a National Government'.[4]

Bettina Cass has provided the best account of the origins of child endowment proposals, locating them in a class and gender discourse about 'family wages' designed to reinforce the dependency of women in working-class families after 1907.[5] Yet while such a feminist account is right to stress longer-term structural contexts, it does not really address the issue of why child endowment was introduced or what its architects thought they were doing. While it is important to

45

acknowledge the role of patriarchy, we need also to acknowledge the role of the historical actors most involved in 1940 and 1941. The 'deep structures' of patriarchy and the specific articulation of laborist policies after 1901 have been recently explored by Francis Castles.[6] He contends the preference of the union movement and of the ALP to protect wage earners' conditions via the Arbitration Court, wage arbitration and restrictive immigration policies goes much of the way to explaining the avoidance in Australia of universal, contributory social security schemes. Equally the preference for a 'basic wage' programme suggests why Australia was interested in child endowment so early.

The relationship between Australia's wage-fixing system and child endowment nicely illustrates Cass' general proposition that:

> . . . the history of attempts to introduce child endowment as a 'social policy' illustrates well the contention that social policy cannot be separated from economic policy and that the political definition of a measure as 'social' very often hides its economic purpose.[7]

The introduction of child endowment also further reveals the political virtuosity of the economists involved in the Finance and Economy committee, who saw in child endowment a weapon with which to fight the enemy of war-time inflation.

Child endowment and the basic wage, 1907–29

The basic wage decision of 1907 by the first President of the Arbitration Court, H.B. Higgins, proved a problematic achievement, if only because it had by 1920 led the way to substantial criticism of his judgement about the adequacy of his 'basic wage'. Higgins' shrewdness in using a legalist interpretation of the Excise Tariff Act of 1906 has long been admired. In the course of refusing H.V. McKay of the Harvester Company a certificate of remission because he did not provide his workers with a 'fair and reasonable wage', Higgins was able to make a ruling about such a wage. Higgins adopted a standard based 'on the normal needs of the average employee as a human being living in a civilised community'. Higgins took the average family to be 'about five people'. After a somewhat cursory examination of some 'typical' household budgets, Higgins ruled that a weekly wage of £2/2/0 would provide that minimum and frugal level of subsistence below which no civilised community could go, hoping that this would also establish what he called 'comparative wage justice' for all workers in any particular industry. (He appears to have used the wage rates being paid by 'good employers' as his indicator.) Higgins' Harvester Judgement 'became the major watershed in the history of Australian wage determination'.[8]

There can be little doubt that Higgins' intentions in delivering the Harvester Judgement involved a partial attempt to place the wages of unskilled labour on a needs basis instead of allowing only market criteria to determine the level of wages. In this he was temporarily successful, even if in the longer term the principle of industry's ability-to-pay returned to the wage-fixing forums. The significance of the Arbitration Court's wage-fixing role, its origins in a political climate sensitive to political and class compromise, and the potential of trade-offs between capital and labour have been well documented and require no elaboration here.[9]

Complaints about the inadequacy of the basic wage had become numerous by the end of the First World War. The Hughes' Government, in announcing its decision to establish a Royal Commission to enquire into the basic wage, did so in the context of the run-up to the 1919 federal elections and amidst a wave of unprecedented industrial militancy by unions. 1919 saw the greatest number of working days lost through strikes since records were first kept, largely in response to significant localised unemployment, falling wages and reduced output as the economy adjusted to peace-time.

Hughes established the Royal Commission on 19 December 1919 under the chair of A.B. Piddington with representatives of labour and capital. It presented its report on 19 November 1920.[10] It was instructed to enquire into and establish a desirable standard of living at the time for a man, wife and three children. It was also to report on the actual cost of living over the last five years. Finally it was to suggest how the basic wage could be automatically adjusted to the rise (or fall) of the purchasing power of the currency.[11]

The life and work of its Chairman, Albert Bathurst Piddington (1862–1945), show him to be an exemplary liberal reformer.[12] He was a zealot for modernity, science and rationality, seeing the state as the servant of inter-class harmony. With a taste for controversy, he supported birth control and sex education, racial and sexual hygiene being linked in his view to the sanctity of the family and the central role of women as the 'guardians of the race'.

Piddington, like many other progressive liberals, was concerned also to promote inter-class harmony. He was convinced that the existing industrial arbitration system was failing: '. . . it is not to be wondered at that industrial arbitration has failed to prevent strikes for higher wages. The wonder is rather that the system has been as much respected by workers as it has been'.[13] Like other liberals, he was able only to locate the problem in the machinery set up to deal with it, which is to say that the logic of his position held that it was a failure in the arbitration system which led to strikes, low wages and the rest. The possibility that the problem lay in the whole structure of capitalist productive processes and relationships was not considered. If there was 'actual insufficiency of existing wages to enable families to live in frugal comfort', then the arbitration system must be improved.

At the centre of Piddington's argument was a view that Higgins' judgement of 1907 was inadequate. The wage of £2/2/0 provided '. . . a reasonable standard of comfort for a married couple with only one child [but] that then and ever since, any larger family has been obliged to live at a standard below what is reasonable'.[14] The Harvester case of 1907 had been heard quickly, he said, with little empirical investigation into the cost of living. Higgins had rationalised a case for a wage of seven shillings a day on the grounds that this was the going rate paid by 'better' employers at the time.

Following a detailed review of current and historical costs of clothing, food and rent, the Commission concluded that if the weekly cost of living for a family of four in 1914 stood somewhere between £3/6/1 (in Hobart) and £3/13/11 (in Perth), then by 1920 the cost of living ranged between £5/6/2 (in Brisbane) and £5/17/0 (in Sydney).[15] Piddington was careful to avoid any explicit claim in that the establishment of the actual cost of living 'according to a reasonable standard of living' need be read as an argument for a basic wage of the same order.

Hughes asked G.H. Knibbs, the Commonwealth Statistician, to establish the costs of using the new 'living standard' as a formula for the basic wage. Knibbs quickly rejected Piddington's 'living standard', arguing that:

> Such a wage [Piddington's average of £5/16/0] cannot be paid to all employees because the whole produced wealth of the country including all that portion of produced wealth which now goes in the shape of profit to employers would not . . . yield the necessary weekly amount.[16]

How Knibbs arrived at this conclusion is not known and how valid it was, given the complete absence of any national income accounts, must remain conjectural.

With this problem confronting him, Piddington devised, in some haste and without referring to his colleagues, an elegant and sophisticated solution to the problem, which he outlined in a Memorandum to Hughes. His object was to salvage as much of his report as possible, but without the disadvantage of seeming to promote higher costs to employers.

Piddingtons' Memorandum began with some elementary analysis. He noted that the living wage was designed to provide a wage level capable of ensuring a minimum standard of living for an average family. However he noted that all families with more than three dependent children suffered from privations, whilst all families with fewer than three children, and all unmarried men, received more than was apparently necessary. He drew on the 1911 Census to indicate the actual diversity of Australian families, as against the imputed average family presupposed by the basic wage. His solution set out to remedy this defect. Disregarding the likely objections from unions, Piddington proposed to redefine the family basis used to calculate the basic wage from its two adults plus three children model, to a family unit of two adults only. With this family unit in mind he proposed a basic wage of £4/0/0 a week. For each child in a family he proposed an additional sum of twelve shillings in the form of a child endowment payment, financed by a tax on employers. (This tax would be a flat tax of ten shillings and nine pence per week per employee, which would produce the £27 900 000 per annum needed to pay the 900 000 or so dependant children their twelve shillings per week.) Employers would, he reckoned, be much further ahead under such a scheme, as they would not have to pay £5/16/0 per employee but only £4/10/0 per employee if their tax was included.

In Piddington's case, disinterested benevolence and an interest in class harmony seemed to blend together, as shown by his observation:

> . . . it is important to remember that all the propogandist material either for strikes or for revolutionary change comes invariably from the privations of the family. It is the wives and the children who as they suffer most, so they furnish the readiest and most poignant illustrations of industrial injustice. . .[17]

The Government of W.M. Hughes was not swayed by Piddington. In November 1920, Hughes firmly ruled out any possibility that a basic wage set at £5/16/0 could be introduced, though he reserved judgement on the scheme contained in Piddington's Memorandum. Hughes and his Government were however sufficiently impressed by the logic of the proposal to use it in their response to a campaign for higher wages by Commonwealth public servants. Piddington subsequently observed of this, 'It silenced all agitation'. It proved to be the end of the road for Piddington's compromise solution. He was led to adopt a more public posture with the publication in 1921 of his book, *The Next Step*, in an attempt to keep the issue alive.

If Hughes had hoped that the appointment of the Royal Commission would be seen by the unions as a token of good intentions, the strategy backfired. The Commission's findings proved a constant embarrassment to Governments and employers through the 1920s. It provided an endless stream of arguments in favour of union claims for higher wages. Piddington's Commission had done its job too well in documenting the gap between living costs and existing levels of wages. This gap was widened by the departure of Higgins from the Arbitration Court in 1921 and by the movement of the Court's judgements towards a 'capacity of industry to pay' principle, finally embodied in the 1930 wage reduction decision.

These industrial relations problems informed the Bruce-Page Government's attempt to use the relationship Piddington had drawn between the basic wage and child endowment. In his policy speech of October 1925, Bruce had casually referred to child endowment and had promised to refer the matter to state arbitration or Wages Board. This reference rebounded on him in 1926 as various welfare and womens' lobby groups pressured him to take more decisive action.

Early in 1927 Bruce indicated in a letter to the Premiers his intention to raise the matter of child endowment and adjustments to the basic wage at a Premiers' Conference scheduled for June 1927. In this he had the support of C.H. Wickens, the Commonwealth Statistician.[18] There can be little doubt that Bruce's interest in child endowment lay in its potential, discussed in Piddington's 1920 memorandum, to simultaneously reduce the basic wage and be seen to support a popular social reform.

The subsequent Premiers' Conference in June 1927 saw a hostile group of Labor Premiers rejecting his appeal for co-operation.[19] That Bruce had linked child endowment and the basic wage was clear from the start. In his opening address to the Premiers, he alluded to the failure to win for the Commonwealth centralised powers to adjudicate Australia's industrial relations. As he put it 'If the powers . . . had been granted [this] would have enabled child endowment to be dealt with on a national basis as part of that system'.[20] However his proposal that the states take on the responsibility to establish voluntarily a unified scheme of child endowment which was tied to some reduction of the basic wage was in hindsight not likely to be successful. Several times he noted that 'Every state of course has power to deal with the basis on which the living wage is determined, and to provide for an alteration to cover child endowment'.

Near the end of his speech he put the proposal which drew on that of Piddington (which had been adopted in NSW in 1926). He called for, '. . . a uniform basis of wage regulation in all states adopting the one family unit, namely a man and his wife, and superimposing provision for child endowment'.

He was proposing a radical alteration in wage fixing. He was suggesting a general reduction of the basic wage for all wage earners without families by making the needs of a man and wife the unit of wage determination and using endowment to 'top-up' the incomes of larger families. But he was in a vulnerable position in leaving it to the states to adopt. He also failed to comment on the likely political disgrace for Labor Governments should they agree to what was in effect a reduction in the basic wage. The Victorian Labor Premier, E.J. Hogan, said to Bruce:

> The only proposal submitted is . . . for the readjustment of the wage level. Whether the Victorian industrial organisations would approve of readjusting the wage unit so that single men would receive less, in order to provide for child endowment, I am not able to say.[21]

It soon became clear that the states would reject the Prime Minister's proposals out of hand, so a face-saving formula, a Royal Commission, was proposed. The Commissioners were formally appointed on 30 September 1927.[22] The Commission was asked to report on whether or not a scheme of child endowment was warranted and if so how such a scheme should be financed.

From the start the Commission was split into factions. O'Halloran, Evans and Mills produced a majority report condemning child endowment, and Curtin and Muscio produced a minority report in favour of it. The divisions within the Commission were undoubtedly serious, and may have affected the quality of the reports, especially of the majority report, which lacks the careful empirical analysis of Piddington's 1920 Report. It firmly rejected any child endowment scheme because 'the additional taxation necessary to finance from public revenue a scheme for full maintenance of dependent children . . . would cause disastrous reactions'.[23] These would include rises in the cost of living and additional unemployment. Relying on the theme of resistance to state intervention, the report continued, 'by removing from parents all financial responsibility for their children, parental responsibility would be weakened, incentive to thrift and effort reduced, and the sense of unity of interest between parents and children lessened'.[24]

The minority report prepared by Curtin and Muscio foreshadowed much of the post-war reconstruction ethos, even as it fully supported that liberalism of Higgins and Piddington which argued that 'some system of Family Allowance is thus the logical corollary of the living wage doctrine which is in theory the principle underlying our present methods of wage fixing'.[25] In many respects their report is a repository of the commonsense of liberalism in the inter-war years:

> The importance of the well-being of children to the nations is not confined to any class: it involves all children. It is the family life that more than any other contributes most powerfully to the development of human beings.[26]

It followed, in their view, that such a vital social function should be supported as a shared cost by the community: 'To differentiate between families, in any system of family allowances because of the occupation of the breadwinner, would diminish the national benefit, and also be unjust to a large number of children'. They were confident that a world of greater 'social security' was at hand. They held that income security must be the necessary basis upon which other projects like better access to health care or housing had to be built:

> . . . the extension of services, whether medical or dental, or . . . the building of decent houses, which benefit families irrespective of their size will do nothing to abolish the hardships of large families as compared with smaller ones'.[27]

Such an argument prepared the way for a recommendation that again largely followed the logic of Piddington's proposal to reduce the family unit (and so the basic wage) to a unit of man and wife, and then top-up with endowment. However, they rejected Piddington's model. They rejected the propositions (adopted in NSW) that industry be taxed by pay-roll tax and that the family unit of the basic wage be reduced. Curtin and Muscio argued that either way such a scheme would discourage higher wages or create 'an unfair burden on industry'. They preferred a simple child-endowment scheme paid for out of increased taxation achieved by lowering the tax threshold on income tax to bring in more lower-income-tax payers. Their own proposal to lower the tax threshold, they believed, would generate the extra £4 500 000 per annum needed for the scheme they envisaged. They proposed taxing those wage earners—without dependants—on incomes down to £200 per annum. Their solution was a prefigurement of the reality of the later welfare state; the costs of the social services were to be borne by taxpayers so that by means of a progressive tax imposed on higher-income earners or on low-income earners without dependants, a benefit could be conferred on large families. In no way was there any impingement on the processes of capital accumulation itself, or the fundamental social inequalities of Australian society.

At one point the two commissioners touched on income inequality. They cited Sutcliffe's estimates that 68.7 percent of breadwinners earned less than £200 per annum, while 4¼ percent earned 22 percent of the national dividend. Yet they showed no interest in asking why such a pattern of inequality should exist or how their own proposals dealt with this income inequality. In any event, the minority report sank quickly from sight, while the majority report reinforced the Bruce Government's stand that as the Commonwealth did not have central arbitral powers it was not interested in child endowment.

At a Conference of State Ministers in May 1929, Bruce requested but failed to persuade the states to voluntarily cede their powers. Bruce replied by proposing not only an end to child endowment but the withdrawal by the Commonwealth from the arbitral field—with the exception of the maritime industries. In the resulting political uproar, his government went to the polls, and Bruce lost Government and his own seat. Child endowment was thus removed from the political agenda. It would not return until 1940.

If in the inter-war years, several lines of argument and policy had linked the problems of the basic wage and proposals for child endowment, there was no guarantee that these lines would intersect and produce any real outcome. The new problems of the war economy, however, were to ensure that child endowment re-emerged on the policy agenda.

Child endowment and the basic wage, 1940–41

By late 1940 the advisers to the Menzies Government had to confront the first real test of their capacity to solve an emerging conflict of policy, which was to implicate child endowment. Child endowment had risen and again sunk from sight in mid-1940 as the search continued for a mix of increased taxation and some social policy sweetener.[28] However, a more pressing problem was to give child endowment a new lease of life.

As Copland and Giblin had been pointing out through 1940, the increases in employment and the growth of real wages were coinciding with a continuous heavy demand for labour and a dwindling supply of (male) labour. This was a labour-sellers' market and a recipe for militant wage demands. Trouble centred on the New South Wales coal fields. Industrial strikes involved a loss of 1 507 252 working days in 1940, of which 1 371 382 had been lost in the coal fields. Production of coal was reduced by 1 800 000 tons for 1940. Industrial action had accompanied the ACTU wage case for an increase in the basic wage, for which hearings by the Arbitration Court began in August 1940. Copland pointed out that, 'Up until October (1940) it could almost be said that all elements of the economic system other than labour had been brought under control'.[29] Labour was free to get what it could under the system, he said, which virtually left it free to strike. Never a friend to the labour movement, he adopted an 'objective' stance when he went on to argue that:

> In many of these matters labour was merely making up for lost time . . . Labour is just as interested or disinterested in the war effort as are the wheat farmers, the great retail stores, the coal owners or the brewers, or in fact any other class.

This appears to have been a rare instance when Copland acknowledged the reality of a class-structured society, and the ongoing conflict of interests which not even war could do much to quieten.

By January 1941, after months of what was seen as an unreasonable delay in hearing the case, unions began a campaign to have overtime wages exempted from income tax. In both New South Wales and Victoria, key unions carried resolutions putting a ban on all overtime. The New South Wales Trades and Labour Council endorsed this ban and condemned taxation of wage earners, 'which reduces the living standard of the working class. We call upon all unions to join in a campaign to compel the withdrawal of this taxation. . .'[30]

It was this which the advisers had anticipated. The unions wanted a wage increase, which would be inflationary, but to not grant a wage increase could have dire industrial consequences and affect the war-effort.

A strategy to remove themselves from this dilemma came from

within the Department of Labour and National Service, and from the coterie of economic advisors, especially from the Office of the Economic Consultant to the Prime Minister, D.B. Copland. The strategy was to defer any increase in the basic wage, and to introduce a child endowment scheme.

It was significant, recalling Bruce's dilemma in 1927, that the linkage of the basic wage and child endowment followed the decision of 16 December 1940 to issue the National Security (Industrial Peace) Regulations. At a stroke these regulations resolved the 40-year-long problems of dual authority in federal industrial relations and gave to the Commonwealth Arbitration Court an undoubted pre-eminence and authority for the duration of the war.

This change was brought about by F and E, which had been advocating the establishment of a Department of Manpower. Following the elections of 1940, F and E renewed its advocacy: 'the establishment of a Ministry of Manpower and National Service was more urgent than when it was first recommended'.[31] As they saw it, '. . . transfers and increases of available labour power were an essential means of reducing the inflationary tendency of the financial programme'.[32]

Their urging coincided with other pressures and Menzies agreed to this advice by creating a Ministry of Labour and National Service under H.E. Holt. Roland Wilson was given the job of Director General of this new instrument of labour planning, which he formally took up on 13 November 1940.[33] In the long term Wilson and his department were to preside over unprecedented extensions in the power to direct labour which amounted after 1942 to industrial conscription. In the short term Wilson became a key figure firstly in extending the jurisdiction of the Arbitration Court and then in the child endowment strategy.

The business of adjudicating wage claims remained in the hands of the Arbitration Court. The Commission had adjourned the Basic Wage Case on 28 November 1940 and gone into recess for Christmas, so giving it additional time to consider its judgement. It is not possible to say what kinds of conclusions, provisional or otherwise, its members had arrived at during the hearings. To read back from their decision handed down on 7 February 1941 to the period before 28 November would be to beg very many questions, especially in the light of certain interventions that were made in December 1940.

Certainly the Government, after the establishment of the Department of Labour and National Service, had made clear its opposition to any wage increase. Wilson subjected the union case for an increased basic wage to detailed and unrelenting scrutiny.[34] The case against any increase to the basic wage was seen entirely in terms of its likely contribution to inflationary pressures. Yet the Government's advisers recognised that politically it was not advisable simply to reject the unions' case out of hand. There was at least one argument before the end of 1940 that the Arbitration Court be encouraged to defer a judgement on the matter until June 1941 with the Government dealing with the political implications of such a move by introducing a deferred pay scheme based heavily on the Keynes plan of November 1939.[35] This scheme did not reappear in any of the subsequent manoeuvres to persuade the Arbitration Court not to grant an increase of the basic wage.

Though not all of the details of what took place in December 1940 or January 1941 are yet available, there is enough evidence to suggest collusion between the Government and the Arbitration Court, in which child endowment became in integral part of the political trade-off. As Labor MHR, J. Drakeford put it, 'A clue to the reasons which actuated the courts' decision may be the fact that the Government announced its intentions about child endowment while the courts' decision was pending'.[36]

Initially the key players were a young economist, Richard Downing, and the aging Chief Judge of the Arbitration Court, George Beeby. Downing was a protege of D.B. Copland and L.F. Giblin. He had come from Cambridge only half way through 1939, having completed a lengthy analysis of Australia's wage-fixing mechanisms and principles.[37] In December 1940 he was on leave prior to taking up a position as Copland's personal assistant in Canberra.

Wilfred Prest recalls that in December 1940 Downing 'was generally thought to be in some sense a consultant to Justice Beeby', adding that Downing 'wrote a memorandum on the relative merits of a wage increase v. child endowment'.[38] It is not entirely clear in what respect Downing was a consultant to Beeby. The evidence, such as it is, suggests that Copland used Richard Downing as a 'go-between' in discussions between the Government and the Arbitration Court in the person of Justice Beeby. Professor H.G. Burton recollects being present in the Beebys' house in St Kilda Road when Downing visited to discuss his memorandum with Judge Beeby. Here, 'Downing put to [Beeby] the case for deferring the increase in the basic wage . . . on condition that the Commonwealth government introduced child endowment paid for by a payroll tax'.[39]

Perhaps Downing was operating under instructions from his mentor, Copland, or acting in the spirit of the F and E discussions, but his intervention seems to have been the catalyst for an extraordinary response by Beeby, who committed himself to a 'private communication' to the Minister for Labour and National Service, H.E. Holt.

In this communication, Beeby identified the concerns which had led him to approach the Government.[40] He outlined six major arguments for deferring a judgement on the basic wage until June 1941, providing that the Government introduced a child endowment scheme. He indicated that his chief concern was to avoid any extension of industrial strife which could erupt should the case for an increase in the basic wage be rejected.

Beeby clearly expressed his own variation on a long standing theme—the problems involved in economic management—so as to secure both the goals of economic policy and the consent of those likely to be disadvantaged by the achievement of those goals. To increase the basic wage would lead to inflation; to refuse the increase might exacerbate the already high level of unrest. As a solution Beeby argued that '. . . a really comprehensive scheme of child endowment would secure industrial peace for a long time. The real source of industrial grievance today is the inadequacy of the basic wage for family allowance'.

The bulk of Beeby's memorandum provided a sketchy proposal for a child endowment scheme (to cost £9 million per annum, based on a payroll tax of 2 percent of wages) to provide a five shillings benefit for each child after the first.

Beeby argued that whilst this would have some inflationary effect, it would be far less than might be entailed if the basic wage were to be increased. He repeated Piddington's arguments of 1920, when he noted that the present basic wage was 'more than adequate for the needs of a single man or a married man and wife', but 'In the recent proceedings it was established beyond doubt that the wage now paid is inadequate for a family unit larger than man, wife and one child'. Likewise his suggestion to use a payroll tax relied on Piddington's proposal in which capital would still be involved in some disbursement of its 'income' to labour, and this, it was hoped, might satisfy the union movement.

Beeby's memorandum received urgent attention from Roland Wilson. He consulted informally with his F and E colleagues, and it was his lengthy report, as Director General of Labour and National Service, which became the basis of Menzies' announcement of 16 January.

Wilson's report agreed that 'a refusal of the present [wage] application would accentuate industrial unrest which is already widespread'. He was less sanguine about the value of child endowment achieving industrial peace 'for a long time'.[41] Even so he strongly supported the logic of Beeby's paper, adding that, '. . . a system of child endowment would initiate a long delayed social reform. . . The "world worth fighting for" should not condemn the children of large families to a lower standard of living . . . than children of small families'.

Wilson did not fail to use the opportunity to return to the theme he and his colleagues had raised in mid-1940:

Another reason in favour of child endowment, and one which will become more important, if production for civil needs has to be more

. . . seriously curtailed . . . is the greater freedom which the Government would have in increasing rates of taxation particularly on the lower incomes'.

Here one of the strengths of the economists is revealed—their persistence in regarding the war economy they were building as a system of interrelated parts. It was this which gave them their flexibility in advocating a number of different options designed to implement the overriding principles of a war economy.

In the second part of his report, Wilson examined Beeby's specific proposal for a child endowment scheme. He recommended that a universal and non means-tested benefit be given to all but the first child, which would be simpler to operate than Beeby's means-tested proposal. However, he suggested a mechanism which once more testifies to the dominant role of fiscal motives in this exercise—that it would be appropriate to link child endowment to 'a revision of the income tax exemptions on account of the dependent children'. By removing certain income tax exemptions for children, the Government would thereby produce an additional £2 700 000 in income tax revenues. This invisible increase in income taxation on families with children would be neatly masked by the child endowment provision. Wilson argued that this was 'administratively efficient' and 'would also contribute materially to the gross cost of the scheme'.

This cost Wilson estimated at £13 million. However, some cost cutting, and the removal of exemptions for children would reduce this cost to £8 million. His attempt to calculate the net gain for income earners with families suggested that there would be some 'vertical' redistribution from big families on large incomes to big families with lower incomes.[42] Wilson admitted that this was likely to be a short-term and therefore nominal effect. He accepted Beeby's view that if a payroll tax were used, sooner or later employers would pass the added cost on in the form of higher prices for goods and services and so nullify to some extent any initial advantage some taxpayers gained. Wilson estimated an actual total cost of £8 500 000 and revenues of £9 million from payroll tax.[43]

In his summary, Wilson returned to the world of political strategy. He argued:

> . . . it would appear that child endowment must be regarded as an alternative to a higher basic wage. If the Court thinks the Government is likely to institute a scheme of child endowment it will *probably* not raise the basic wage. If it follows this course, the Government will find it difficult to give sound reasons for refusing child endowment.
>
> . . . The chief judge's advocacy of a 'bold move' therefore appears to be based in part on the sound strategy that a bold move is one of avoiding a kick in the rear. (Wilson's emphasis.)

Although MacFarlane of Treasury objected, Menzies and Holt appear to have seized Wilson's initiatives, with the full support of their other economic advisers.[44]

Menzies could not have been unaware of the political bonuses which would accrue to his Government. The establishment of a War Advisory Council had been designed to secure greater co-operation between the Government and the Opposition by providing positions for the Opposition, but its performance so far suggested only ambiguous costs and benefits. Menzies knew of Curtin's interest in child endowment in 1928, just as he knew of the ALP's commitment to it during the 1940 election campaign. Copland had not hesitated to remind Menzies of the political gains to be won:

> In a recent memorandum submitted by the Financial and Economic Committee to the Treasurer . . . it was suggested that agreement might be reached with the Labor Party about increases of taxation, if certain taxes, politically acceptable to the Labor Party were offered as an inducement to [it] to agree to substantial taxation on lower incomes. I suggest that the inclusion of child endowment in the expenditure planned may be an additional bargaining factor in obtaining acceptance of an increased programme of taxation.[45]

Menzies made his decision to announce the Government's intentions without consulting Cabinet, and against the advice of the Secretary of Treasury. There was some element of risk in this as later UAP and Country Party backbench responses suggested, though he had very clear and strong recommendations from Wilson and other F and E members. (The possibility that Menzies and Copland had together initiated the contact by Downing in December cannot be dismissed.)

Holt's submission to Cabinet blended altruism with political expediency and the desire to legitimate an anti-inflationary policy. He stressed the '. . . desirability of giving some concrete evidence of the sincerity of our desire to make the world we are urging people to fight for a world they will be anxious to fight for.[46] In this respect, 'The actual proposals made are far from revolutionary, but they would go some distance at least towards assuring to the family, a basic economic standard commensurate with family responsibilities'.

The underlying political and class interests received uncommonly clear expression when Holt observed, 'Promises of a greater measure of social justice after the war have been very prominent in England, and there is reason to believe they have not been ineffective in securing the willing co-operation of the British Labour Movement in the war effort'. If Cabinet needed reminding of the Australian context of industrial strife, Holt did not hesitate to do so: 'So far we have not given the same clear expression of our determination to create a better social order in Australia. Our omission to do so, is not without value to the industrial trouble-makers'. Cabinet had no trouble in supporting Holt's submission.[47] A relatively rapid process of policy making now ensued.

F and E members dominated these proceedings as F and E was given the brief to prepare the all-important 'policy and financial' aspects of legislation. MacFarlane was excluded.

F and E was adamant that allowances be paid to all children after the first child and that the benefit be set at five shillings per week. They also supported Wilson's proposal to withdraw income-tax exemptions for all children, and made it clear that a payroll tax should be a temporary measure only. As might be expected, they argued that 'the burden should be shifted as much and as quickly as possible on to taxes which fall on surplus individual income'.[48]

By 7 February a comprehensive proposal had been put together which the Cabinet sub-committee was able to take to Cabinet. The latter gave the task of drafting the Bill to F.H. Rowe, seconded to the Department of Labour and National Service from the Repatriation Commission. The leading role assumed by Labour and National Service and the subordinate role given to the Department of Social Services is further testimony to the general subordination of social policy to fiscal policy and to the specific linkage between a wages policy and child endowment.

The Child Endowment Bill was introduced into the House on 27 March 1941 and had a fast passage through Parliament. It attracted hostile comments from some sections of business but in general was well received. The legislation provided a flat five shillings benefit for all but the first children of a family, without any means test. Children of parents in higher income brackets ceased to be income-tax deductions. Since it was for the 'maintenance, training and advancement' of the child, the benefit was paid to the mother, thus affirming certain expectations of motherhood. Theoretically it was not to be considered as part of any wage determination, though H.L. Anthony was not so careful to maintain this fiction. He pointed out, '. . . it is a logical adjunct of the wages system, the money required to pay it is a logical addition to payroll costs of employers'.[49] It was in more ways than one a measure of its time; longer-term doubts about its role as a redistributive measure would linger on into the 1960s.

Its immediate strategic success was undoubted. Beeby in his announcement on 7 February 1941 indicated that a deferment of a decision would be in effect until June 1941, when the position regarding the basic wage would be reviewed.[50] With respect to winning the support of the labour movement, Menzies' decision to make a 'bold move' was equally successful.

J.H. Scullin, the elder statesman of the ALP, greeted Menzies' January announcement as 'a social reform long overdue' and one to be 'heartily welcomed'.[51] This was the view of most of the labor movement, which felt it had forced an anti-Labor Government into adopting the measure 'rather than be replaced by a Labor Government'. Yet residual suspicion of the Menzies' Government lingered. In late January, the *Labor Call* editorial (which usually reflected Victorian ALP Central Executive views) saw Menzies' announcement as 'a smokescreen to cover other moves which will have far less appeal to the workers'.[52]

When Beeby made his announcement there was a vehement reaction from the union movement but the connection between the decision to defer the case, and child endowment, was more puzzling. Don Cameron noted, *a propos* Beeby's decision, that '. . . the workers were metaphorically deluged by a barrage of legal reasons why the war effort must not be interrupted and why national income must be maintained'.[53] Even Curtin was led to remark that 'the judges are as wrong as their predecessors have been through all the history of the Court'.[54] The puzzle was neatly expressed thus:

> For the Arbitration Court to deliver a severe rebuff to the organised trade union movement's basic wage requests and then for the Acting Prime Minister to inform the employers that they. . . are to bear the cost of a child endowment scheme. . . comes as more than a surprise. Where is the trap?

Though the ACTU-led campaign for wage justice would simmer on for a few more months, the strategy outlined in the last months of 1940 had worked. The Government and the Arbitration Court had removed themselves from the horns of a profound dilemma. Child endowment had been found capable of fulfilling a wonderful range of tasks.

Its evolution as a policy measure points to important continuities in fiscal policy already dealt with in the previous chapter. In particular, members of F and E had become much more concerned about the risks of inflation and the political problems involved in getting the precarious Menzies' Government to enact appropriate policies. The pressure since August 1940 from trade unions to increase the basic wage was seen as a dangerous threat to fiscal stability. The liberal planners were not insensitive to the ideological potential of child endowment as a reform which might better integrate the working class into 'the whole' and so consolidate 'national unity'. In late 1940 it seemed child endowment was at least as much the product of pressing fiscal imperatives as it was evidence of the Government's desire to make Australia 'a place worth working and fighting for'.

4

'The light on the hill': Social Security and the advent of Labor, 1941

> We have a great objective—the light on the hill—which we aim to reach by working for the betterment of mankind.
>
> J.B. Chifley, 1949

1941 had begun with the establishment of child endowment. It would end in the rout of the non-labor parties. Menzies tendered his resignation as Prime Minister on 29 August 1941, leaving his coalition partner, A.W. Fadden, with the wreckage. On 25 September, as Treasurer, Fadden presented the 1941–42 budget to Parliament. Eight days later, the two Independents, A.W. Coles and Alex Wilson, voted with the Opposition to reject the budget and so bring down the Fadden Government.

In office only weeks before the Japanese Empire initiated the Pacific War, the Curtin Government has become in the eyes of many commentators one of the great governments in Australia's political history, and certainly the most successful and long-lived Labor Government. R.M. Crawford wrote, '. . . the period of Labor rule from 1941–49 stands out . . . as one of the decisive epochs in the shaping of the Australian community'.[1] Jill Roe observed:

> A major component in such assessment has been the Labor Government's achievements in extending the social services. Following from the conservatives' introduction of child endowment in 1941, came Commonwealth widow pensions (1942), new maternity allowances and funeral benefits (1943), unemployment, sickness and special dependency benefits (1944), and then the promise of free medicines and free hospital treatment.[2]

Any answer to the question of how the welfare-orientated consensus was achieved must not begin by assuming, as so many historians

61

have done, that social policy is an autonomous expression of a special set of motives, like altruism. An examination of the origins and early work of the Joint Parliamentary Committee on Social Security under both the UAP and ALP governments illustrates something of the context and the continuities of social policy, as well as some of the ideological themes that dominated post-war social policy. Regarding the character of the Labor Government and its committment to social reform, it will be suggested that the most significant aspect of the Curtin Government was the *rapprochement* achieved between Keynesian liberalism and Australian laborism, a *rapprochement* that remains potent 40 years on.

The Menzies Government and the Joint Committee on Social Security, June–August 1941

T.H. Kewley's account of the origins of the Joint Committee on Social Security is consistent with his view of an inevitable and benevolent linear sequence of welfare reforms:

> Early in the course of the Second World War, the Commonwealth Government, like many other Governments, declared that social security was to be a major objective in the Post-War World. With this in mind, the Menzies Government in July 1941 established a Joint Parliamentary Committee on Social Security.[3]

Missing from such an account is reference to what in July 1941 had become an increasingly turbulent political environment.

The Menzies Government had fallen by mid-1941 into a deep political morass, and the establishment of a Joint Committee on Social Security was designed as a kind of life line to political survival. Menzies attempted to rally both his own back-benchers and the electorate with a call for 'national unity' on 17 June 1941. Menzies took his draft of the 'all-in' speech to the War Advisory Council. This Council, symbolically an expression of 'national unity', was more frequently a venue for the ALP to harass the Government, consolidating the image of Government drift. In the discussions of Menzies' draft speech on the morning of 17 June, Curtin intervened to suggest that the greater weight of the burdens forecast by Menzies would fall on labour, and accordingly, ' . . . some indication should be given that their efforts and sacrifices were going to result in making social conditions better'.[4]

Curtin followed this up with a suggestion that the Government appoint a parliamentary standing committee to report on social reforms. Menzies subsequently amended his speech that night by including a reference to social security as an issue which a parliamentary committee might consider.[5] There can be little doubt that

Menzies' decision was basically oriented to securing greater political unity by pacifying Curtin and the Opposition and restoring some unity to Parliament.

Within days Sir Frederick Stewart, Minister for Social Services, seized on the opportunity to submit a paper to Menzies which suggested enlarging and specifying the terms of reference for the proposed parliamentary committee. Menzies agreed to Stewart's proposals, which were included in the motion to establish the committee on 3 July 1941. On that day, Parliament established the membership of the committee and it was agreed that the Joint Parliamentary Committee was to be attached to the Department of Social Services and that it would report to the Minister, Sir Frederick Stewart.

Stewart's Cabinet submission epitomised his own liberal committment to welfare as a tool to secure social solidarity. Stewart iterated the liberal conception of a social contract between the state (as the essence of 'community') and the individual, and claimed history as a partner: 'This is undoubtedly the goal towards which we have been tending for fifty years, and we shall continue to move towards it willy-nilly.'[6] The spirit of progress, he asserted, was abroad in the world: 'What the Australian Government can do is to go ahead of public opinion and reap the immense advantages in morale of a plan conceived in the words of John Maynard Keynes, 'in a spirit of social justice . . . [and] towards reducing inequalities'. He called for a 'full programme of social security' and listed five areas for inclusion in such a scheme on a priority basis:

1 Widows' and orphans' pensions
2 Unemployment insurance
3 Contributory pensions
4 A national housing scheme
5 A comprehensive health scheme, including
  a Child welfare
  b Maternal welfare
  c Nutrition
  d Community health service

In the brief discussion on each of these areas, Stewart's commitment to a contributory basis for 'social security' remained as strong as it had been in 1936. In making this Cabinet submission, Stewart was presumably not expecting anything more than that Cabinet would refer his proposals to the new Committee, which it duly did. The comprehensive social security scheme provided the specific terms of reference for the Joint Committee. This memo forms yet another link in the chain of policy making connecting the UAP Governments of Lyons and Menzies to the ALP Government.

With the exception of the commitment to a contributory insurance basis for his social security programme, Stewart had no less comprehensive a vision of the post-war world than Chifley. He used the essential rhetoric of the 'new order' which Chifley and his liberal advisors would turn to such good effect in the later years of the war.

The Joint Committee's chairman was J.A. Perkins (UAP), the deputy chairman Senator R.V. Keane (ALP), and H.C. Barnard and M.M. Blackburn were selected by Caucus on 26 June. From the Government backbenches came Senator W.J. Cooper and Colonel R.S. Ryan.[7]

Thus was established the Joint Parliamentary Committee on Social Security. A result of the frenzied need to contruct a political consensus, it proved to be astonishingly long-lived. It would survive until the end of the Seventeenth Parliament in 1946, and produce nine major reports, five of them before October 1942. It was largely insignificant in terms of directly shaping any piece of major social policy or social legislation. Treasury and the Government's economic advisers retained too tight a control for this to happen. Indeed, leading members of Government, especially in the Labor Government, took steps to remind the Committee of its marginal role in policy making, such as when Chifley reinforced Treasury's role over and against that of the Department of Social Services. Crisp recalls that Chifley left H.C. Barnard the ALP Chairman of the Committee 'in no doubt that [Chifley] was strongly opposed to the Committee's being 'used' as a means towards the aggrandisement of the Department of Social Services'.[8]

The Joint Committee has not had a good press. M.A. Jones summarised the general view when he wrote that the Committee's 'reports were unimaginative. In the tradition of Australian Social Security they are almost devoid of philosophy and lack the wholeness of vision of the British debate on Social Security at the time'.[9]

However, rather than criticising the reports as lacking a 'philosophy', it is more to the point to see them as working within the taken-for-granted themes of inter-war liberalism. The Committee worked out of a widely shared consensus requiring little in the way of explicit 'philosophical' articulation. It is equally misleading to suggest, as Jones did, that the Committee's reports lack 'objectives'; it is perhaps more remarkable that this Committee produced as many detailed recommendations as it did. However, it is true that the Committee lacked that influence which might have ensured that its recommendations would be taken more seriously.

Ultimately the significance of the Committee's work is that it functioned as a kind of ideological lens. It gathered and focused a considerable amount of information. It was one of the main public mechanisms for expressing views about a 'new order' and to this extent confirmed the growing status of social reforms. Needless to say it also gave an impression that things were being done, something governments frequently wish to convey.

Prior to its first formal meeting Stewart lent his secretary, Roy Rowe, an experienced administrator, to service the Committee.[10] He also engaged as research officer a youthful and unabashed 'socialist', Ronald Mendelsohn, then at the start of a long and distinguished career in the public service.[11] The collaboration of Rowe and Mendelsohn symbolised the links between liberalism and laborism after 1941. As Mendelsohn in a 1941 essay had insisted, 'socialism' ultimately depended on the possession of managerial technique: 'Development of the technique of managing a Socialist State may seem a superfluous task, but the lack of that technique is the principal factor preventing the introduction of socialism forthwith'.[12] It was entirely compatible with that approach that Mendelsohn should see himself as a 'social engineer' and claim membership of the 'socialist egalitarian' tradition of Sidney and Beatrice Webb.

The development of the Committee's first report typifies the uses and abuses to which such committees are often subject. Constrained by time, the Committee was dominated by Mendelsohn. It was he who prepared the basic working tools, set the parameters for the Committee and wrote its interim report (which was accepted with only a minor demur).

At its first formal meeting in Sydney on 21 July, the extent of Mendelsohn's influence was already apparent.[13] Keane in his opening statement urged that the Committee accept Mendelsohn's appointment, his questionnaire, a list of witnesses for the following day, and a paper by Mendelsohn on Social Security in Australia.[14] The size of this task and its urgency doubtless predisposed the members to an appropriate degree of affability. Mendelsohn's position paper was as eloquent a statement of the liberal position as anything else written in the war years. It began with an observation that the improvement of social and living conditions was the 'most fundamental problem of modern Government'. Mendelsohn went on to outline the liberal view of the experience of mass unemployment, and the challenge thrown up by competing political systems. He noted that Communist and Axis countries were also in pursuit of a fundamental improvement in living conditions which opened up, in the broadest way, the political functions of social reforms:

> The Committee may make such recommendations as will promote social justice, strengthen our people for their war effort, and disarm extremists who might be tempted into the error of trying to create a just order by means of injustice and violence.[15]

Mendelsohn's 'socialism' was essentially indistinguishable from the liberal doctrine of civic rights and duties in the social contract:

'. . . from each of us in his station, the community may rightfully expect a performance of his duty, and to each of us, the community owes a living sufficient to enable us to realise our possibilities as civilised human beings'. Discussion of Mendelsohn's paper probably took up most of the first day's meeting.

With little more than three weeks at its disposal, the small Committee was still able to visit four capital cities (and Launceston) and to take submissions from, and question, a total of 66 witnesses. By 24 September J.A. Perkins was able to present the Minister with a ten-page interim report.

The production of the first report depended little upon the evidence presented by the witnesses, of whom about one third were public servants, while academics made up another significant group. Fewer than one third of the witnesses provided evidence concerning anomalies in the existing range of Commonwealth legislation, and their advice was directly incorporated into the first report. More to the point, Mendelsohn seems to have used the evidence—much of it in the form of general views—to confirm the position already sketched out in his first paper, while he opened up areas which might be controversial or where his account was at variance with the bulk of the evidence. But there can be no doubt that Mendelsohn made the most decisive use of his position to present his report, which later became the Committee's Report.[16] In this he was aided by the distractions afforded by Menzies' political demise in August.

In its confident opening paragraphs, the first report was solidly based on the consensus of evidence that the time was ripe for a social security scheme. It accurately summarised the views of most witnesses in calling 'for a plan against poverty, a plan of social development': 'There is still far too much malnutrition and bad housing: there are still people who must struggle from day to day to provide themselves and their children with the bare necessities of existence. Nor are these people few in number'.[17] If Australian governments had once sought to redress such abuses, 'no longer [could] we sustain the claim that Australia [was] the social laboratory of the world'. What was needed was 'a campaign against poverty' and its chief agent, unemployment, and for this to be successful 'an Australian outlook' was needed. It was 'essential that a national policy be developed'.

The report recommended that there be 'a plan of social security to be embraced by a Commonwealth Social Security Act'. Here Mendelsohn acknowledged the influence of New Zealand and American legislation as well as the advice of witnesses. Such an Act would 'include those measures now in existence and those to be enacted from time to time as part of a Social Security Plan in Australia'.

As to the precise form of such a plan, the report carefully avoided any overt rejection of the insurance principle. At the same time, where it specified an attitude it remained wedded to the common-sense of a contributory-based social security scheme. Mendelsohn had earlier spelled out his own views on this matter in his first paper to the Committee. He had argued that in effect there was no distinction between contributory and non-contributory schemes because, 'No-one escapes paying for social services: whether the workers pay more through a social insurance scheme than through a non-contributory scheme will depend on the steepness of the progression of the taxation system'.[18] Perhaps he persuaded the Committee. Certainly a singular feature of the report is the absence of the usual glowing references to a contributory scheme. What appears instead is carefully worded advocacy for a rational and comprehensive social security scheme with no indication of how it would be financed.

The report's immediate achievement was in the field of specific recommendations to overcome anomalies in existing legislation. It made several recommendations to alter the amount of income which old-age pensioners could earn. It also suggested that Aboriginals living in 'civilised circumstances' should become eligible to receive old-age, invalid and maternity allowances. These and the other minor amendments recommended by the Committee had the requisite specificity and good sense for them to be implemented immediately. However, the very political context which had given birth to the Joint Committee finally caught up with the Government which had established it. Only a week after the report was tabled, the Fadden Government fell from office.

The new government moved to implement the small scale recommendations with commendable speed. Public reaction to the first report was sufficiently favourable to suggest that the Committee would have some political future. Press reaction was especially favourable. For some of the more prosaic tabloids like the *Argus*, the report was seen mostly as 'a catalogue of allowance and pension proposals'.[19] The *Sydney Morning Herald*, however, saw it as a 'social reform charter': 'A new charter of widespread social reform is envisaged in the comprehensive Interim Report of the Parliamentary Joint Committee on Social Security'.[20] Equally, not every paper went to the trouble of the *Labor Call* when it reprinted the report, seeing it as an endorsement of ALP calls 'for an immediate start to social reforms commensurate with the needs of the war'.[21] With the coming to office by the Labor Government on 3 October 1941, the opportunity was now at hand for Labor to realise its 'historical mission'.

The Curtin Labor Government in 1941

The elections of 1940 had left the Menzies' government dependent on two Independents. In terms of *realpolitik*, the Fadden Government fell in October 1941 because the two Independents who held the balance of power believed it was no longer worth supporting. To a lesser extent it also fell because the Labor Opposition was no longer prepared to sit on its hands. The pressure on Curtin to challenge the Coalition Government became so great that his own position may have been in jeopardy had he not acceded to that pressure. Ostensibly the excuse for defeating the Government was provided by the budget, presented by Fadden on 25 September.

The Fadden Budget and the ALP's opposition to it is significant on three counts. Firstly, it was largely the work of those key economic advisers in F and E who had been preparing the budget since June 1941, and who would continue to advise the new Government after 1941. Secondly, the Chifley budget of October 1941 was essentially the Fadden budget which Labor had opposed. Finally, this posed recurring problems for Labor in Government when they found themselves receiving advice reliant upon the very same fiscal principles they had rejected. In particular, their opposition to taxation of low incomes in 1941 had somehow to be reconciled with persistent advice that this was vital if inflation were to be constrained.

The defeat of the Fadden Government confirmed what the economists in F and E had long known about the vulnerability of governments to unpopular taxation policies. For the economists this was an unpalatable and excruciating truth since the taxation weapon was crucial to their war-economy armoury. They had therefore but one course of action open to them. They had successfully persuaded the weakened Fadden Government to impose taxation on low incomes with a trade-off in the form of compulsory savings, inspired by Keynes. They would now have to persuade the largely unknown Labor ministry of the wisdom of the same political and fiscal course. The grand irony of the defeat of the Fadden Government was to be revealed twenty months later when the Labor government imposed taxation on low incomes in a way even the Fadden Government had shied away from. That story, which properly belongs to the next chapter, raises the larger question of what it was that the new Labor government brought to office in terms of its predispositions and commitments.

Central to Labor's self-portrayal is an image of its mission to provide reform, change and progressive policies. Brian Dickey underlines this popular view:

> . . .the Labor Government positively welcomed this access of power and set about not only winning the war, but winning the peace too. Here at last was the opportunity to set right the social inequalities the labour movement has endured. . .during the 1930s. Power in Canberra meant for Chifley, not just winning the war, but the opportunity to embody some of the Australian Labor Party's aspirations for greater equality and better care in the community in permanent legislative form. It was for

Curtin, Chifley and their colleagues . . . as much a matter of redistribution as it was reward, when they addressed themselves to questions of social welfare.[22]

How much reliance should be placed on this and similar judgements?

If the UAP-CP Government was tired, divided and demoralised after a long period in office, the new Government was united, and exhilarated by the prospect of office. Curtin led the ALP with a firmness which has never been equalled. He enjoyed respect both within his party and amongst the new Opposition, and come to be regarded as a great war-time leader.[23] He had a largely inexperienced but enthusiastic and talented cabinet. Caucus, vindicating the principle of elective Ministries, largely chose well.

Most of the strength went into the War Cabinet—with Curtin, Chifley, Evatt, Forde, Beasley and Makin, and with Dedman joining on 11 December. Curtin's most inspired choices, apart from Chifley for Treasury, were probably the selection of Eddie Ward, MHR for East Sydney, as Minister for Labour and National Service (which won much support from the unions) and Dedman, the ex-Indian Army Officer,[24] for the increasingly important War Organisation of Industry position. Social Services went to E.J. Holloway, a senior and respected trade unionist.

Chifley's selection as Treasurer provoked considerable surprise amongst contemporary commentators. His performance in Parliament following his return in 1940 had hardly been auspicious. He had remained silent in this first year of his second parliamentary career. He did not figure in any of the journalists' lists of likely ministers before the Caucus election. Yet he came fourth in the ballot, behind Curtin, Forde and Beasley. Both Curtin and Scullin fought hard to give him the Treasury against the well-established claim of the Deputy Prime Minister, F.M. Forde.

As Crisp indicates, Chifley was in fact well placed to become Treasurer. Aside from being one of the few ministers with ministerial experience—that experience had been as Assistant Minister to E.G. Theodore—he was widely respected for his conciliation skills. Like his mentor Scullin, Chifley had spent a decade mastering public finance, which, he said, 'was the heart of government'. Crisp wrote that his was ' . . . a remorseless rather than a darting intelligence. His power lay in his capacities for tenacious pursuit of problems . . . for tireless sifting of the issues in terms of his labour objectives'.[25] He also had, in Crisp's view. 'a remarkably keen, if largely self-tutored intellect, with a zest for administration and a first-class political temperament'. Perhaps his great strength also lay in being able to 'surround himself with men of the greatest talent and in a capacity to reach decisions quickly in order that 'we may get important things expeditiously done'.

Crisp's assessment of Chifley's personal conversion to Keynesian economics however raises some central questions about this Labor government. Writing of Chifley in 1936, Crisp noted that, '. . . Chifley in a broad sense became a 'Keynesian-of-the-first-hour', a fact of enormous significance for Australia in the years after 1941'.[26]

Even allowing that Chifley's Keynesianism involved degrees of adaptation and selection, the general thrust of Crisp's judgement is accurate. Later, however, Crisp modified this judgement when he wrote, 'Chifley, the planner with his eye fixed on 'Labour's light on the Hill', was a Treasurer of a new, positive dispensation—part Keynesian, part socialist'.[27]

Leaving aside Crisp's blending of analytically and historically disparate themes, he implicitly challenges the historian to establish both the character of the ALP's programme before 1941 and its commitments in Government after 1941. Was it a socialist Government with a working-class base, pursuing socialist reforms? Or was it a liberal progressive party pursuing a theme of inter-class reconciliation by means of timely social reform? Answers to such questions may in turn help us to establish whether the 'welfare state' legislation after 1941 involved modification, abolition or consolidation of key aspects of Australia's capitalist formation.

The problem is most decisively revealed when considering the commitment of the Labor Government to Keynesian-style economic management policy, from its first budget of November 1941 to the commitment to full employment in the white paper of 1945. Did the demonstrable convergence between liberalism and the Labor Government after 1941 entail the betrayal of socialist virtue by Chifley and his ilk? Was it merely the realisation of a previously undisclosed affinity between the ALP and inter-war liberalism?

Several points will be developed here. Firstly there is evidence to show that there was indeed a convergence between important elements within the labor movement and the liberal programme, which after 1941 enabled the Labor Government to win the active support of Australia's middle classes.

Yet this does not entail an argument that after 1941 the ALP 'sold out' its socialist or radical legacy. The fact is that the ALP has always been characterised by a basic indeterminacy in its identity as a political party. The very multiplicity of identities and interests which have been carried by the ALP will not sustain an argument that the ALP after 1941 sold its birthright. Perhaps all political parties exhibit an indeterminacy. Yet the agonies of self-examination the ALP has often indulged in are perhaps one result of indeterminacy within a party variously defined as reformist, radical or even socialist.

Socially and historically, the ALP has been for most of the twentieth Century a trade union party, a working-class party, and a multi-interest party.[28] Its origins and its subsequent organisational and structural development alone are testimony to its failure to achieve a coherent and solid identity. On rare occasions, this would be acknowledged within the party; as Curtin ruefully allowed *à propos* New South Wales Labor in 1937, 'Never in the history of the party has there been complete unity'.[29] The oldest political party in Australia, the ALP's relationship to the working class has always been ambivalent.[30] It has been both the main vehicle for working-class political activity and the target of accusations of betrayal of that class.

For if the ALP had its origins in working-class concerns to establish an authentic voice of its own, it was also from the start a major vehicle for middle-class reformers and utopians.[31] The ALP has been host to many working in the major left traditions of reformists and revolutionary socialism, just as it has been host to the crank utopians and their panaceas of vegetarianism, Douglas Credit or alternate modes of child rearing.

As a consequence, both the ALP and its trade union base have been the site of recurring ideological conflict. As the standard bearer of the Mythos of social change, in all its varied and contradictory forms, it is hardly surprising that the ALP should demonstrate a proclivity for self-destruction and bitter doctrinal debate, or that it should exercise so powerful a fascination for journalists and intellectuals.

If it is difficult to say what the ALP essentially has been, or is, it is less difficult to say what it has *not* been. It may be doubted whether the ALP has in any rigorous sense ever been either a socialist or a social democratic party.[32] Popular and/or conservative vilification notwithstanding, there is nothing about the evolution of mainstream Labor theory or practice to suggest it was ever a socialist party.

In the sense that both socialism and social democracy entails the theoretical repudiation of the central institutions and practices of capitalism, the ALP has been neither socialist nor social democratic. In spite of all the energy spent looking for a 'final' definition of socialism, it is still the case that socialists everywhere have agreed on the rejection of the private ownership of the means of production, proposing instead public or social ownership.

If the ALP's history reveals anything it reveals congeries of theoretical orientations, intellectual inheritances and political performances which have been orientated at best to reform and to change within capitalism. To this extent the ALP is a reformist party, but the question remains whether its programmes were to benefit the working-class or all Australians. This dilemma is central to the evolution of the ALP and here it is seen as the tension between the idiom of a national party and a radical working-class ethos. Around this dilemma there were common agreements: that state intervention was a 'good thing', and that fairness and co-operation were decent values.

A commitment to equity, to fair play, and to progressive improve-

ment of the living standards of ordinary people has always been at the
heart of the labor vision. As Albert Metin wrote in 1901:

> In appearance [the labor parties] constitute what we know as a *class
> party* leading the struggle against the bourgeoisie. In practice they accept
> private ownership and the wages system, seeking simply to ensure good
> working conditions in the world as it is.[33]

Ben Chifley at the end of 1949 provided his own exegesis on labor
doctrines in his famous 'Light on the Hill' speech:

> If the [Labor] movement can make someone more comfortable, give to
> some father or mother a greater feeling of security for their children, a
> feeling that if a depression comes there will be work . . . then the Labor
> movement will be completely justified.[34]

The war years between 1914 and 1918 had seen the basic contradiction of whether the ALP was a working-class party or one for all the
people surface with a vengeance. The war years gave a great impetus
for Labor's leadership to give serious consideration to Labor's role as
the party of all the people. The second great crisis, the Depression,
did also. It was then that the ALP confronted itself. The party apparatus, the trade union movement and the Conference crumbled in the
search for the core of the Labor movement, expelling Premiers,
condemning Labor governments and any who degraded the ALP's
mission by compromise or defeatism.

In 1939 the potential for a re-opening of this debate lay concealed
beneath the appearance of a party emerging from the wilderness,
cleansed and healed. If anything the declaration of war in 1939 revealed the depth of the commitment to national leadership without in
any way bypassing the class-based perceptions of the ALP. Labor
patriotism was to sustain six years of 'equality of sacrifice' rhetoric.

Yet whatever Curtin's intentions, Australia remained a class society
and the ALP a part of that class society. However much the national
party tradition within the ALP hoped for a harmonious society
where a Labor government might govern in the interests of all the
people, this hope remained fantastic. It was well intentioned and persuasive: it activated great policies and brought Curtin unimagined
fame, but a fantasy it remained. The Curtin Government and its
successor—most tragically in the confrontation with the miners in
1948–49—would have to encounter and deal with the political con-
tradictions which were the chief legacy of the ALP's history.

Regarding the relationship between the ALP and the liberalism of
the 1930s, it would be too much to claim an identity between the two.
If anything, there was an affinity between the ALP and the planners
which became a working partnership in the war years.

This affinity which grew out of common responses to the Depression and out of a shared belief in the efficacy of planning and state

intervention. There was also a common vision of a harmonised society, purged of disruptive class conflict by progressive improvements for all who were the victims of capitalism's anarchy of production and consumption. This affinity would never entirely overcome the divergent class experience of middle-class planners and the trade union members of the ALP. Yet after 1941 it made for a union in which Keynesian liberalism merged with the commonsense of the Labor 'mission' to secure a just 'new order'.

The precise extent to which the Depression marked a watershed in the history of the ALP may always be open to debate. However, there can be no dispute that the Depression reaffirmed much of the ALP's view about the degradation unemployment wrought. In this respect the ALP shared with the 'new liberals' of the 1930s a common view that mass unemployment must never be allowed to recur.

The commitment to theories of credit expansion and to spending one's way out of depressions, of the kind developed by Theodore as Treasurer in 1930, provided a useful basis for moving towards Keynesian economic management strategies. In this respect Keynes gave the ALP the techniques whereby it could become, in Gollan's words, 'the party of controlled capitalism'.[35] State intervention and planning to impose equilibrium thus formed an important point of intersection. Regulation and planning were central themes in labor views through the 1930s. ACTU President A.E. Monk explained in 1937: 'We feel that unemployment insurance does not sheet home the blame for unemployment where it belongs, that is, in the unplanned state of our economic system'.[36] Only planning, Monk argued, could give the worker what he truly wanted, 'employment assurance'. What became the doctrine of full employment after 1944 Labor spokesmen were outlining in the 1930s. It provided a basis for the blending of Labor and liberal policy themes after 1941.

While the ALP's lack of a clear ideological identity was precisely what allowed this alignment with the 'new liberalism', it also concealed deep and ongoing tensions.

The ALP and social reform

It would be fair to suggest that the greatest concerns of ALP spokesmen in the second half of the 1930s were the imminence of war and the dangers posed by fascism. Even so, the political significance attached to social policy by the new Curtin Government was noted early by journalists, who commented on the allocation of the Social Services and Health portfolio to a senior minister. Later historians have concurred in ways already alluded to, with this estimation of the significance of 'social reform'.

The self-portrayal by ALP ideologues involved a similar estimate that it was the party uniquely equipped to launch social reforms. As numerous speeches by John Curtin as Opposition Leader indicated, Labor was that party 'with a particular and deeply felt commitment to victory and a just peace'.[37] If the other parties were the parties which 'represented and defended capitalism', then the ALP was 'the only party with a forward looking policy'.[38] Frequently Labor ideologues had recourse to quasi-religious language to describe the character of the ALP's 'mission to spread a social gospel'. Yet even here, tensions lurked beneath the surface of confident pronouncements. For some, this quasi-religious language expressed a class view of Labor's commitments to social justice.

In J.J. Holland's 'Gospel of Labor', social justice meant justice for the poor and those on the basic wage, if necessary at the expense of the wealthy or of capital itself. Labor's 'special mission' was in Holland's view a commitment to social justice, but only if social inequality could be banished. The social philosophy of Labor, he averred:

> . . . is based on social justice and its object is social security and the abolition of social injustice . . . The first great evil is poverty which Labor will attack all along. Poverty can be abolished if unemployment is banished . . . Today, as ever, we see in our nation an enormous inequality of wealth . . . at one end thousands of families are struggling with economic difficulties . . . at the other end, people are surrounded by every conceivable comfort and luxury.[39]

The answer for Holland was planning: ' . . . the nation's economic life must be sensibly planned, in order that employment and rising wages shall be provided for every worker'.

What became less and less clear was the degree of commitment by the ALP to a radical redistribution of income to improve conditions for the poor and unemployed. Such a class view had underprinned Labor's rejection of the contributory principle of National Insurance in 1938–39. Curtin, who in 1938 had defended this commitment, was by 1940 stressing class harmony and 'equality of sacrifice' under a truly patriotic national government.[40]

The themes of 'victory and justice' were strikingly outlined by Curtin in policy speeches and radio broadcasts in 1940. The goal of a 'world worth fighting for' was spelled out in Curtin's campaign speech of August 1940, when he vowed that 'The ALP is committed to a new social order based upon democracy and the rights of all men and women to enjoy the fruits of honest toil'.[41]

The theme of class harmony achieved by technocratic planning informed Curtin's view that ' . . . tragic poverty and economic disorder will disappear when we are bold enough to mobilise the confidence and good will of scientist, technician, trade unionist and industrial leader for the tasks of peace'. Planning, that key theme of the interwar liberals, was also claimed as such by the ALP: 'We have to plan with the entire resources of this nation to win the war, and we must also . . . plan with the entire resources of this nation to win the peace'. Though the rhetoric was bold, Curtin was unable to deal with the tensions between a programme of social reforms and the need to balance the interests of all classes.

Undoubtedly one of the more striking convergences between the ALP and the inter-war liberals was the shared conviction that poverty was directly linked to and explicable in terms of mass unemployment. Logically such a connexion implied that the abolition of mass unemployment would lead by and large to the abolition of poverty. It was, in the context of the thirties, an understandable link. For most, like Don Cameron, it was commonsense:

> There are about 800 000 [men, women and children] in Australia living on sustenance rations, fat and bread, jam and bread, no adequate housing, rotten social facilities, having ragged clothes. They are not basic wage earners. They are the unemployed.
> . . . Mass unemployment is a basic feature of Australian capitalism and until it is vanquished, poverty will shadow the lives of many Australians.[42]

It was here, in the perception that mass unemployment sustained mass poverty, that the real blending of Keynesian liberalism and Australian Laborism took place. Out of this perception would come Labor's commitment to 'full-employment' achieved by a variety of Keynesian economic techniques. This would become Labor's 'welfare policy' and its answers to the profound inequalities of Australian capitalism. It would eventually prove to be an entirely problematic solution. Even in the first months of the new Government's life, the work of the Joint Committee on Social Security and the persistent advice coming from the economists of the Finance and Economy Committee underlined how much fiscal considerations would continue to shape the kind of social policy likely to be implemented.

The Joint Parliamentary Committee under Labor, 1941–42

The new Labor Government was not long in assigning tasks to the Joint Parliamentary Committee. On 4 November, Cabinet had dealt with a perfunctory two-page memo from E.J. Holloway supporting a proposal to introduce unemployment insurance.[43] The proposal entailed a truncated scheme to cost the Government about £2 million per annum. Holloway provided no detailed argument in favour of the scheme apart from some vague references to cushioning post-war unemployment. Cabinet remained unimpressed and Holloway was asked to refer the matter to the Joint Parliamentary Committee.[44]

The Joint Committee, now under the chairmanship of H.C. Barnard, made unemployment insurance the subject of its second and third reports. These two reports were atypical. First, they were produced as a result of a request from Cabinet for a narrowly-focused report on unemployment insurance. Second, while the committee continued to take evidence from a wide range of witnesses, the production of the second and third reports was guided by only a handful of submissions from within the public service.[45] Once again Mendelsohn's submissions and his control of the production of the reports were crucial, though a submission from a junior adviser, J.F. Nimmo from Treasury, also proved quite decisive.

Mendelsohn's submissions to the Joint Committee are significant because of its shift away from a contributory social security tax base. He provided a very clear summary of unemployment insurance principles and the shortcomings of all existing schemes, which were not designed for the relief of mass long-term unemployment, 'but to tide workers over during short periods of joblessness'.[46] British experience in particular suggested that a scheme of relief for unemployed workers needed to be built alongside the unemployment insurance scheme to catch both non-insured workers and the long-term unemployed once their eligibility for benefits had expired. Equally, he argued that by itself unemployment insurance was only a small part of the larger framework of employment policy. As he indicated, if the committee wanted to recommend such a scheme, it would need (in order to make recommendations about scales and durations of benefits) to make intelligent guesses about the post-war level of unemployment.

He then reviewed the merits of the traditional state, employer and worker contributory insurance system against those of a single tax basis for unemployment 'insurance'. Mendelsohn came down firmly for the latter.[47] The real problem for tripartite schemes was the exclusion of so many people, including 'farmers, small entrepreneurs, shopkeepers and independent workers'. To this was added the chance for employers to pass on their contribution costs to everyone else in the form of higher prices. A 'general insurance [sic] tax' levied on all income earners had its problems, not the least being that all taxpayers could claim benefits, but it avoided the exclusion of so many groups. In addition, 'a tax on incomes stops where it is levied and cannot be passed on at all'. On the whole, '. . . the method of a general tax is to be preferred because it distributes the burden more equitably . . . every part of the community is called upon to make a sacrifice in order to stablilise the income of each individual'.[48]

If Mendelsohn ably summarised the economists' views on unemployment insurance, the contribution by J.F. Nimmo was equally significant. Nimmo's paper made its greatest impact in its insistence on an immediate policy to deal with war-related problems. (This led to the decision to split the first draft of Mendelsohn's report into what became the second and third reports.) Secondly, Nimmo's analysis clarified the basis for rejecting an insurance scheme while retaining a strong contributory principle through a new taxation base.

The formal status of Nimmo's submissions was not clearly revealed. He said, 'None of the opinions which I may place before the Committee are intended to express the views of the Department of Treasury in which I am employed'.[49] However, Nimmo's submission received attention from many Treasury officials and from economists working in F and E, and revisions were made in the light of their comments. It seems to have been very much in the way of a 'floating of balloons' by Treasury. With its broad-ranging concern to establish a 'national minimum', it would be in evidence in later policy-making. In its own way it is as fine a statement of liberal social policy of any of the submissions by more senior officials or of any of the published work during the later years of war. It should give Nimmo a small but secure niche in the history of liberal ideology and the making of the welfare state.[50]

Nimmo's memorandum opened by reflecting the generalised anxiety in the weeks after Pearl Harbor:

> The immediate possibility of air raids and of other forms of physical warfare in Australia, and the existence of some transitional unemployment unavoidable when there is a speedy and substantial transfer of resources from civil to war production make it urgent to extend the scope of the social benefits provided by the State.[51]

Nimmo, as a good Keynesian, held that where people's standards of living were affected by war, or by Government policy, Government was obliged to ensure that no one fell below a minimal subsistence level.

War provided one basic rationale for his proposals; administrative comprehensiveness the other. He observed that currently the Commonwealth and State Governments had already assumed responsibility for some groups of people to be kept on a minimum level of subsistence. Logic dictated that the gaps be filled:

> The next step in social policy is to fill in these gaps 'in order to make impossible the occurence to anybody of extreme want'. This is but the logical extension of the present practice of guaranteeing a minimum income to the aged, the infirm and widows.

To these two basic rationales he added a third. If coupled to a suitably planned taxation scheme, the guarantee of a minimum income to all needy people '. . . would probably strengthen the hand of the Government in curtailing non-essential production'. In terms which would not resurface until the 1960s, Nimmo proposed nothing less than that 'the Commonwealth Government immediately guarantee a minimum income to *all* persons in Australia'. Such a guarantee would ensure freedom from want in time of war, and 'would become the basis for a more comprehensive post-war scheme'. It was clear that Nimmo was not contemplating a contributory insurance scheme. Proposals to use a means test for the minimum income, and a strict work test for the unemployment benefits scheme, pre-empted any resourse to an insurance scheme. The economic rationale for this proposal—and it was the only kind offered—must have pleased Giblin immensely. Nimmo accepted, with Giblin, the need to reduce the supply of goods and services available to civilians. Equity demanded that the sacrifices entailed in this be shared, and that those with higher incomes be asked to sacrifice more of their available income. Although Nimmo set his minimum income fairly low, he gave powerful support to those of Giblin's persuasion seeking to tax those on all but the very lowest incomes with a view to reducing excess demand. As Nimmo put it:

> Persons with incomes in excess of £5 000 are already paying more than two-thirds of their incomes in [tax] . . . Something more can be obtained from those with incomes £1 000–5 000 and a good deal more from those with incomes £400–1 000, and, if increased social benefits are to be offered, persons with incomes £150–400 can reasonably be asked to contribute more.

Here was the very political and fiscal core of Chifley's National Welfare fund proposals of February 1943. It was legitimated by the notion that there was a form of income redistribution going on from all those in incomes of £140 upwards to those on incomes under this level.

Nimmo chose as his minimum income level the then current old-age pension of 23 shillings and sixpence per week.[52] He was at pains to reassure his audience that the total cost of his programme would not add more than £11 million to the existing social service outlays for 1942–43. This he suggested was 'a relatively small price to pay for a very necessary increase in social security'. The means to pay for this increase lay in adopting 'a progressive income tax based on a widely accepted principle of ability to pay. . . ' It was assumed that the '. . . only means to finance any scheme of social security . . . is by transferring income from those whose income is in excess of some given minimum to those whose income is to be augmented and those without an income'. Here in its original form is the policy assumption which pre-empted any possibility of genuine income redistribution through the war-time 'welfare state'. What Nimmo foreshadowed was nothing less than the institutionalisation of poverty in post-war Australia, which R.F. Henderson would 'discover' in the 1960s. At a time when the Commonwealth's 'basic wage' and various State 'basic wages' in 1941 were around £210 per annum, Nimmo was proposing to reach down well below that level to secure taxation revenue. At the same time, like most of his generation, he silently incorporated the principle of 'lesser eligibility' into the level of benefits, ensuring that benefits would never even begin to be more than a fraction of the then 'basic wage' income. Nimmo's rationale presupposed that his national minimum would be the income of Government beneficiaries, which would be financed by all income earners beginning at an income threshold barely above that of Commonwealth pensions. The very low level at which the tax threshold on incomes would start seems not to have worried Nimmo or his colleagues. As he saw it, the problem was 'to determine the most equitable means to transfer income from the relatively well-to-do to the relatively destitute', when people on incomes as low as £150 per annum would be taxed.

Nimmo disregarded the 1907 Harvester Judgement that a basic wage should be the base line for subsistence. He was prepared to argue for an income set variously at between a third and a half of the 'basic wage' as his baseline for subsistence.[53] The notion that the basic wage in 1943 constituted the beginnings of being 'relatively well-to-do' may have struck its recipients as strange. But in all of this he was merely restating the received wisdom of a century or more which had held, since Bentham, the necessity of maintaining the principle of 'lesser eligibility' in the disparity between wages for work, and income support for those not in the labour market. To be fair to Nimmo, the proposed scales of benefits, especially those for unemployment benefits, were marginally better than those available in the late 1930s. (In Victoria, for example, in 1937, the 'dole' was worth seventeen shillings and six pence for an adult male, compared with Nimmo's suggested rate of twenty-two shillings and six pence.) Equally his suggested scale for a minimum income reflected a slight increase on the existing old-age pension rates.

Nimmo indicated that the rate of taxation could be considerably increased over that obtaining in 1941–42 and to do this the Commonwealth would have to seize the tax powers from the States. He suggested a short-term alternative social security shilling tax on incomes beginning at £150 per annum for the longer term, into the post-war period:

> . . . it is recommended that a separate social security tax on a progressive basis be imposed to finance all Commonwealth Social Security payments. This tax would be levied conjointly with ordinary income tax, but the Social Security collections would be paid into a separate fund.

This proposal likewise has an uncanny resemblance to Chifley's 1943 National Welfare Fund proposals.

Though an 'unofficial' paper, Nimmo's submission had the support of the Governments advisers. It was a prescient document, pointing to the logic of the National Welfare Fund exercise of 1943. For the time being however, the Joint Committee had to get on with producing its next reports, in which only parts of Nimmo's paper appeared.

The Second Report of the Joint Parliamentary Committee focused very closely on the problems of war-time unemployment, and their recommendations reflected the considerable anxiety that Australia would be directly affected by war: '. . . the certainty of further and probable large scale attacks upon this continent have created new aspects of individual insecurity'.[54] The intensification of war, the committee argued, entailed not only enemy action but also Government action, which produced economic and employment disruption. In this the committee iterated the premises of Nimmo's paper. It was 'imminent peril' which led to recommendations to provide protection 'against distress arising from the war'. Accordingly, it argued that Government take action immediately to provide a scheme of benefits for workers unemployed because of the war.

Nimmo's influence was also evident in the prescriptions for financing the scheme. It is significant that the committee took up Nimmo's long-term plan and not his proposal for an immediate levy of one shilling per pound on all incomes. It accepted his view that 'The simplest and most equitable plan . . . is to impose a general tax on every income earner in the community with the exception of those on the lowest scale'.

It would be best, they suggested, to have progressive tax, and, without specifying it, would presumably have had in mind Nimmo's scale of tax beginning on incomes of £150 per annum. The scale of benefits proposed had no explicit foundation in Nimmo's proposals since the committee was not developing his benefit scales either for guaranteed minimum income or for unemployment benefits. They recommended unemployment benefits close to Nimmo's minimum income beginning with 50 shillings for adults, 25 shillings for wives of unemployed men and 5 shillings for children.

In the final paragraphs the committee dealt with the vexatious issue of administration. F.H. Rowe had been much exercised both by Nimmo's implicit criticism of his department and his preference for joint Commonwealth-State administration. Their own recommendation suggest they were swayed by Rowe's views. The committee recommended that the Department of Social Services administer the scheme, ensuring that it remained a responsibility of the Commonwealth Government.

There appears to have been little delay between the presentation of the report to Holloway on 6 March 1942, and his memorandum to Cabinet of 14 April. The Cabinet submission reveals few significant changes to the committee's recommendations. On 20 April 1942, Cabinet discussed Holloway's proposals for a scheme of unemployment benefits for those unemployed as a result of War Organisation of Industry regulations.[55] Holloway recommended that benefits of £2/10/0, £1/5/0 and 5 shillings per week be paid respectively to married men, wives and each child. It was suggested that the scheme would require a very strict work-test, but only a 'liberal' means-test since it was designed mainly for regular workers. The scheme would be temporary, though Holloway did not specify time limits.

He also followed closely the Joint Committee Report regarding the financial basis, suggesting that '. . . the time has arrived when serious consideration should be given to financing social services on a national basis'. He went on to suggest that if uniform income tax was agreed upon,

> . . . certain amounts should be set aside for social service payments so that eventually the present non-contributory system would be gradually replaced by one somewhat similar to that in force in New Zealand, but one which if graduated, would by comparison fall less heavily upon the lower incomes.

Here the older Labor animus against low-income workers being taxed to sustain an unemployment benefits scheme had re-emerged— and with it an acute recognition of the principles upon which the much vaunted New Zealand social security system rested.

A relative degree of tough mindedness seems to have been present in War Cabinet discussions of Holloway's proposal. (He was not included.) On 5 May, War Cabinet accepted the thrust of the scheme, but reducing the proposed maximum benfit from £2/10/0 to £2/0/0, as Dedman had argued successfully that the unemployed should not get paid more than the average soldier. War Cabinet also imposed a stringent means test. A final twist of the knife came when the War Cabinet recommended that the Department of Labor and National Service administer the scheme, rather than the Department of Social Services. This decision reinforced the 'traditional' role Social Services had come to play as an utterly subordinate Department in regard to both Treasury, and Labour and National Service, a relationship which the coming years did little to alter. All in all, these decisions, ratified by full Cabinet on 6 May, represented a significant political defeat for Holloway. Even more sobering was the failure to implement the scheme; as far as can be established no benefits were paid out under it, and Australia waited until 1945 for something more comprehensive.

The second report and its companion third report signified a major shift in the premises underpinning the fiscal mechanisms of social services. Advice from the Joint Committee suggests why this was so. In its third report presented on 25 March 1942, the revised assumptions represented in the arguments of Mendelsohn and Nimmo are to the fore.[56] The rejection of insurance based social services is strongly defined.

The report made an initial plea for consolidation of existing social service legislation. This seems to have been prescribed as a step to be taken in lieu of considerations of more comprehensive proposals for national medical and health services, housing schemes and the like. In this the committee merely reiterated its recommendation, in its interim report, for a Social Security Act.

Likewise its second recommendation and discussion merely re-stated the arguments for a 'comprehensive authority to co-ordinate all war time social measures', possibly in the shape of a Social Security Commission. Similarly it recommended that the Department of Social Security be given responsibility for civil emergencies, involving after care and amenities for people evacuated from bombed or in-vaded areas.

Its major focus was on unemployment policy. Here the committee argued that planning both for war-time unemployment and for post-war unemployment needed to begin immediately. Planning and the provision of a national system of labour exchanges was seen as a pre-liminary step, as was acceptance that different kinds of unemploy-ment might need different solutions. The report chose one particular group of unemployed, 'hard core unemployed', who required 'voca-tional training to fit them for appropriate training', suggesting that the Directorate of Manpower might take on this work. For most of the short-term unemployed, the committee followed Mendelsohn and Nimmo in arguing that short-term employment difficulties could be solved by improved organisation of the labor market, 'using an efficient system of employment exchanges under Commonwealth control'. These exchanges would provide information about where jobs were available and apply a work test preparatory to payment of unemployment benefits—where unemployment was defined, in Mendelsohn's terms, as 'involuntary worklessness'.

In four paragraphs, the report discussed the deficiencies and merits of unemployment insurance. While the report accepted that insu-rance schemes needed no means test, there were basic problems in insurance-based programmes. As a quasi-actuarial system, benefits and contributions had to balance, which could be a problem especial-ly if unforeseen unemployment were to occur. The report added, borrowing heavily from Mendelsohn's paper, that should long-term unemployment be a problem an insurance scheme would simply col-lapse and require a system of supplementary benefits. Finally, insu-rance schemes usually excluded self-employed workers and farmers. The conclusion represented a far-reaching break with traditional poli-cy regarding unemployment: 'Our problem can be solved only by providing work or maintenance for every unemployed person in the community as a right, for the full period of unemployment, it being understood that compliance with a work test is a condition of the payment of maintenance.' The committee then underlined its rejec-tion of the insurance principle by suggesting that both for the war period and the post-war period, unemployment benefits be based on

. . . the principle of a graduated tax on incomes . . . as the most equitable means of financing unemployment benefits and any similar measures. The purpose of which is to maintain a minimum of subsistence for disemployed persons or those suffering from want of the necessities of life.

Here the committee emphasised most clearly its indebtedness to Nimmo and his notion of a 'national minimum' or 'guaranteed minimum income'. The truly radical gesture contained in such seemingly innocuous phrases as 'and any similar measures' surely is worthy of a prize for understatement.

The committee accepted that employment policy should utimately be given priority over unemployment policy. Their suggestion was a hint of things to come:

[We should] have in readiness public works projects which can be commenced as soon as unemployment increases . . . Such a policy has a great advantage in that we can use a period of adversity to improve our capital equipment such as forests, unified railway gauges, telephone and telegraph services, water supply and irrigation, bridges, roads, aerodromes, sewerage systems, housing and slum clearance, hydro-electric schemes . . .

It was a vision of a thoroughly Keynesian kind, entailing a planned approach, designed ' . . . to operate over the period of a trade cycle so that it is accelerated at the first signs of economic depression and slackened when the demand for labour and materials recovers'. They gave special attention to a national housing scheme which could simultaneously absorb labour and meet the need for additional housing. It was a brilliantly condensed statement which the committee and subsequently the Department of Post-War Reconstruction, would restate and expand on in later policy documents and reports.

The papers which went into the preparation of the second and third reports of the Joint Committee have some significance as indicators of shifts taking place in conceptions of social policy. What remained less clear was how these analyses would be turned into practicable policy. We must now turn to the major revision of the federal pattern in Australian politics, entailed in the accomplishment of uniform taxation, and the role played by social policy in the Labor Government's fiscal policy. Here we may more clearly grasp the Labor Government's contribution in these years to the making of a 'welfare state'.

5

'Stealing a sheep and giving the trotters away in charity': Labor and the national welfare fund, 1942–43

On 11 February 1943 Treasurer Chifley unveiled the outlines of what was to become the Australian 'welfare state'. His announcement of the establishment of a national welfare fund appears to confirm in striking fashion the special place of the Labor Government in the history of welfare. He also foreshadowed, with great effect, a comprehensive scheme of unemployment and sickness benefits, family allowances, a national health service and other social measures, all to be funded from the welfare fund. With this announcement, Chifley affirmed the ALP's traditional status as a reforming party and earned it a reputation as the architect of the welfare state.

However, the proposals were in one sense another step to refine the fiscal machinery of a total war economy. They were also a device to resolve a political problem. The Curtin Government had vowed publicly never to tax low-income earners. That pledge, instrumental in bringing down the Fadden Government, had been reaffirmed during the campaign to secure uniform taxation in 1942. Yet the advice which the Government received indicated that sooner or later it must break its pledge. The origins of the national welfare fund are to be found in the complex evolution of fiscal and budgetary policy between June and September 1942. In this period the Government held out against advice to adopt an anti-inflationary policy which involved an extension of income tax to those on less than £400 per annum. A striking and comprehensive package of welfare policies became part of the solution to these difficulties.

With the onset of the Pacific War in December 1941, the Government's advisers found the resistance to more comprehensive economic controls melting away. A wide range of measures talked about in 1941 were implemented in the first months of 1942, including manpower controls, controls over production, prices, wages and commodities, as outlined in the national economic plan of 1942.[1]

Crucial to the speed with which the final stages of a war economy were constructed was the collaboration, at personal and policy levels, between the economists of Finance and Economic Committee and the new Government. The Government proved itself even more willing to accept the advice coming to it than its predecessors had done. The themes which had exercised the liberal-Keynesians since 1939 were restated with greater force after Pearl Harbor, and the new Government seemed more than willing to accommodate them.

This *rapprochement* is signified in a major policy statement drawn up by Copland for John Curtin on 16 November 1941. It is essentially the Keynesian programme, underpinning the completion of a total war economy and the evolution of the 'full-employment' doctrine. The Keynesian idiom informs even the first sentence: 'The fundamental aim of the Australian Labor Party . . . is to secure the fullest and most advantageous use of Australia's resources of men, materials and capital, in the best interests of the community as a whole'.[2] This involved a shift away from Labor's traditional concern with bank credit to a Keynesian view of 'real resources'. As Copland put it. 'What we can do is limited only by our real resources, monetary considerations are secondary'.

There was a clear warning that the Government would henceforth not 'print more money' to secure the diversion of men from civilian to military activity, since this would produce

> . . . an inflation disastrous to the interests of the whole community and especially the workers . . . The transfer will not be held up by the efforts of civilians to retain the services of these men by using their spending power. The Government will either remove or immobilise any excess spending power that threatens . . . inflation.[3]

The paper foreshadowed additional taxation of those incomes with excess spending power as well as direct controls on consumption like rationing. The statement signalled acceptance by the Labor Government of the central tenet of Keynesians that the maintenance of 'effective demand' directly affected the level of employment: 'Insecurity in peacetime arises from the inability of an unregulated free enterprise economy to employ all who seek work.' Unemployment occurred because ' . . . of the unwillingness of the country as a whole to spend a large part of its aggregate income on the purchase of consumption goods'.

The Keynesian blending of individualism and state regulation was also affirmed: 'Our aim will be to see that each individual is given the best possible opportunity to secure his own ends insofar as these ends are consistent with the maximum welfare of society'.

Any commitment to a socialist programme was simply rejected. Nationalisation was not on Labor's agenda since the state, by providing rational control of financial policy, increased regulatory powers and better and longer-term budgetary planning would, they believed, solve the problem of periodic depressions. Thus was established the liberal political-economy that would become post-war orthodoxy.

The continued development of the war economy proved a triumph of the first order for the Australian economists. It resulted in consolidation of economic hegemony over large tracts of policy terrain in the post-war period. After an initial period of mutual suspicion, Treasurer Chifley came to place increasing reliance on the Finance and Economic Committee. It seems that F and E's meetings were neither as frequent nor as crucial *per se* to policy development as they had been in 1940 or 1941. Rather it was the collectivity of individual advisers, with their access to ministers and their informal meetings, which allowed them to exert a continuing directive role over policy. In particular, Giblin and Coombs established a close relationship with Chifley.

The membership of F eand E had not altered much since 1941. Giblin remained Chairman of a regular group, including Wilson, Copland, Melville, Walker and Coombs. On the fringes, young R.I. Downing and to a lesser extent, J.F. Nimmo, proved themselves adept writers of memoranda. The rapid pace of administrative change from January 1942 affected the frequency of meetings and attendance. The Committee accepted that 'the Government has frequently to make decisions before all aspects of a given problem can be investigated thoroughly'.[4] Through 1942 it continued to play a major role in formal policy deliberation, though its importance declined after the formation of the Department of Post-War Reconstruction (which became the new home for many of the key economic advisers).

A clear indication of the policy line adopted by F and E provided by Giblin's review in February 1942. For fiscal policy the problem remained much as it had been defined in 1940 and 1941:

> . . .incomes and purchasing power have increased greatly with consequent increased demand for all goods, both for investment and consumption. If we rule out inflation, demand can only be equated to supply by the transfer of purchasing power from private to public use by loan or taxation.[5]

Giblin did not, on this occasion, express his views concerning the need for taxation, preferring instead to concentrate on stricter controls on consumer goods, sterling exchange, and imports. Giblin's paper anticipated the kind of controls which would characterise the total war economy of 1942–45.

Even so, it was as clear to Giblin as to his colleagues that sooner or later the taxation bullet would have to be bitten. And in that eventuality, welfare policy could well play a vital role. The economists certainly wasted no time in trying to persuade a government with a major military crisis on its hands that social policy could be an important adjunct to war economic policy.

Something of the general rationale for social services had been spelled out by D.B. Copland late in 1941. In a memo to Curtin on 10 December 1941, Copland had rejected the notion that there was an intrinsic conflict between 'developing the social services and prosecuting the war'.[6] He argued for a distinction between social services which could interfere with the war effort, and those which did not, and which might not even assist it. In the category of 'interfering' social services he placed 'an ambitious housing or slum reclamation scheme', since they diverted precious labour and material resources away from the war. Schemes like unemployment and health insurance he argued could be introduced immediately without affecting the war effort. Indeed, if an employment insurance scheme was introduced on a contributory basis 'it will help the war effort by increasing saving and reducing the demand for non-essential goods'. The distribution of benefits to unemployed and low-income earners would enable them to buy better food, 'an aid to primary industry and beneficial to the health of the people'.

Copland took up these some themes in a paper circulated to Finance and Economic members early in 1942. Combining a certain level of humanitarian insistence on equity with a harder-edged committment to planning, he noted there was a case for protecting those people who were comparatively badly off before the war and who could now be worse off. He accepted that it was 'the Government's responsibility to ensure that the distribution of goods and services is as equitable as possible', that is after the necessary diversion of non-essential goods to the war effort had been achieved.[7] These were strong arguments for a health service scheme and for unemployment insurance. With respect to pensions the ambiguities of his position—and that of his economic colleagues—is more clearly revealed. Increases to pensions involved 'the transfer of marginal income from people who would normally save a large part of it . . . to people who will spend a large part of it, using up resources which would otherwise be available for the war effort'.

However, all was not lost: 'Insofar as [pensioners] would demand more clothing and fuel, this could be controlled if . . . rationing schemes were introduced'.

The new Labor Government was happy to receive this kind of advice. It moved swiftly to honour its pledge to increase invalid and old-age pensions, though this only came about after revised Treasury estimates showed that it would not be possible to grant all of the proposed increase straight away. After that slight setback in October

1941, Holloway, Minister for Social Services, was able, in April 1942, to raise pensions by an additional one shilling and six pence per week.

Echoes of the economists' framework can be heard in Holloway's justifications. Considerations of humanity coincided happily with 'aiding the war effort'. Holloway urged the House not to forget 'that a large section of our population is undernourished, badly housed and too frequently unemployed', adding that the increases 'will mean an improvement of national morale, and will stimulate and increase the vigour and tempo of our war preparations'.[8] The liberalism of the 1930s was evident in his view that:

> . . . it is true that the totalitarian Governments have given their peoples a large measure of social security at the expense of personal liberty . . . Upon the free nations rests the responsibility of showing that the democratic way of life is the best, and that in such a society there can be not only social security but also liberty of action and freedom of speech.[9]

These were, however, minor sorties into social policy. A far more important task was at hand. The problem of taxation which confronted the war economists was in part connected with the historic pattern of Federation and the responsibility shared between the Federal and State governments for taxation. Until the Commonwealth had central control of tax powers, the war-economists believed no effective bulwark against inflation would be possible. Their answer was uniform taxation. The taxation issue was also connected with the problem of persuading a nervous government of the efficacy of a new, heavy regimen of taxation reaching down to the lowest-income earners.

Both problems were to stretch the political ingenuity of the war-economists, though, as it turned out, the seizure by the Commonwealth of central tax-powers was relatively simple compared with the problem of using that power in the second half in 1942.

Taxation and social policy: the case of widows' pensions

If there was one point at which relative balance of powers between the Federal Government and the States altered, it was at the passage of uniform taxation legislation in May 1942. At one stroke the Commonwealth Government acquired 'an effective monopoly of income taxes'; all Australians were now to be dealt with 'by one simplified tax administration scheme'.[10] The use of the 'defence power' by the Commonwealth had already given the central Government a new role in the lives of Australians, which uniform taxation made into a long-term reality. The decision by the Commonwealth Government to remove the States from the tax field was above all a political exercise, and a risky one with no guarantee of success.

Though the political credit, or blame, for achieving central control of the taxation power belongs to the ALP, its progenitors were the economic advisers who, since January 1941 at least, had been promoting the cause of uniform taxation. In this the magisterial support of Keynes himself had been important in July 1941,[11] whilst J.F. Nimmo had in January 1941 spelled out an elaborate policy and strategy for achieving uniform taxation.[12] All this planning came to nothing in the political turmoil of the Menzies and Fadden Governments.[13] But as a Treasury paper in January 1942 observed, there remained powerful arguments in favour of uniform taxation, notably the savings in the cost of administration, the capacity to increase taxation from as yet untapped sources, and a simplification of a complex and 'unscientific system'.[14]

It is not clear who made the decision to initiate another attempt to win uniform taxing powers. Giblin and McFarlane were involved in the discussions with Chifley which led to the decision to go ahead with uniform taxation.[15] By January 1942 it was agreed that a three-man committee would meet and Giblin finalised the terms of reference for the committee, made up of R.C. Mills, E.S. Spooner and J.H. Scullin.[16] All of these men shared Chifley's conviction that 'nothing short of complete control by the Commonwealth during the war will meet the huge demands that have to be faced. National rights must take preference over state rights'.[17] The report did not disappoint Chifley[18] when it recommended the adoption by the Commonwealth of uniform taxing powers to begin on 1 July 1942.[19] However, one important problem remained, which turned the Government's attention to widows' pensions for a partial solution.

Even before the committee had completed its draft report, Copland had alerted it and Giblin to a potential line of criticism.[20] It was almost certain that Victoria and New South Wales, as the wealthiest States, would end up paying more to the other States than they might receive in Commonwealth compensation. In what was purportedly a report for MacFarlane, Giblin observed that 'financial unification should be considered only in conjunction with unification of expenditure or at least of standards of expenditure. As the proposals [for compensation] stands, it is against all sound political principle . . .[21]

Two things had perturbed the advisers. There was the failure of the Committee's report to take into account diverse social benefit expenditures between the States. Secondly, as Giblin commented to McFarlane, 'The report is noticeable for the omission of all explanation of how the same revenue can be attained by generally lower rates of taxation. The concealed additional taxation needed to be disclosed and its equity considered.[22] Giblin was somewhat blunter in his comments to R.C. Mills: 'Your Committee's scale for Uniform Taxation has got us into the trouble anticipated. It looks as if a number of Ministers had snatched at it, as an easy way of avoiding the difficulty of increased taxation.[23] Three days later, Giblin observed again to Mills that 'the Government is getting into a mess over the business'.[24] With the Premiers' Conference due to begin in six days, the States' reactions confirmed Giblin's and Copland's doubts. It was decided at this juncture to prepare a suitable bait, a scheme for widows' pensions, to which in March Cabinet had happened to agree in principle. Though it proved abortive, this proposal again testifies to the political utility of social policy measures.

Widows' pensions had long been on the agenda of liberal reformists and of the ALP. The ALP had prevaricated between 1908 and 1915 before writing it into its platform. Non-labor parties in government had come close on two occasions to enacting legislation, but on each occasion, the issue had been decided in the context of the larger measure of which it was part. By itself it was regarded as an admirable idea, as had been indicated by the Joint Parliamentary Committee's first report which had recommended a pension scheme providing twenty-five shillings a week to widows over 50 years of age, plus ten shillings per week for any dependant child not covered by child endowment.[25]

E.J. Holloway had taken it upon himself in late January 1942 to raise the matter of widows' pensions with Cabinet and with the Prime Minister.[26] Holloway made good use of the Joint Parliametary Committee's Interim Report which had recommended a widows' pension of twenty-five shillings. He reminded Cabinet of the history of previous attempts to legislate on the matter, as well as the Labor Party's long commitment to the principle. The scheme he reported would cost about £1 500 000.

Holloway's motives seem relatively clear cut. He had received a commission from Cabinet to prepare a submission on the increases to old-age and invalid pensions in October 1941. He seems to have been guided both by Curtin's policy speech pledge of 23 August 1940 regarding widows' pensions and by the Joint Parliamentary Committee's report. He proposal was accepted by full Cabinet on 24 March 1942.

Although it is clear that the ALP Government was prepared to introduce a measure for widows' benefits irrespective of any overriding political or fiscal motives, it is interesting that Chifley and Giblin decided to use widows' pensions as the bait for uniform taxation. It was a decision with few risks. The Government had little to lose, and the prize might be voluntary co-operation from the States.

At the opening of the Premiers' Conference in Melbourne on 23 April 1942, Chifley dangled his bait:

> We propose to ally with uniform taxation what might be called, perhaps a modest scheme of pensions for widows . . . That proposal will cost the Commonwealth Government approximately £16m . . . I want you to

keep that in mind when considering the position of each State as the result of the adoption of a proposal for a Uniform Tax.[27]

The linking of the two proposals may well have surprised the Premiers but they lost no time in rejecting both. As Albert Dunstan, Victorian Premier, put it: 'I am disinclined to accept the bait . . . particularly when the plan violates a principle inherent in the constitution. Such a plan is wrong; and it cannot be made right simply by adding a widows pension scheme to it'.[28]

In retrospect, the bait seems to have been too meagre to overcome the Premiers' suspicions of the Commonwealth's intentions. They may have seen, like William McKell, Labor Premier of NSW, that uniform taxation required the surrender of State sovereignty.[29] The States were not only miffed by the apparent failure of the Commonwealth to consult with them. They argued that uniform taxation would not assist the war effort.[30]

Chifley's political strategy failed. The Government subsequently introduced the legislation for widows' pensions only one day before its package of uniform taxation legislation was introduced on 15 May 1942, with no relationship between the two.

Widows' pensions were described as a civilised measure when Holloway introduced the Bill: 'Almost every civilised country has recognised that the premature death of the breadwinner is one of the major causes of poverty.' Even so, the Minister allowed that 'It would be unreasonable to expect the community at large to support every widow regardless of age and economic circumstances'.[31]

In spelling out the criteria of eligibility, Holloway said benefits were to be paid to three kinds of widows: to those with at least one dependent child, thirty shillings weekly; to those without children and aged over 50, twenty-five shillings weekly; to those without children and under the age of 50 in 'necessitous circumstances', twenty-five shillings weekly. A good deal of hostile comment from the guardians of public decency greeted the definition of 'widow', which embraced not only widows but *de facto* wives, wives whose husbands had deserted them at least six months before, divorced women who had not remarried, and a woman whose husband was in a hospital for the insane.[32]

In the first year, 1942–43, a total of 38 308 women received assistance under the scheme. By and large the legislation as a whole was well received by the press and by the Labour movement. A minor reform, adding £1 800 000 to Government expenditures, it nonetheless seemed to confirm that the ALP was living up to its electoral pledges.

Meanwhile the problem of enacting uniform taxation remained, as did the larger problem of harnessing its potential to the fiscal programme of the economists.

Taxation and social policy: the national welfare fund

Following the attempt to secure voluntary evacuation by the states
from the tax field, the Curtin Government now moved to take by
compulsion what it failed to obtain by consent. Appropriate legislation was introduced and passed in the Parliament. The subsequent
appeal against the legislation by the States to the High Sourt of Australia was rejected by the justices who held that the Commonwealth
had a clear superiority over the states, irrespective of the war and
defence powers given to the Commonwealth by the Constitution.[33]
Even before this historic judgement had been handed down on 23
July 1942, planning for the next budget had been under way for more
than a month. In this planning process, crucial political questions remained to be answered about how best to use the new powers which
the Commonwealth government had seized. On 22 June 1942, Treasury Secretary McFarlane estimated the gap between expenditures
and revenues for the next fiscal year at £45 million.[34] The prospects
for a further expansion of credit and voluntary savings programmes
seemed reasonable, but a further increase in taxation did not. That
this should have been so was due entirely to the Government's own
actions, because in early June 1942, Curtin had pledged not to impose
higher rates of taxation in the event uniform taxation prevailed,[35] an
astonishing action at a time when control of taxation was passing into
the Commonwealth's hands. Presumably it was aimed at reassuring
electors that it would not be an excuse for higher taxation. Curtin had
also hammered home this point inside Cabinet on 9 June, firmly in-
dicating that budget planning would continue on the basis of the
existing scales of direct tax visualised by the uniform tax legislation.

The economists' reactions to this can only be guessed at, given that
their chief rationale for uniform taxation was its promise of gaining
more taxation revenues. This was not the war-economists' only problem with the Labor government's attitude to taxation 'reform'. There
was also Labor's longer-term resistance to taxation of low-income
earners, used to defend the overthrow of the Fadden budget in October 1941.

Central to the ALP's opposition to Lyon's National Insurance Act
in 1937 had been the view that workers should not have to pay out
their wages for a social security system. Curtin's 1938 pamphlet had
clearly outlined this class view of social services, envisaging a tax
yield of £20–50 million based on heavy taxation of middle- and high-
income earners, pay-roll taxes, and a variety of wealth taxes.[36] The
principle of 'making the rich pay' underpinned a redistributive policy.
Official Labor policy held that social security should be based on the
taxpayer's ability to pay, using 'a graduated tax equitably distributed
throughout the community'.[37] Some Labor men went further, oppos-
ing even a general tax basis. Radix argued that 'All that this taxation

does is to redistribute wages paid to workers among a great number'.[38] Radix preferred a wealth tax and a company tax.

In this respect, a class view clearly implied that an insurance levy or a contributory scheme was inimical to the interests of the workers. The ALP, by rejecting such financial bases to the social services, implied a commitment to a more radically egalitarian and redistributive tax base.

Arising out of the mainstream Labor commitment to equity and 'fair play', there had always been support for the notion that ability to pay and progressive taxation would inform ALP tax policy. Don Cameron argued in 1937:

> Labor's policy is to provide wherever possible free social services to all . . . Such social services, although made free to all in the same sense as our public roads, parks and libraries, would be paid for indirectly by all, according to the ability to pay. The rich would pay more . . .[39]

Such a view informed the ALP opposition to attempts made by the Menzies and Fadden Governments to reach down to the lowest-income earners for taxation revenue. In Labor reactions to the 1940 and 1941 budgets, a class view had been strongly to the fore; the Trades Hall Council in Melbourne in January 1941 fought the Fadden budget, which one delegate described as a 'ruthless, anti-working class budget which would ruin low income families'.[40] In the subsequent campaign, some unions not only rejected the budget, but were opposed to any increases in taxation. The Sheetmetal Workers Union urged 'a reduction of all direct and indirect taxation until such time as the interest-free money from the Commonwealth Bank is used to . . . . finance the war'.[41] The Labor reaction to the second Fadden budget of September 1941 was as vehement: 'The Budget is . . . a most outrageous attempt to dragoon the lower-middle basic wage and lower wage earners, into a conscript army of compulsory savers'.[42] There could be no doubt in 1941–2 that both tradition and the trade union movement called for redistributive taxation policies, which was in direct conflict with the persistent advice coming from the members of F and E.

With respect to the formation of the 1942 budget, Treasury and the war-economists regretfully accepted that Curtin's pledge to not increase taxation would have to be complied with. Notwithstanding several ingenious exercises devised by the war-economists to slip in lightly disguised new taxation measures, the budget exercise held firm, and Curtin's pledge was upheld. The result was a budget, delivered in early September 1942, which made no increased demands on taxpayers' income. It was, however, vulnerable to criticisms about its failure to control inflation.

Inflation, which had for so long been largely a theoretical problem, had by mid-1942 assumed some form with increases in food and clothing prices. Detailed analysis by Giblin indicated that an inflationary gap close to £195 million was likely, which would be 'three times as great as that filled in 1941–42 in a temporary and precarious way'.[43]

The Opposition, while it had neither the intention nor the ability to reject the budget, was able to make a critical point about the gap between expenditure and tax revenue of nearly £300 million. 'Where', asked Fadden as Leader of the Opposition, 'does the honorable gentleman propose to secure the financial reinforcements to close this gap?'[44] Fadden shrewdly pressed the very points made by F and E members: 'the huge volume of spending power in the hands of the section of the people which receives about 70 percent of the total personal incomes . . . is practically untouched'.[45] He made his point in terms that could have been borrowed from Giblin: '. . . the group receiving incomes up to £400 a year are the repositories of the remaining taxable capacity, and, the greatest consumers of the remaining labour and materials which can be diverted to war purposes'.[46] This criticism touched some raw nerves and amounted, in McFarlane's selective judgement, to 'serious political opposition . . . which amounted to a crisis in confidence'.[47] This overstated the case. The budget, unlike the previous coalition Government budgets, provoked neither crisis nor any reversal of policy, passing smoothly through the Parliament.

If the budget was largely uncontroversial it was because it had not attempted to implement the revenue and anti-inflationary measures being urged on it by Treasury and by the members of F and E. Yet sooner or later the potential of uniform taxation would have to be called upon, but in such a way that the drift away from traditional ALP views about taxing low incomes would not be noticed.

Even as the final steps were being taken to present the budget, Chifley returned to Cabinet on 26 August. Acknowledging that no change could be made of a budget then in the hands of the printers, Chifley indicated, somewhat cryptically, '. . . that in view of the increases in the Government's commitments, more revenue would be needed'.[48]

It seems clear that Clifley had come under intense pressure from his advisers and from the Commonwealth Bank to find more revenue both for war purposes and to soak up excess cash by way of an additional £40 million in direct income taxes. There is no record of what decisions, if any, Cabinet made on this occasion, or whether Chifley was merely seeking implicit support for the steps he would take over the next four months that would lead to increases in taxation tied to the fiscal foundations of a welfare state.

Only three days after the presentation of the Budget, F and E held a two-day meeting. Their point of departure was the need to find an additional £40 million. The meeting began with consideration of post-

war inflation, before Giblin asked the members to assess the usefulness of an additional £40 million in taxation. Copland, Coombs and
Walker argued that by itself £40 million 'would do no good, excess
spending would have to be checked by direct controls'.[49] However,
they also agreed, on balance that 'if controls were introduced and
maintained, adequate to close the entire gap, an extra £40 million of
taxation and post-war credits would be very useful in simplifying and
facilitating the administration of the controls'. Of all the members,
only R.C. Mills was 'unequivocally in favor of extra taxation', while
Giblin expressed 'no definite views' and Roland Wilson did not vehe-
mently oppose extra taxation, he just did not think it particularly
useful. Ultimately the committee agreed unanimously that taxation
would be useful provided that full direct controls were imposed. The
committee could not at this stage say where the extra £40 million
would come from. Even so, there was basic agreement that 'general
taxation could play a useful part in making the controls easier to
administer and in allaying fears of inflation'.

Sometime between the F and E meeting of 5 September and mid-
October, a number of economists and Treasury officials began to
work on proposals for finding that 'additional tax revenue' Chifley
had raised in Cabinet on 26 August.[50] It was out of this variety of
policy considerations that a strategy to link increased taxation to a
scheme of social security was made. The key actors in this process
appear to have been R.I. Downing working for Copland, and H.C.
Goodes and Frederick Wheeler working in Treasury on a 'social
security tax'.

Downing attempted to calculate the base income which Government policy should aim to leave in individual hands. He suggested
that the ideal average expenditure for a family of four should be
around £216 per annum. 'Our problem', he said, 'is to get people
down to spending only this bare minimum'. Perhaps more to the
point, 'somehow or other, whether by taxation, borrowing, rationing
or inflation, everyone must come down to this level'.[51] The restriction
of civilian spending, he admitted, could be brought about by 'taxation
and compulsory borrowing'. Yet 'drastic taxation [was] likely to produce political objections'. Downing's consideration of heavy taxation
ran parallel to the work of his colleagues in Treasury, hard at work on
a proposal to reduce overall civilian income by that magic figure, £40
million.

There appears to be no extant evidence identifying whose idea it
was to devise a scheme of taxation tied to the smokescreen of a social
security system. Almost certainly it was an exercise in collaboration
involving Chifley, Wheeler and Goodes in Treasury. Chifley's role in
the policy somersault requires some attention. Crisp suggests only
that

> . . . from considerations of social justice and equity [Chifley] preferred
> to base the social security programme on a National Welfare Fund
> financed from progressive taxation, rather than on the insurance princi-
> ple, which weighed proportionately more heavily on those with lower
> incomes.[52]

On almost all counts Crisp gets it wrong. He implies that the national
welfare fund was the central element of policy and that Chifley had to
make decisions about how to fund it. Enough has already been said to
indicate rather that the crucial issue was how to introduce heavy new
taxation without undue or unpleasant political repercussions. Crisp
accepts the 'commonsense' that a progressive tax was to be preferred
on the grounds of equity to the apparently regressive insurance principle. However, as Chifley's own advisers pointed out in 1942, more
money could be got from the proposed national welfare fund tax rates
than from a flat one shilling in the pound social insurance rate.[53]
Given that the basic priority informing the exercise was to tap all
income levels and to scoop off more income from the lower-income
groups, this could hardly be surprising. We may never know what
went on in Chifley's mind over these months. We may only be sure
that he accepted his advisers' recommendations that the need to tax
lower-income earners remained as urgent as ever, and that he accepted the political solution of his advisers, especially Wheeler and
Goodes.

Both Goodes and Wheeler belonged to that group Crisp has called
the 'off siders', that 'smaller number of younger economists and
administrators, protégés of one or other of the senior men, for whom
they did much of the initial and detailed sifting, drafting and liaison
work'.[54] There appeared to be some agreement on certain principles.
It was understood that the Government would be open to charges of
betrayal and hypocrisy. There was also the anxiety over the general
election which would have to be held in 1943. Even by the end of
1942, as the fear of Japanese invasion receded, there was less confidence about the electorate's willingness to heed further calls for
sacrifice. (Curtin's call of 19 August 1942 for an austerity campaign,
J.J. Dedman's 'victory suits for men', and Curtin's suggestions for an
austere Christmas, provoked a mixture of hilarity and resentment.)
The traditional volatility of taxation as a political issue must have
weighed heavily on Chifley and his advisers.

Between October and November 1942, Goodes, Wheeler and
Chifley worked through a series of draft proposals.[55] It was Wheeler
who came up with a proposal to soak up the required extra revenue
by establishing a new tax rate which would raise revenue to be placed
into a social security fund:

> . . . a separate social security tax would create administrative difficulties
> and be confusing to the taxpayers. As an alternative it is suggested that

the rates of uniform taxation be increased to provide an additional £40 million.

The separate identity of the social security tax could be maintained by providing that 30 percent of the tax levied shall be paid to the social security fund. This proportion could, if desired, be shown on each notice of assessment.[56]

It was a bold proposal. It did not avoid the issue of being seen to compromise the Government's pledge not to increase uniform taxation. Rather, by confronting it head-on, Wheeler hoped to avoid any opprobrium that might result. He also indicated that this proposal was not only simple to administer, but had advantages over the alternate schemes like a flat one shilling tax on all incomes over £100 per annum. (He took comfort in the taken-for-granted principle that progressive taxation was always more equitable than a flat tax.)[57]

Even so, the long-term goal to seek big increases in tax contributions from the lowest-income earning group was now in sight, with the 'burden of sacrifice' about to rest on the shoulders of those on incomes down to £100 per annum.

Wheeler of course was simply realising the potential, hitherto unused, of the uniform tax legislation. Wheeler had come up with a 'practical' solution to the 'practical', i.e. political, problem of how to use uniform taxation to reap an increased tax harvest. Whatever the rhetoric about equity these proposals were designed to tax low-income earners both for the first time and with a degree of severity. Far from the conventional image of Chifley and the Labor Government as benign and benevolent, Chifley's acceptance of this advice marks him out as a hard-nosed realist. Far from being oriented to the values and practices of egalitarianism, the fiscal foundations of Australia's welfare state were about reaching down to the very lowest-income earners in the name of preventing inflation.

It was a bonus to the Labor Government that this proposal would in a few months' time enable it to announce the initiation of a 'new order'. The creation of a 'social security tax' within the uniform tax framework must have helped Chifley to reconcile any cognitive dissonance he may have experienced. After all, it had only been a matter of weeks since he had vetoed any increase in income tax.

Between 23 November and 15 December Treasury officials and Chifley worked over the final elements of this new policy intitative. Coincidentally this took place even as John Curtin approached the ALP Federal Conference meeting in Melbourne on 16 November to seek approval for the introduction of overseas service for conscripted soldiers in the South West Pacific Theatre. This move offended further party principles and led the Government and the Party to yet another political precipice. Though the immediate crisis was over by 26 January 1943, when Cabinet accepted Curtin's move, the proposals to announce a national welfare fund acquired an extra significance during these days as the ALP groped for renewed affirmations about its 'historic mission' as a party of reform. Chifley's national welfare speech of 13 February could not have been better had it been planned; that it was a matter of coincidence did not lessen its political utility at a time of considerable anxiety for the ALP.

On 18 December Chifley had presented his arguments for additional tax revenues to Cabinet. The political strategy underlining the proposals received its first test in an increasingly strained political environment. He began with a lengthy account of the financial requirements for the rest of the financial year.[58] It was clear, he said, that the recent budget had provided for only small increases in taxation. With a view to controlling excess spending power he recommended that 'consideration be given to the imposition of further income taxation at the rate of £40 million per annum'.

If this was the bitter pill he was asking Cabinet to swallow collectively, he had the sugar coating at hand. In another two-page memorandum, Chifley dangled the carrot of a welfare state.[59] Rather than suggesting immediate implementation, this was more a kind of grocery list compromising 'a comprehensive system of social services in Australia'. It referred to unemployment benefits, housing subsidies, free health, medical, hospital, dental and pharmacy services, sickness benefits, maternity benefits, marriage allowances and funeral benefits. It was a dazzling array. Wheeler had estimated, for Chifley's benefit, that this package would cost £50 million, on top of the existing social service outaly of £36 500 000. The estimate was exaggerated. For example, the unemployment benefits scheme assumed a 10 percent unemployment rate costing £20 million at a time of almost no unemployment. The rationale adopted was presumably that the proposal to establish a social security fund would be designed for the post-war period. But there remained the need to find extra revenue for war expenditure.

The third Cabinet paper contained proposals designed to gather the tax bounty provided by the instruments of uniform taxation. Essentially Cabinet had a choice between the three options Goodes and Wheeler had worked on since October. There were proposals for a wages tax, a flat-rate tax, and a plan for increased uniform tax rates coupled to the invention of a new 'social security fund'.[60] Detailed summaries of the rates of tax, the likely yields and the merits of each, were provided. It was argued:

> If the additional revenue is obtained by increasing the rates of uniform taxation, all the disadvantages of the wages tax will disappear . . . If it is clearly stated that 30 percent of the tax payable will be for social security purposes, and that 30 percent of the collections will be credited to a social security fund, identity should be preserved.

Interestingly, there was no statement in the detailed tax scales of what proportion of the new taxes would be borne by taxpayers on incomes between £104 and £400 per annum, where in fact over half of the additional tax yield would come from. These analyses existed. It may be that they were withheld from the Cabinet to ensure that no political opposition would surface at this stage.

Plainly Cabinet was concerned, and any immediate decision was deferred for a month. Some of the ministers wanted the tax proposals tied to the Government's reconstruction planning.[61] (Curtin said that he was indeed thinking of establishing a Ministry of Post War Reconstruction—which he did four days later.) Other ministers wanted to wait until there was a clearer statement about reconstruction and the social services. Yet another group suggested that 'it would be unwise to link any proposals with the additional finance required, which was mainly for war work'. After considerable discussion, it was agreed that Chifley's proposal to increase uniform taxation rates tied to a social security fund be adopted. It was agreed to defer further consideration of the 'social service side of the submissions' until after the New Year. With this, the tax proposals passed their first major political test.

One month later Cabinet returned to these matters. The Cabinet meeting of 16 January 1943 began with Chifley observing 'that a sum of about £40 million would be collected from the new taxation. A considerable portion of this would require to be allocated to a social services fund.'[62] The question was how much would be spent and on what. Chifley foreshadowed the final decision of Cabinet when he suggested that increased maternity allowances, funeral benefits, and pensions to dependants of old-age and invalid pensioners should be introduced immediately. Unemployment benefits, he suggested, would take at least five months to prepare, while the complex of health measures 'could wait until later'.

On the issue of maternity and funeral benefits, and allowances for the dependants of pensioners, Cabinet followed Chifley's recommendations to introduce them immediately. These schemes together would consume an estimated £5 million. With regard to housing subsidies, free health, medical, hospital and dental services, conservatively estimated at costing at least £15 million, Cabinet agreed that Holloway investigate the schemes with special reference to the 'administrative', i.e. political, issues involved, a clear reference to the likely opposition from the BMA. As for any public annoucements, Cabinet agreed that 'the matter be referred to in general terms, i.e. something to the effect that the Parliamentary Committee on Social Security has given attention to these matters and the Government will consider them in the light of the Committee's recommendations'.[63]

All of this seems clear enough, on the surface at least. However, while Cabinet had agreed to allocate £30 million to a welfare fund, it had also agreed to earmark only £5 million for immediate expenditure. There was no discussion of unemployment benefits. Designed in principle to expend £19 million, there was so little unemployment that this allocation would remain a fiction. The minutes certainly fail to reveal what discussion, if any, took place on the linkage of taxation to a welfare fund. There is no way of establishing to what extent individual ministers had to suspend doubt or criticism under the imperative to maintain political fiction.

The next step was to take the measures into the Parliament. There Chifley's only advantage was his opinion that Fadden and the Opposition would be likely to support any moves to lower the tax threshold. His only concern would have been his own backbenchers. That test came on 11 February 1943 when he made his financial statement to the House. The statement was something of a political masterpiece. He was careful to reveal all the good news before the bad. He situated the specific proposals in the broadest possible context of the Government's commitment to and involvement in planning for a better world in which improved labour standards, economic advancement and social security would all be pre-eminent.

In at least one respect there would be a unifying and powerful theoretical (or rhetorical) continuum between this speech and the Government's White Paper on Full Employment—which provides the capstone to the 'welfare state'. As Chifley put it:

> Broadly, our post-war aim must be the physical development of our country linked up with expanded production and increased population. Measures directed to these ends must aim at ensuring a high level of employment which is fundamental to economic advancement and social security.[64]

By implication, though this is not fully spelled out, social services provided a safety net below the labour market. Here Chifley only suggests the need to 'ensure further minimum social standards'. With this in mind, 'The Government now proposes to lay the foundation of a comprehensive scheme of National Welfare . . .' After running through a list of the plans for further development, Chifley moved on to the announcement of a national welfare fund, the provision of a new maternity benefit, and funeral benefits for old-age and invalid pensioners, costing a total of £2 250 000. In addition, dependants of old-age and invalid pensioners would receive allowances for wives and children worth an additional £640 000.

Regarding revenue, Chifley outlined the imposition of new rates on uniform taxation and the lowering of the exemption rate (for single-income earners) from £156 per annum to £104 per annum with a tax of six pence in the pound on incomes of £104 rising to eighteen shillings and six pence in the pound on incomes over £5 000. Of the link between the new tax proposals and the national welfare fund, Chifley said, 'The Government proposes to finance the National Welfare scheme by taxation. The most equitable way in which this can be done is by increasing the tax on individuals'.[65] He was not content to rest his argument for increased taxation only on the welfare proposals, and he acknowledged the goal of restraining excess spending. Here he took a calculated risk, possibly feeling impelled to demonstrate to the Opposition that a Labor Government could take its fiscal responsibilities just as seriously as they.

The public response to the speech largely vindicated the strategy outlined by Chifley's advisers. What controversy attended the passage of the legislation arose not out of its content so much as out of the tactical decision to 'tack' the Income Tax Assessment Bill (1943) and the National Welfare Fund Bill (1943).[66] The resultant constitutional crisis was resolved when a joint session of both Houses met to secure a compromise, ensuring passage of both Bills.

It is clear that the Opposition understood the intent behind Chifley's programme, but lacked the political will or power to press its point home to any effect. E.S. Spooner summarised his concern, noting that the tax measures were '. . . harnessed to a national welfare scheme that obviously is introduced at this stage only to obscure the necessity to impose more taxation upon the lower groups of income'.[67] The proposals failed 'to give such groups the benefits of post-war credits', as Fadden's Budget of 1941 had proposed. Spooner argued that the Government was obliged to accept the foundations of Fadden's budget proposals—which was essentially true—but was doing it in 'a manner calculated to mislead taxpayers'. He suggested that the Government admit 'that about £4 250 000 of the proceeds of this new taxation is required for some social benefits and the whole of the balance is required for war finance . . . The two things have no connexion with each other, other than a possible book entry'.[68]

Sir Frederick Stewart was equally concerned about this aspect, noting that he was generally sympathetic to social legislation initiated by the Labor Party. 'This measure however leaves me cold . . . it is a deliberate confidence trick, a sham practised on the [working] class . . .'[69] He called on the Government to make up its mind: 'This new tax either is a contribution by the workers to their own social services or a war tax'. He also observed that Labor members had fought national insurance on the grounds that it was wrong to expect workers to pay for social services:

> Under the Government proposals, the man on £3 a week will have to pay a tax of 3/- a week as a contribution to future social services . . . The man on the basic wage of £5 a week will have his tax increased from 8/- a week to 13/6 a week, an increase of 5/6 a week, which is about three times the amount he was to have paid under the national insurance scheme.[70]

Chifley, however, made no reply either in defence or rebuttal.

On the Labor side some fairly sharp things were said, although Caucus unity held sway. Calwell and the other Labor backbenchers voted to support the measures, agreeing that if Chifley had 'stolen the sheep' at least he was 'giving back the trotters'.[71]

Initial Parliamentary reactions were positive. Many commentators linked uncritically the social security proposals to the broader appeal of post-war reconstruction planning which the union movement had been pressing for. On 24 December, C.A. Crofts, Melbourne THC President, eulogised Chifley's proposals: 'The aim is nothing less than to provide economic security from the cradle to the grave. This scheme is far ahead of the Beveridge plan'.[72]

By mid-February however, Labor reaction was no longer so simple. An anonymous article in *Labor Call*, headed 'Taxation in Excelsis', analysed the taxation proposals in Chifley's financial statement. It concentrated on the higher tax rates on big incomes and—misleadingly—suggested that no new taxes would be imposed on lower incomes. It counselled patience until the details of the social security had been worked out. Brian Walkinshaw in a radio speech on 3KZ was not so kind. He drew a comparison between the Beveridge Plan and Chifley's proposals in these terms: 'The Beveridge Plan . . . is based upon private enterprise for profit . . . The ALP plan is not better than the Beveridge plan. If we do not pay insurance we will pay taxes'.[73] Even when such plans were implemented, he said, the basic social conditions which caused the problems of ill health, unemployment and poverty would persist.

Such criticism, especially that from the Labor movement, stung Chifley into an uncharacteristically bitter attack on his critics: 'The authors of some of the statements I have seen, particularly the statements by the Member for Richmond, H.C. Anthony, have exhibited all of the characteristics of the accomplished liar'.[74] He also accused Walkinshaw of uttering a 'mass of inaccuracies' which 'was a disgrace' to the Labor radio station responsible for it. Yet for all that, he failed to provide a clear rebuttal of the essential arguments against his proposals. He was not obliged to, and the severity of his response suggests that some of the accusation had hit home.

However, the war-economists had finally achieved the kind of comprehensive income taxation scheme which gave them economic controls they had long sought, and Chifley's political strategy was vindicated. He had succeeded in achieving a *de facto* reversal of long-standing ALP policy concerning taxation of low incomes, and he had not even had to go to an ALP conference to do this. He had constructed a political framework in which he could keep faith with his advisers, and he had steered Cabinet towards accepting both the taxation proposals and a longer-term commitment to introducing a range of social security schemes. He emerged having appeared to confirm the reality of Labor's special mission. In politics the 'big lie' sometimes triumphs, but that it should have lingered for so long is perhaps somewhat more amazing. It was perhaps Chifley's greatest political performance and one against which to measure his later failure in the banking legislation and his Government's industrial relations policy in 1948–49.

The unemployment and sickness benefits legislation was more than twelve months in preparation before its submission to Parliament on 12 February 1944. In July 1944, after the legislation had been passed, a conference of Commonwealth and State officials was held to discuss the consequences of the legislation for the States. Another Conference in October 1944 failed to resolve questions of who was to administer the scheme. In March 1945 Dedman, introducing the Re-establishment and Employment Bill, announced the Commonwealth's intention to administer unemployment and sickness benefits itself. Responsibility was to be shared between the Department of Social Services and the Department of Labour and National Service. The scheme finally came into operation on 1 July 1945.

The range of health, hospital, medical and pharmaceutical measures envisaged by the Government were variously enacted in the 1944 Pharmaceutical Benefits Act of 1945 and the National Health Service Act of 1948. The political travails consequent on these measures deserves a separate study.

We shall turn now to the Labor Government's commitment to welfare in the larger movement of ideas and policy associated with post-war reconstruction. It was here that the convergence between Keynesian liberalism and Australian laborism became historically significant.

6

Reconstruction, full employment and the welfare state, 1943–45

On 30 May 1945, the Minister for Post-War Reconstruction, John Dedman, tabled the Government's White Paper on Full Employment, calling it 'a charter for a new social order'.[1] This official commitment to full employment was crucial to the evolution of Australia's welfare state. The association between a 'welfare state' and an 'interventionist state' committed to securing full employment would soon enter into received opinion regarding welfare states.[2] But perhaps the issue is more complex than that.

While many writers have stressed the significance of the White Paper and post-war reconstruction attitudes, its relationship to welfare policy has received little systematic attention. Irrespective of how much the White Paper and/or subsequent Government policy actually shaped the period of growth and full employment in the post-war period, numerous questions remain open. What light does the full employment doctrine shed on the relation of capitalism to the inequalities which social security ostensibly aimed to ameliorate? Was the White Paper the capstone to the welfare state or its nemesis? Did it presuppose the annihilation or subordination of the social services in a revitalised capitalism? Jill Roe has suggested that by the end of the 1940s 'reforming zeal had petered out . . . social policy ceased to share the centre of the stage . . . the social services were judged adequate for the post war period'.[3] Yet the assumptions which sustain that judgement are questionable. Had the social services ever been in the centre of the stage? Was it 'reforming zeal' which had, all by itself, spurred on the growth of social services?

The origins of the reconstruction ethos

Hasluck provides a compelling account of the commitment to post-war reconstruction, which he claims 'had been in formal official use since the end of 1942 but became part of the currency of Australian political life . . . during 1944 and 1945'.[4]

Perhaps it is more accurate to locate at an earlier date the formal origins of what became so powerful a *leit motif*. There can be no doubt that the Depression years were the crucible in which old liberal themes were tested. The interest in planning and the systematic re-course to state-sponsored rationality in the 1940s was a legacy of the 1930s. The clearest evidence of this is to be found in papers given at the Second Summer School of the Australian Institute of Political Science held in Canberra in January 1934. The theme was national economic planning, and there was general agreement that the De-pression was a symptom of some irregularity in Australian capitalism. What civic virtue and education had been to pre-war liberals like Anderson and Deakin, the idea of planned capitalism was to the liberals in the Depression. If the Depression ultimately provoked no widespread radical estrangement from capitalism, it certainly re-sulted in an urgent desire to make it work better. Few of those present at the summer school had any illusions about *laissez-faire* capital-ism. As G.V. Portus[5] put it, 'Ours is no longer a competitive system of free enterprise, automatic and unplanned. Free enterprise has been placed under controls, sometimes imposed by society as in the cases of protectionism, factory laws and labour codes . . .'[6] Yet it was not enough. The indictment against the present order held that 'unemployment and insecurity [was] inherent in the system, and not mere excrescences that can be pared off from it'.[7]

For Roland Wilson, a young economist working then in the Bureau of Statistics, the last four years provided plain evidence of the prob-lems of capitalism: 'Idle hands, rusting machines, rotting ships and silent factories, slumps, ignorance and empty bellies. A world praying for poor harvests. These are the things that have turned men's minds to planning'.[8] For Wilson the only choice now left was between wise and unwise planning. But he rejected socialism and its 'authoritarianism' in favour of a compromise between planning and capitalism, which he called 'the newer planning' associated with Salter and Keynes. This planning allowed

. . . the retention of the existing framework of private enterprise. The profit motive will continue to be utilised as the most effective driving force for securing that provision of variety, and regulation of detail which lies beyond the power of conscious direction. Competition will not be eliminated where it is required to hold self-interest in check.

But private enterprise will be subject to more conscious supervision
and will be afforded more adequate guidance than has hitherto been
available.[9]

This statement summarises the liberal commitment to planning which
the 1940s set in place.

E.R. Walker, one of the young economists who would embrace
Keynesian macro-economics with enthusiasm, anticipated the recon-
structionist ethos of the 1940s when he asserted that the goal of planning was

> . . . the maintenance of high incomes and steady employment, and a
> more equal distribution of incomes than we have in our present relative-
> ly 'free' economic system. So long as people are in want, there is to be no
> unemployment or idle machinery and no vicious circle or deflation will
> be tolerated.[10]

W. McMahon Ball shared Wilson's optimism that in planning there
lay the hope of social reconciliation through an agreed social-
economic goal: 'the interest of the whole community must always be
the test'.[11] The question which rarely surfaced was whether such a
test made much sense in a capitalist class-society where systematic
exploitation was a structural precondition for the survival of the
order. W.G.K. Duncan made this point obliquely when he observed
that

> Planning means sacrifice; and it is highly important to ask who is going to
> bear the sacrifice. I suggest to you that it will be the politically weak . . .
>   In Fascist Italy organised workmen have voluntarily accepted wage
> reductions . . . Now who is going to bear the burden in Australia, or
> in Great Britain or in America? Not the powerfully entrenched
> interests . . .[12]

Critical observations such as these would become fewer in the
1940s. The realities of mass unemployment perhaps encouraged a
tougher view. Lloyd Ross, then a Marxist, was convinced that Wilson
'had failed to give any indication of what were the specific things in
capitalism that were breaking down'.[13] Wilson had pointed to the
symptoms of breakdown, but not their source. The liberal planners
provided a less than total diagnosis, with the hope that only a less
than total remedy was needed.

This left a major problem which would be buried under the confidence and optimism of planning for the post-war period. The problem, which the vague approbation of planning from most of the
speakers failed to deal with, was the extent to which the prerogatives
of capital would be hampered. G.V. Portus had certainly raised this
question in the first paper: '. . . a growing number of intelligent people are no longer satisfied to leave the evolution of modern industrial-
ism in the hands of unchecked private capitalism'.[14] This, however,

raised 'the question of whether the adoption of economic planning means the supersession of private capitalism'.

Lloyd Ross provided the only challenge to liberal ideology at this conference when he categorically stated:

> . . . all plans must be inadequate that do not interfere drastically with private property, that do not socialise the main methods of producing and distributing wealth, and that do not enforce on all departments of economic life the measures that are necessary to eliminate unemployment, wars and poverty.[15]

Ross had 'no limiting bias towards private property', which he accurately understood to be the case with his conference colleagues. He saw in the Bolshevik experience the necessary ruthlessness and capacity to call on the enthusiasm and creative abilities of 'the masses', which he believed the Australian crisis required. Against the pragmatic idealism of the other speakers, Ross could offer only an apocalyptic idealism. Like them, he eventually became part of the Australian state in the 1940s, committed to realising the visions of planning which animated the 1934 conference.

Like other elements of social and fiscal policy already dealt with, reconstruction planning had its origins in the first years of war under the UAP government. The first signs of a committment to post-war reconstruction are discernible even in October 1940. In this month Roland Wilson of Labour and National Service established a small reconstruction division. At least one of the motives was the desire to placate H.V. Evatt, a member of the new War Advisory Council who was insisting that the Menzies Government should take more seriously its intention to implement the war aims of the Allies.

To this new division came a small but representative group of liberal planners and ALP sympathisers. Arthur Tange came from the Bank of New South Wales,[16] L.F. Crisp from Oxford,[17] Pearce Curtin from the London School of Economics,[18] and Gerald Firth from Melbourne University.[19] As Coombs indicates, there was support from Richard Heyward in Labour and National Service,[20] whilst John Burton in External Affairs expressed interest in reconstruction.[21]

In an attempt to further the work of this division, Cabinet, early in February 1941, approved the formation of a Commonwealth Inter-Departmental Advisory Committee on Reconstruction with H.E. Holt as Chairman and Evatt as Deputy Chairman.[22] It was from the start unwieldy, representing fifteen departments, but the planners saw its usefulness as a research forum leading to the formulation of policy.[23]

It was in this setting that the advisers first outlined the theme which would recur with increasing emphasis in the rhetoric of reconstruction, the theme of full employment. Copland had early identified the need to ensure that unemployment was controlled in the post-war period. By early 1941, he was developing the Keynesian project of maintaining effective demand by Government stimulation of public works:

> General spending power [must be] distributed throughout the whole community by a big programme of public works. The infusion . . . of this spending power will maintain many other people in work who would go out of work if it were not for a new plan.[24]

For most of 1941 and 1942 the Inter-Departmental Committee met as frequently as it was able, leaving individual departments free to contribute their own initiatives. During 1941 specialist committees and study groups attempted to identify post-war objectives with primary emphasis given to the re-establishment of servicemen and munitions workers. The doctrine of full employment was animated by the fear that the demobilisation of servicemen would involve a return to pre-war levels of unemployment, as it had done in 1919. This would be the crucial test of the Keynesian faith in planning, and the planners would never tire of reminding themselves and their political masters that this was the central problem awaiting solution. It was a sign of the times that even Treasury officials had accepted this definition of the central problem. As Treasury Secretary McFarlane noted in late May 1941:

> The fundamental aim of post war society should be the maximisation of the community's social welfare . . . We can take it that the maximum feasible Real National Income . . . is an essential pre-requisite . . . If the making of roads which are at present unnecessary is the *only* means of providing employment, then it is desirable to make these roads'.[25]

However, if the early work on reconstruction established the central goal of post-war policy it did little else. Most of the meetings of the advisory committee ended with requests for more information. Administrative overload kept Wilson from giving it all his attention. The seminar-style meetings and the absence of a clearly identified policy process encouraged a discursive approach to the issues. The onset of the war in the Pacific after 7 December 1941 ended this exploratory phase in post-war planning and not until mid-1942 would a renewal of activity take place.[26]

Post-war reconstruction and social policy

When, in mid-1942, post-war reconstruction returned to the policy-makers agenda, considerable energy was devoted to the question of which department should be responsible for it. Treasury, Social Services, and Labour and National Service each made a bid to control reconstruction planning. The outcome was significant for more than symbolic reasons: it demonstrated the ongoing subordination of welfare considerations to macro-economic policy.

The issue was largely fought out before the Joint Parliamentary Committee. Wilson, as Director General of Labour and National Service, argued for the *status quo*, i.e. an inter-departmental committee serviced by his reconstruction division. He was convinced that reconstruction planning could not be handled by one Government department.[27]

Ranged against Wilson and the *status quo*, however, were arguments from administrators, economists and the labor movement for post-war planning to be carried out by a single authority. Frank Rowe, Director General of Social Services, wanted that authority to be an expanded social services department. Rowe was seeking approval to

> provide a scheme of social security covering the whole of the people, but more particularly those whose incomes . . . may fall below the basic wage at any time. Eventually steps will have to be taken to arrange something in the nature of a national minimum.[28]

Rowe here was clearly referring to the notion of a national minimum outlined by J.F. Nimmo in January 1942. Ideologically this proposition ran counter to the already powerful view that a revitalised capitalism with an interventionist state to guarantee full employment would better ensure social security than any scheme of social services. In this respect Rowe and his Minister, Holloway, had little or no chance of winning the infighting over responsibility for reconstruction. Key liberals allowed only a subordinate role for social services, as shown by the victory of Treasury in winning *de facto* control of reconstruction later in December 1942.

Outside of the administration, the Labor movement was adding its voice. At its Federal Conference of June 1942 the ALP had called for an 'early outline of general principles of post-war reconstruction' and for the establishment of a National Council, including representatives of Labor to prepare for post-war reconstruction. From the start, Labor spokesmen tended to promote the idea that a post-war order must be a 'new order'.

In ALP discussions of that 'new order', full employment figured as a central element. War did little to alter the traditional responses to unemployment within the ALP, and this assisted the acceptance by the Labor movement of concepts promoted by the planners after 1941.

In November 1939 at an ACTU Conference on Unemployment, the President of the ACTU, Albert Monk, had identified unemployment as a problem requiring a national solution. The war provided the union movement with new arguments to sustain traditional commitments and union leaders like Albert Monk proved to be important

and persistent advocates for reconstruction. Monk participated in the
26th Conference of the International Labor Organisation in New
York in October 1941.[29] His statement to the conference envisaged a
three-stage process to bring about the new order: immediate social
reforms through out the war; post-war long-term planning; and the
abandonment of private property and the establishment of social
ownership. Monk's report to Evatt, as Minister for External Affairs,
referred to the ILO Resolution which called for the establishment of
'special reconstruction agencies to be set up to study the social and
economic needs of the post-war world'.[30]

By June 1942, the Labor movement was again raising the issue. In
June, Denny Lovegrove of the Melbourne THC argued:

> The fear of economic insecurity must be banished from the lives of the
> common people. They must be better fed, better housed and better
> clothed. . . Post war planning that can be done without interfering with
> the war effort should be done now. . . Post war planning is essential.[31]

The ACTU now began to campaign for the establishment of a Tripartite Committee, with Commonwealth ALP and ACTU representatives, to consider reconstruction planning. Monk mobilised the THC
and the Victorian ALP Executive to argue for such a committee at
the forthcoming Federal Conference of the ALP in Melbourne on 16
November.

The Federal ALP Conference of 16 November 1942 in Melbourne
was much agitated by Curtin's surprise announcement of his intention
to seek approval for the merger of AIF and AMF units. Even so,
Monk's lengthy campaign on behalf of reconstruction was brought to
fruition. Conference agreed to press the Government to appoint a
minister

> . . . whose sole duty it should be to proceed immediately with the prepa-
> ration of a comprehensive scheme of post-war reconstruction and to co-
> ordinate all Federal and State government agencies working or capable
> of working for the solving of this problem.[32]

If union pressure appeared to be decisive, Coombs' account of the
origins of the Reconstruction Department emphasises that planning
for the new department had been underway for 'several months'
before the November Conference.[33] Coombs believes that the real
point of departure for the Government was its concern about civilian
morale. 'Reports of the crumbling will to resist at the time of the
bombing of Darwin' led Alf Conlon and General Thomas Blamey to
urge on Curtin the 'need to do something'.[34] The subsequent committee of 'distinguished academics and intellectual leaders' emphasised
the need for positive and creative objectives with which the public
would identify'.[35] Perhaps Hasluck's view that this committee had 'no
effective influence' on anything is accurate. Coombs, however, links

its interim report to Curtin's interest in post-war reconstruction as a 'morale booster'. Coombs writes:

> . . . some months [before November] Curtin had told me that he planned to establish an agency independent of existing departments to concentrate on planning for the post-war period and that as soon as I felt able to hand over rationing to someone else, he proposed to appoint me to head this agency.[36]

Accordingly Coombs held discussions with Chifley and with Roland Wilson, prior to presenting a memo to Chifley in October 1942 outlining a possible structure for the department.

Whatever the mix of motives, on 22 December Curtin announced that a Ministry of Post War Reconstruction would be set up and that Chifley would become the new Minister whilst remaining Treasurer. On 15 January 1943 H.C. Coombs was appointed the first Director-General of Post War Reconstruction. Suggestions in Coombs' October paper to Chifley seem to have shaped the pattern of the new department—a small secretariat 'designed to exercise a unifying philosophic influence on the work' of other sections.[37] It became a kind of 'brains trust' to Chifley and Cabinet, generating ideas and providing a good deal of co-ordination. It remained one of the smallest of the war-time departments, and had few routine administrative functions until after 1945. It worked as a secretariat, carrying out research and providing publicity.

It was a small, coherent and youthful department. The Canberra office of 21 senior appointments had an average age of 35, whilst Coombs was only 36. The department recruited heavily from the old reconstruction division of Labour and National Service: Crawford, Curtin, Crisp, Firth and Tange. In addition Coombs recruited James Nimmo, Ulrich Ellis, P.A. Dorian and H.S. Wyndham. He was not loath to recruit controversialists like Lloyd Ross.[38] Crisp recalls that both Coombs and Chifley 'were receptive men with wide human sympathies. They positively attracted ideas and people with ideas'. As for the staff, Chifley joked about some of them as 'long-haired men and short skirted women. . . [It] was not backward looking nor dominated by memories of 'what had been done last time'.[39]

Not unnaturally there was much criticism of the link between Treasury and reconstruction in the person of Chifley. The ALP Federal Conference of December 1943, for example, while it appreciated the Treasurer's work, urged 'that a separate Minister should be appointed to devote the whole of his time to post-war planning and construction'.[40]

The Opposition, through H.E. Holt, was critical of the prominence given to Treasury:

> . . . it is notorious that the job of the Treasury is not to put forward progressive schemes, such as we would expect from the Department of

Post-War Reconstruction, but to scrutinise closely the proposals of other departments. Its policy is invariably one of retrenchments.[41]

Crisp's defence of the appointment rightly suggests that Chifley was no pawn of Treasury, but it avoids the central thrust of Holt's charge. The linkage of Treasury and reconstruction ensured the dominance of economic considerations over other criteria, as Coombs was not averse to pointing out: 'Basically the whole problem of reconstruction is finance. That is why the Ministry of Reconstruction is allied to the Treasury and the portfolio is held by the Treasurer'.[42] Such a statement invites a re-evaluation of certain long-held views about the intentions of the post-war planners.

While it is clear that the planners were intent on refining their liberal impulses, it is not clear what those impulses meant in terms of a social programme. Against the frequent attribution of reforming or egalitarian impulses, a close examination of reconstruction policy reveals a more ambiguous set of commitments.

C.B. Schedvin is not alone in seeing an egalitarian bias at work in the Reconstruction Department:

> Social equality was . . . the keynote of the department's philosophy. This was drawn partly from Labor Party doctrine and partly from personal conviction. Most of those who joined post-war reconstruction had reached maturity through the depression . . . a number had been attracted to economics . . . because of a desire to understand and to eventually modify the workings of the economic system.[43]

Coombs is another protagonist of the doctrine of egalitarian reform, writing 'most of those involved shared a general acceptance of modest social reform and greater egalitarianism as broad social objectives'.[44]

There can be little doubt that the liberal planners believed deeply in the redemptive power of reason to transform and harmonise a brutal and unjust social formation. Coombs for one never made any secret of his own commitment to Keynesian reformism. He believed that post-war reconstruction was 'compatible with the maintenance of a free enterprise system—indeed it was believed it would make a healthier and more vigorous private sector'.[45]

This observation seems to have been widely shared by the other economists who, like Downing, believed that if the old, unreconstructed free enterprise economy had lacked anything it was enterprise: 'One can talk glibly about the virtues and social advantages of enterprise, but it sounds pretty silly in the face of the almost universal urge of entrepreneurs to restrictionism and consolidation, the very antithesis of enterprise'.[46]

Yet the will to plan sooner or later encountered a contradiction within the liberal terrain; the symbolics of 'freedom' and the brute facts of an inequality deemed necessary. Downing was 'perpetually worried by the real economic need for planning and the at least apparent social and political need for freedom'.[47] In this residual lament for the virtues of 'freedom', he acknowledged that under socialism perhaps 'all the fundamental decisions would have to be made by the central planners'. Worse, and in terms strikingly like those used by Keynes in his defence of liberalism, there was the *need* for social inequality: 'I know all the things I hold dearest seem to rest on inequality'.[48]

Given their class culture and expectations, the most that might have been expected from the planners was what Coombs had called a commitment to greater equality. The new reconstruction ethos sought a refurbished capitalism with jobs for all and a safety net underneath the labour market for those who fell through. What was not clear was the extent to which the commitment to social security also entailed a commitment to egalitarian social policy.

The commitment to the objective of full employment concealed a fatal flaw in the programme of the liberal reconstructionists. The alliance of state and capital (with an enhanced capacity for rational management and monitoring of the levels of aggregate demand), was the central expression of the liberal commitment to harmony. Yet this alliance was not one in which the structural power of decision by capital over economic enterprise was in any way to be eroded. It was the inability of the liberal planners to escape their own ideological rules which proved to be the fatal legacy of this period. The state aspired to be the guarantor of full employment whilst lacking the power of decision over economic matters that would enable it to achieve this goal. In numerous ways the liberal dispensation failed to conceptualise the structural relations of state and capital that would make full employment a viable political goal for the state to fulfil. Indeed, the liberal achievement at this time generated a new set of ambiguities and tensions. Privately-owned capital continued to be the chief foundation of economic enterprise and was the basis upon which the state's vastly increased hunger for revenues continued to rely. The state thus became dependent for its revenues upon a source of income largely outside its control. To some extent therefore, it became embroiled in trying to ensure that profitability and economic development continued to be the norm while its capacity to influence economic decisions remained limited. The state apparatus, in making exaggerated claims about its capacity to deliver economic growth and full employment, created a long-term credibility problem. In the endless debates about the nature and extent of controls to be maintained in the post-war period, the planners fell back in ideological disarray before the banners of 'freedom' and 'the play of market forces'.

Equally significant was the liberal failure to adequately explain the problems planning was supposed to solve. The Joint Committee on Social Security reported in 1942:

In simple terms, our social objective may be described as the attainment of a better standard of living for the great majority of the nation, and in particular for the lower wage earners, and protection against the hazards which life presents—poverty, unemployment, ill-health, malnutrition and bad housing.[49]

If the implied distinction between achieving a 'better standard of life' and 'protection' is significant, so also was the failure to identify the source of 'the hazards of life'. The great—and fantastic—hope of the liberal planners was that planning could by itself obviate the worst of these unexplained hazards. What was missing was any realistic attempt to understand what it was about the patterning of social relationships that gave rise to the reproduction of fundamental social inequalities. It was far easier to subscribe to the notion that there were certain 'hazards of life' than it was to identify the specific sources of poverty and unemployment.

From the point of view of the political arm of the state, post-war reconstruction had to be stripped of any hint that it was a socialist plot. As Prime Minister of a Labor government, Curtin was careful to stress this:

There is no threat to private enterprise. It languished and was in continual difficulties before the war. It could not survive on its pre-war basis . . . Proper control and development can launch private enterprise in an expansion greater even than was brought about by the industrial revolution.[50]

In this way, Curtin demonstrated the liberal failure to grasp that if the state's partnership with capital prevented the state from making major economic decisions then that partnership was largely illusory. In war-time the state had achieved far more extensive powers of direction—which infringed the prerogatives of capital—than could be contemplated in peace-time. In peace, planning without the power of decision could only render the state an ineffective agent of social harmony or economic development in the interests of all.

Curtin also provides us with an exemplary statement on the relationship between the commitment to full employment and the commitment to social security. The distinction he drew between the normal mechanisms of the labour market and the social security system as the basis of protection for those unable to sell their labour is a vital one. Social policy would be directed, he said, 'to providing guaranteed minimum standards *for those unable to support themselves*, through old age, invalid and widows pensions, child endowment, maternity allowances, unemployment insurance, and allowances to others *unable to work*'.[51] (My emphasis.) Work for wages would again, in this schema, become the chief agency for securing welfare. The institutionalisation of poverty for those not able to work was the consequence of this programme, however well-intentioned it was.

J.B. Chifley reiterated this proposition about the relation of employment policy to social security. In a series of newspaper articles in December 1943, Chifley clearly identified the Government's central post-war goal when he said, 'The primary aim of our post-war economic policy must be a high and stable level of employment'. The Government was

> . . . determined to see that work as well as being available to all, is adequately rewarded and directed towards worthwhile ends. These ends are rising living standards. Only on that basis can this country develop its resources fully and build up its population.[52]

Chifley clarified the relationship between full employment and social security in his last article. The theme of mutual interdependence was stressed even as Chifley also indicated the role which social welfare programmes might play in maintaining 'aggregate demand':

> [Full employment and social security] is ultimately indispensable to the other. Even at the best of times there will be many calls upon each of Australia's social security services. Comprehensive and adequate provision against these calls will sustain purchasing power which is half the battle in maintaining full employment.[53]

Yet Chifley was careful also to caution against giving undue significance to social security, in terms that have not received due attention: 'Social security services are at best palliatives to the world's economic problems, and they should be less and less necessary as economic problems are mastered, full employment maintained, and national incomes maintained'.

This insistence on the subordinate character of the social services was if anything reinforced by Chifley in his use of metaphors. On the psychological security afforded trapeze artists by the presence of a safety net; he said: So it is with social security. The modern ideal is that there should be social security provisions to protect every citizen in his or her emergencies, from the cradle to the grave.[54] Yet once again he insisted

> . . . of course, our objective is not primarily social security but the much higher aim of full employment of manpower and resources in raising living standards. In other words, the main function of reconstruction will be positive,—to create conditions in which palliatives will become less and less necessary.[55]

He may have sought to deflect attention away from his Government's social policy, but he cannot have been ignorant of what his own advisers knew, namely that the taxation basis of the much-vaunted welfare fund was regressive and had a major impact on low-income earners.

Regarding the substance of the new taxation measures and their relation to the proposals for welfare services, there is no well-argued defence of the claim that the tax basis of the national welfare fund, considered as a component of 'fiscal welfare', was an egalitarian or redistributive measure.[56] Chifley was content to make vague noises about the tax basis being 'more equitable'. The Government had rejected an insurance basis because the flat rate of contributions 'weighed far more heavily on the lower income groups'.[57] Conversely, the national welfare fund was 'raised by means of direct taxation, [and] the burden is being distributed in strict accordance with ability to bear it'. In a later pamphlet, Chifley added that progressive taxation meant 'the richer man pays not simply more than the poorer man at the same rate in the pound as in New Zealand, but since the tax scales are graduated, he pays at a progressively higher rate in the pound as his income rises'.[58]

While all of this may have been true in principle,[59] Chifley failed to deal with the objection that under the UAP scheme of national insurance, low-income earners would have paid less than they were to pay under the 'progressive' tax basis of the national welfare fund.

Furthermore, the taxation proposals associated with social services, which did not become real until after the war, entailed a major new tax imposed on lower incomes and an increase in the tax rates. This was made possible by what Downing called 'the confusion of thought' at the time:

> Other tax devices designed to reduce the political stigma of raising tax rates were the description of part of income tax as a Social Service Contribution, the establishment of a National Welfare Fund . . . and the shift of the base year for tax assessment from the previous to the current year . . . From the point of view of government revenue [this] had two advantages. It shifted the tax base from the year 1941/42 when income was £1255m. to the year 1942/43 when income was £1431m. Moreover, the Government took advantage of the occasion of the shift to add one quarter to all tax assessments, and in the confusion of thought that reigned at the time, was able to get away with a description of its 'steal' of tax on three months income as a 'forgiveness' of tax on nine months income. The painful impact of this playing with words can however be moderated by regarding the policy in its true light—as a 25 percent increase in tax rates, eminently justifiable in view of the need to reduce excess spending power.[60]

The point Downing makes is the one already spelled out—that the primary goal of fiscal policy in early 1943 was to reduce excess spending power by taxing all but the very lowest of incomes.

Any comparison between national insurance and the 1943 proposals is not entirely fair, since the intended benefits in 1938 and 1943 were different. However, under both schemes likely beneficiaries were paying for their benefits, and under Chifley's scheme they were possibly paying more. In the case of the 1938 proposal, all wage earners conferred benefits upon themselves; the 1943 scheme anticipated benefits would be paid from all income earners beginning on incomes of £104 per annum. There may have been a modest degree of redistribution somewhere, but it has yet to be demonstrated what it was. It is likely that in the post-war period, when all the schemes were operating, there was modest redistribution going on from wage earners to non-wage earners who were dependent on Government benefits by reason of old age, youth, gender or unemployment.

Also, the taxation schemes introduced by the ALP were regressive for low-income earners. The average amount paid by income earners on £0–200 and £200–500, was 3.5 and 3.3 times respectively higher in 1949–50 than in 1938–39. The corresponding increases for income earners on £501–1000 and £1001+ were only 2.6 and 2.7 times higher. Certainly the proportion of total income tax paid by the lowest income earners fell, from 2.0 percent in 1938–39 to 0.7 percent in 1949–50, but so also did the proportion for the highest income earners. The real 'victims', using this measure were income earners of between £201 and £1000 per annum.[61]

Finally, from a broader view, there certainly was an increase in expenditure on social services, much of it due to Labor Government initiatives. Thus social services which consumed 2.78 percent of GNP in 1938–39 had risen to 4.22 percent in 1949–50.[62] Yet it is doubtful whether an adequate minimum income had been established. Certainly existing benefits and those which would come into effect after 1944–45 were only half of the proposed 'national minimum of real income' preferred by the Sydney economists in 1941 to the Joint Committee on Social Security. Then they had called for a 'national minimum' only 'a little less than the basic wage'.[63] However, Treasury—and the Government—had preferred Nimmo's suggestions which were based on existing old-age pension rates, and which offered rates of benefits only slightly in excess of pre-war levels.

None of these considerations are in line with the traditional view of these measures as unequivocally 'progressive' or redistributive. There seems to be little basis for believing that Chifley's tax scheme of 1943 was an egalitarian measure, even if it did set in motion some moderate horizontal redistribution of incomes. All in all, full-employment was the real mainstay of Chifley's 'commitment to welfare'. In this way, the ALP became the major proponent of Keynesian liberalism.

The goal of full employment signified a major accommodation with the basic character of Australian capitalism, with a view to ensuring that capitalism worked well enough to guarantee work for all. Wage labour remained the essential provider of happiness. It became, in Chifley's hands, 'the ladder of opportunity', with a Labor Government steadying that ladder. In this respect Chifley was far from being at odds with the Labor movement. Indeed, his rapprochement with war-time liberals was only one instance of the larger accommodation

between the ALP and liberalism which took place after the onset of
war. On occasion, socialist rhetoric might be resorted to, but war-
time labor generally found the political and ideological appeals of
liberalism too seductive. Far-reaching programmes of change remained outside the Labor Government's agenda, while any possible
stimulus from a socialist or progressive culture was dampened by the
obsession of local Marxists with winning the war and supporting
Russia.[64]

Perhaps the most striking instance of how much the political
ground had shifted in the war years is found in the conversion of the
sometime 'militant' and socialist, Lloyd Ross. Familiar with Marxist
literature, with a background in both the CPA and the ALP, Ross
provides a clear example of what the new laborist middle ground in
Australia's political culture looked like at this time.[65] As a sometime
communist, and a publicist for the Department of Post War Reconstruction, Ross provides a clear example of the revision of laborism in
liberal terms. In 1944 he wrote:

> The major political parties (in 1914–18) were led by men who rightly saw
> that a new order would have meant an interference with private prop-
> erty, and wrongly decided that private property was so strongly en-
> trenched that no conciliation was possible.[66]

For Ross in 1944, the reconciliation of private property to the com-
munal good, so as to achieve social security and full employment,
would be the outstanding achievement of the planners: 'The device of
using the control of investment to obtain full employment is not Utopia, but a series of conditions that will save Utopia'. Keynes, as he
pointed out, was 'no silly young undergraduate' since he 'believes in
the possibility of winning full employment'. To those who feared
state planning and limitations on the free use of private property,
Ross urged that they consider the alternative, and 'that alternative at
the end of the way can be fascism'. The compromise was inevitable.
Ross perhaps went further than most of his colleagues when he held
that 'We want full employment—but this means increasing gov-
ernmental control. We are prepared for control—but we may hesitate when we . . . have to interfere with rights of ownership. Yet we
will accept this also, for we want full employment'.[67] Of the union of
liberalism and moderate collectivism; Ross wrote:

> The 20th century can find room both for constructive experiments in the
> technique of collective organisation and also for the freedom and
> dynamism of private enterprise. The essential is that both principles
> should be allowed to develop their positive merits . . .[68]

The wider process of union between liberalism and the ALP, with
all its ambiguities, came with the Labor Government's adoption of a
full employment commitment.

Labor and full-employment

That commitment is woven through the extended policy process which produced the White Paper of 1945.[68] From the start the makers of the White Paper presupposed few, if any, infringements of the prerogatives of capital. Indeed, in the development of policy after 1943, the planners were careful to avoid direct assaults on the power of capital. The White Paper surely represents a major retreat on the part of the Government from a willingness to maintain those controls believed to be vital for an easy transition to a peace economy. From 1943 the evolution of the full-employment policy required only that the state underwrite total volumes of expenditure so as to maintain the required levels of employment productivity and aggregate demand. For most of 1943–44 the economists and advisers were content to outline the doctrine of full employment.

From the onset of reconstruction planning, the problem of post war unemployment was at centre stage. Much of the policy leading up to the White Paper presupposed a post war unemployment rate of approximately 5 percent of the labour force.[69] Against the pessimism of colleagues like Copland and Giblin, E.R. Walker believed that a clear commitment to extensive planning built around a community consensus in peace time of 'freedom from want' was both possible and desirable.[70] For Walker this translated into a preference for direct economic controls over production, involving the setting of quotas on the Soviet model, a preference which set him apart from most of his colleagues. Apart from this difference however, Walker shared most of the assumptions of his colleagues. He agreed for example, that a mixed economy was both desirable and a reality which Australia already possessed. He was keen to argue against the prospects of a 'muddled economy', and saw in the mythos of consensus and the community of interests, the basis for an efficient and an equitable 'mixed economy'. His great fear was that 'sectional interests' would rise up to destroy consensus. However, establishing a common goal for the community like 'freedom from want' might prevent that from happening, and on this basis government could maintain or even extend its planning controls.

Walker spoke of the possibility of setting production goals by giving, targets for private enterprise and where necessary, to provide guaranteed prices, subsidies or contracts for producers. . .[71] While it had something of the Soviet style of planning about it, Walker stopped short at actually suggesting the abolition of the prerogatives of capital over prices, labour or investment. It was to this extent only a small step beyond what most of his colleagues accepted as prudent controls. For most of his colleagues, pump priming and fiscal policy would suffice to secure their goal of full employment.

In his discussion of the post-war controls needed to achieve full

employment, Copland, for example, shared the view that the maintenance of high or full employment would not require any far-reaching
imposition of state authority over the prerogatives of capital. It
needed only that degree of regulation which would variously ensure
that the aggregate demand

> . . . does not exceed available supplies at current prices, (b) that spend-
> ing power is distributed . . . on a reasonably equitable basis, (c) that fac-
> tors of production are sufficiently mobile to permit progress, and (d) that
> the price structure is not distorted by the influence of monopoly.[72]

Such criteria suggested that a range of controls and tools of policy
would be required, but none that would constitute any affront to
capital. Taxation would need to remain at a high level, as would some
forms of rationing, to control the level and distribution of 'spending
power'. Controls over some resources like timber for housing, a
strong credit policy under central bank direction, Government contracts to encourage production, labour exchanges to encourage and
to rationalise 'labor mobility' and the retention of price controls were
all part of the armoury of the planners. For all of his jeremiads
against unregulated capitalism, nothing here indicated any willingness on Copland's part to infringe the autonomy or power of capital.

The Government's own record on the matter of post-war controls,
while it generated considerable public debate and disquiet over the
Powers Referendum of 1944, could only be called ambiguous. Most
of the public debate centred on the alleged intention to retain post-
war industrial conscription powers, a claim which put the Labor Government on the defensive.[73] Certainly the most wide-ranging power
which the Commonwealth Government sought for the post-war
period was that which entailed the provision of employment and the
relief of unemployment 'by any and every method which the Parliament thinks appropriate'.[74] Yet as Evatt indicated it was power only
to determine the terms and conditions of employment, including
wages and hours, industrial relations, and industrial disputes. No interference with the basic prerogatives of capital was intended by the
request for an extension of war controls into the post-war period.
However, the referendum proposals were defeated and the issue of
post-war controls became essentially hypothetical.

The 1944 Summer School on Reconstruction provided a significant
instance of the developing opposition to the minimal controls being
proposed for the post-war period, and of the economists' cautious
and conciliatory tone.[75] The conference reminded the economists of
what they already knew, that political opposition to 'socialist' controls and planning could wreck their post-war planning projects.
Even though the liberal reconstruction consensus appeared to inhabit
the centre ground of the political culture at this time, opposition to
centralised government controls, which for many conservatives was

identical to socialism, was also being refurbished, notably by the resurrection of R.G. Menzies and his invention of a Liberal Party. The revival of free-market ideas was to make even the planners mild forms of intervention seem but a hair's breadth away from making Australia a Soviet republic.

An older liberalism which was concerned only with maintaining the rights of property was much in evidence when a Mrs Glencross spoke on behalf of aggrieved high income earners: 'There is a new poor, including the person who had an income of £1500 a year and who is now only left with 18 pence in the pound on which to live . . . We are wondering when will we have relief from paying higher taxes'?[76]

Coombs, now very much in the public eye as Director-General of Post War Reconstruction, did his best in the 1944 Fisher Lecture to reassure the aggrieved middle class that the will to intervene on the part of the state would not go beyond 'influence':

> Where intervention [by the State in the past] has been social—for example, concerned with the welfare of the members of the community—it has been merely protective, that is, negative. Now however, intervention is proposed which is both positive and social—it is designed to influence the workings of the economic system so as to actively increase human welfare—and to subordinate the workings of the system to the purposes of welfare.[77]

Such a view conflated economic and welfare criteria, effectively obliterating welfare values as an autonomous set of criteria for evaluating the quality of life. It also entailed that from the start of the 'welfare state', the welfare aspects of state policy were effectively subordinated to the overarching goals of economic growth and development.

This achievement was already in place from the very start of the lengthy process of policy making which issued forth in May 1945 in the White Paper. Initiated in June 1944, and primarily the work of a group led by Coombs, and including Downing, Firth and Nimmo, the White Paper went through numerous drafts before it was eventually ratified by Cabinet.[78]

The White Paper began succinctly: 'Full employment is the fundamental aim of the Commonwealth Government'.[79] The Keynesian premises sustaining this responsibility were spelled out simply. 'The amount of employment available at any time depends on the volume of production . . . This in turn depends on the demand for goods and services—that is, expenditure by individuals, firms, public authorities and overseas buyers'. The role of public capital expenditure was thereby immediately indicated: 'Public capital expenditure is the principal type of expenditure that can be readily varied to offset variation in the unstable parts of expenditure . . .' Indeed, the White Paper suggested that relatively small increases in public expenditures and banking policy could be used to expand the total expenditure and thereby increase total employment. Employment breeds employment:

> The essential condition of full employment is that public expenditure should be high enough to stimulate private spending to the point where the two together will provide a demand for the total production of which the economy is capable when it is fully employed.

If the earliest prefigurations of the White Paper had sought consensus through a conciliatory tone, the White Paper avoided almost any reference to post-war controls. The stress was very much on the benefits for all 'sections of the community':

> To the worker, it means steady employment, the opportunity to change his employment. . . To the business or professional man, the manufacturer, the shopkeeper, it means an expanding scope for his enterprise, free from the fear of periodic slumps in spending. . . To the people as a whole, it means a better opportunity to obtain all the goods and services which their labour. . . is capable of producing.

Dedman's Ministerial statement, made when he tabled the White Paper on 30 May 1945, summarised the political uses to which liberal reformism could be put in the hands of a Labor Government. He brought to the task his own inimitable style, relying on something like the language of Old Testament prophecy and his Government's faith in the potency of Keynesian macro-economic technique.[80] He announced to Parliament 'that this White Paper constitutes a charter for a new social order'. The triumph of liberal themes was everywhere apparent in his speech, as was his acceptance that welfare would be best achieved by giving access to the labour market: 'The world is well on the way to the acceptance of this profound truth, that the welfare of all the people depends primarily on full employment'.

The subordinate and residual concept of welfare was given clear expression when Dedman went on to observe that: 'At the same time the Government recognises that this needs to be supplemented by social security measures which protect the less fortunate from hardship and supplement standards of living of those in greatest need'. The Keynesian commitment equally received a clear and simple affirmation: 'The policy outlined in the paper is that the Commonwealth and State Governments should accept responsibility for stimulating spending on goods and services necessary to sustain full employment'.

It is beyond the scope of this book to assess the extent to which the White Paper policy informed either Government post-war policy or the subsequent economic history of Australia.[81] But it is clear that the White Paper proposed no basic change to the fundamental relations of economic power within the Australian capitalist order. It proposed only a new set of functions for the state, primarily to do with monitoring economic performance and underwriting fluctuations in the total level of expenditure. Politically it held out a grand new promise that action by governments could substantially, influence activity and so prevent the recurrence of mass unemployment. So powerful was the faith of the liberal economists, and so great the urge to believe on the part of the majority of Australians, that even now this promise continues to haunt contemporary Governments.

There were some doubts at the time. Economists like J.M. Garland expressed reservations about the impact of Government action on private investors, suggesting that perhaps private investment would remain too volatile a matter to be easily controlled.[82] J.S.G. Wilson claimed that 'the measures advocated are insufficient to guarantee full employment'.[83] He noted in particular the lack of argument for controls over private investment, observing that the British White Paper at least proposed some action by Government to encourage planning of capital expenditures in conformity with a general stabilisation policy.

The promise of a 'new order', alleged to characterise the White Paper, was perhaps more apparent than real. Between 1943 and 1945 there was a steady retreat by the economists even from partial attempts to impose direct controls on capital. Admittedly, the economists must have been dismayed at the failure of the Commonwealth Government to win approval for an extension of its war-time powers. But even if those powers had been granted, it remains unclear how much of the ALP's erstwhile socialism would have been put into effect.

The ALP had wallowed in the Keynesian deluge. Complicity between the ALP and the liberal programme preempted any possibility that a working class policy for change would be attempted. There was no attempt, for example, to 'equalise incomes and wealth', which Curtin had promised in 1938. Nor was there any sign that the Government would take over vast areas of profitable private industry or introduce major changes in the distribution of control *within* industry. Both labour policy and the programme of the liberal planners accepted the limits of a refurbished capitalist economy. Perhaps the complicity between labour and liberal themes depended on the hope that the state could actually deliver full employment and so reconcile the interests of labour and capital to a 'new order' in which the state underwrote private sector activity. Only since the collapse of full employment after 1974 has the possibility that there were fundamental flaws in the theory been drawn to our attention.

Likewise, the primacy accorded to the policy of full employment is really only an indication of liberalism's commitment to planning and rationalising capitalism's 'market mechanisms'. In such a framework social services became a subordinate, occasionally useful political device to soften the blows of harder-edged fiscal policy. If this suggests anything, it is that the commitment to full employment merely reaffirmed the traditional role of wage labour and the social relations of a capitalist formation as the essential measure for achieving 'human welfare'. The adequacy of the provision made for those unable to enter the wage market, for whatever reason, barely entered into it.

Conclusion

If there is anything of value at the heart of the historical imagination it surely is the critical dissolution of the myth that history is only the record of how things came to be the way they are. Good historians remind us of the possibilities inherent in any given moment in the past, as well as analysing how some of those possibilities arose. Good history also describes how particular people laboured in particular social relations and social contexts, making choices not always in circumstances of their own making.

I have tried in this book to describe the interplay between circumstantial constraints, the options open to political will, and the quirks of serendipity in the making of social policy after 1935. If Sir Frederick Stewart had not been prepared to force the issue, national insurance may well have been denied entry into the political agenda. If the medical profession had not been torn by internal rivalries, its opposition to national insurance may have been converted into acceptance of it. If the slide into war had been delayed until 1941, perhaps the implementation of national insurance may have taken place in 1939.

Even more forcefully does the interplay between choice and constraint appear in the course of Australia's war effort after 1939. It is too facile to see war as forcing governments in political, economic or social directions that would otherwise not have been taken. Yet it is unlikely that the welfare and taxation policies which have been examined here would have been implemented without the war.

I have stressed the political character of those persistent efforts to achieve the ideal war economy. I have tried to describe the difficulties encountered by the advisers in persuading their political masters to

implement difficult policies. From this narrative comes a picture of
how the Australian 'welfare state' emerged in a recognizably modern
form. It is a picture somewhat at odds with the image of it as a child of
a great reforming party or as a product of a benevolent historical
process. This book stresses not the novelty of the ALP but the continuities between 1939 and 1945; it stresses not the role of politicians
or parties but the persistent, quiet and ultimately effective role of a
small group of determined economists and advisers whose work profoundly shaped the post-war political culture of Australia. In particular I have stressed the similarity between the Lyons, Menzies and
Curtin governments in their recognition of the role welfare reforms
can play in masking fiscal motives.

In the 1930s concern about the growing fiscal burden of non-
contributory old-age pensions was a key reason why the Lyons Government became involved in the national insurance adventure. In the
radically altered context of a war economy, welfare measures entered
into alliances with fiscal strategies designed to both fund the war
effort and prevent inflation by stripping 'surplus' income away from
all but the poorest Australians. A continuity is thus visible in the
advice tendered to successive governments. In 1941 child endowment
played an analogous role when it was insinuated into a strategy for
resisting inflation. For the Labor Government brought to office by its
rejection of taxation on low incomes, welfare measures promised to
solve the fiscal and political dilemma in 1942–3.

In stressing the significance of a small group of civil servants I have
tried to avoid a simplistic structural account which sees the liberal
reforming impulse as only a cover for less worthy objectives. The
liberal reformers, especially those who entered public service after
1939, certainly had a strong commitment to limited measures of social
justice and equity. There was integrity in their vision of the state as an
agent both of rationality and compassion. It is too easy to be cynical,
to see men like Downing or Coombs merely making timely conces-
sions to secure working-class loyalty to an unjust order. Yet, finally,
there is a zealotry for change, however limited it may have been, a
zealotry oriented to a partial vision of equity. Manning Clark's historical metaphysic suggests that all of us are flawed both by our very
historicity and our passions. This seems more realistic than those
Marxian accounts which insist on seeing the architects of the welfare
state only as agents for ruling-class interests, or those earnest liberal
accounts which stress the practical benevolence of the makers of
welfare states. Somehow the historian has to reconcile the complexity
of personal motives with the structural implications of human actions.

It is to be hoped that this book casts doubt upon some of the current myths about the welfare state. In 1986 it is still widely believed
that the welfare state was or is an instrument for achieving equality.
In a 1986 EPAC Council paper, for example, we read that 'the prin-

ciple objective [of social security] is to enhance various forms of economic and social equality".[1]

Given the ongoing crisis in the economy and in the relation between our governments and that economy we need to be reminded that even T.H. Marshall acknowledged the problem of trying to run a redistributive welfare policy on the basis of an unequal labour market income framework. As Marshall put it, 'the belief that in normal times it is particularly sensible to try and mix the principles and run an egalitarian real income system side by side with an inegalitarian money income system seems to me simplistic'.[2] As the evidence from the past 40 years suggests cash benefits do little if anything to substantially redistribute incomes to the lowest-income earners. If anything, the lowest-income earners of the current decade have a smaller share of national income than they did in the 1940s. Any advocate for a welfarist system of income redistribution has to come up against the facts of the unequal distribution of income within the labour market and of wealth within the ensemble of property relations. As Michael O'Higgins trenchantly puts it: 'A substantial reduction in inequality therefore requires either a reduction in the role of the market, or a reduction of inequalities within it'.[3] So long as the welfare system is mostly bounded off from the labour market, providing benefits to people outside that market, it cannot by itself achieve egalitarian redistribution. This point is fundamental.

For 40 years we have laboured with the metaphor bequeathed us by Ben Chifley of the welfare state as a safety net strung out under the labour market to catch those who fall through. That labour market, as Chifley and the architects of the White Paper on Full Employment (1945) acknowledged, was to be the primary allocator of human welfare. It is not surprising that then, as now, the primary concern of macro-economic policy has been the problem of maintaining or restoring full employment, a commitment which ensured that welfare policy could only ever be a second-order priority. The privileging of the labour market which this requires ensures that there can be no acknowledgement of the fundamental inequalities, which even a fully employed labour market requires, or reproduces. Hence I suggest the origins of the current crisis lie not in 1974 and the return of mass unemployment but are to be found in the 1940s and the assumptions on which the 'welfare state' was built.

In effect, as John Ferris suggests, the post-1974 crisis simply revealed the precarious foundations on which the post-war state had grown. The crisis revealed that the Keynesian interventionist state could not deliver full employment as it lacked both the legitimacy and the power to restrict the prerogatives of capital. It revealed too the fundamental fracture lines in a society deeply divided along class and gender lines, fractures which the post-war planners had fervently wished would go away. Now a watered-down 'new right' economics

seems to occupy the policy mainstream. As Ferris suggests, the failure of Keynesianism and of the welfare state is built on a primary
'failure of moral vision'.[4] He argues that the appalling ease with
which the 'new right' flowed into the intellectual and policy vacuum
left after 1974 was not just because Keynesian theory seemed no
longer to make any sense. Rather it had to do with the blindness of
the Keynesian welfare state to the market-based inequalities.

It also had to do with the long-accepted perception by successive
governments that welfare provisions were simply pawns for use in the
great game of winning elections. As Ferris puts it, the relative success
of the Keynesian welfare state lay not in its actual extension of egalitarian social provision, but the capacity of capital to sustain economic growth for 30 years. In this period all groups got some benefits
but not in equal measure. Governments and parties came to see welfare and incomes policies as counters in the game of electoralism, a
perception encouraged by the various major players. What Gellner
has called the 'social bribery funds' of the welfare state encourage a
degree of amorality and cynicism amongst all the major stake hold-
ers. At the same time the illusion was encouraged that the situation of
the poor could be improved without redistribution or taking anything
away from the 'haves' simply on the basis of full employment and
endless economic growth. (This is precisely the premise of the socialist left's current 'welfare policy'.)

It seems to me, at least, that after 40 years of the Keynesian welfare state that it is time for a change. We must re-establish our moral
and political priorities. For 40 years the essential goal of the welfare
state was a residualist conception of security, and not a commitment
to social justice or equality. The Social Security Review established
late in 1985 can play its own role in the regeneration of our political
culture, if it too insists that these are the two options we as a community should debate and choose between. It might even be possible
for the Review to demonstrate why it is high time to move beyond
security and towards social justice and equality.

Notes

Introduction

1 B. Howe, Minister for Social Security, *Press Release*, BCH 76/85, 17 December 1985.
2 J. O'Connor, *The Fiscal Crisis of the State*, New York, 1974.
3 R. Mishra, *The Welfare State in Crisis*, London, 1984, p. xiii.
4 Milton and Rose Friedman, *Free to Choose*, London, 1983.
5 See I. Gough, *The Political Economy of the Welfare State*, London, 1979, and J. Galper, *Politics of the Social Services*, Englewood Cliffs, 1975.
6 See J. Baker, 'Social Conscience and Social Policy', *Journal of Social Policy*, Vol. 8 (2), 1979.
7 B. Dickey, *No Charity There, A Short History of Social Welfare in Australia*, Melbourne, 1980.
8 B. Howe, 'Power, policies and social Reform', *Labor Star*, February 1986, p. 7.
9 Ibid.

1 The origins and strange death of national insurance, 1935–39

1 J. Roe observes of the period 1915–1939, 'If there had been innovation and State experiment before 1914, it had somehow come to a halt.' J. Roe, *Social Policy in Australia 1901–1975*, Melbourne 1976, p. 103.
2 M. Atkinson in F.K. Crowley, (ed.), *Modern Australia in Documents*, (Vol. 1), Melbourne 1973, pp. 345–346.
3 J. Rydon, 'The Conservative Electoral Ascendancy between the Wars' in C. Hazelhurst (ed.), *Australian Conservatism: Essays in Twentieth Century Political History*, Canberra 1979, p. 51.
4 See J. Macallum, 'The Economic Bases of the United Australia Party' in L. Louis and I. Turner (eds), *The Depression of the 1930's*, Melbourne 1968, p. 153.

5 In general most of the theoretical and research interest has been in the political character of the ALP, which is not surprising given the tendency to see it as the party of initiative. As is well known, W.K. Hancock in his *Australia* Brisbane 1961 first edition 1930 celebrated this model in convincing fashion. The other tendency which originates in this model is to treat non-labor parties as pragmatic and non-ideological. See, for example, L. Overacker, *The Australian Party System*, New Haven 1952, p. 197. For discussions of 'initiative/resistance' themes see H. Mayer, 'Some Conceptions of the Australian Party System, 1910–1950', in M. Beever and F.B. Smith (eds), *Historical Studies: Selected Articles*, (Series 2), Melbourne 1967. See also articles by H. Mayer, M. Goot and D.W. Rawson in *Politics* 4, May and November, 1969.

6 J.G. Duncan-Hughes, 'The Prospects of Nationalism in Australia', *Australian Quarterly*, 3, June 1931, p. 74.

7 F.W. Eggleston, *Reflections of an Australian Liberal*, Melbourne 1953, p. 144.

8 L. Overacker, *The Australian Party System*, p. 197.

9 C. Hazlehurst, *Australian Conservativism*, p. vii. This is close to G. Kolko's concept of conservatism as 'a commitment to preserve existing power and social relationships'. G. Kolko, *The Triumph of Conservatism*, New York 1969, p. 2.

10 P. Hasluck, *The Government and the People 1939–1941*, Canberra 1965, p. 109.

11 See P.R. Hart, 'J.A. Lyons: A Political Biography', PhD Thesis, ANU, 1967.

12 *Sydney Morning Herald*, 12 September 1934.

13 P.R. Hart, 'J.A. Lyons', p. 153.

14 In 1934, Bland was equivocal about the emergence of a social service state threatening 'a new despotism' which could well 'substitute discipline and security for political liberty and economic individualism'. F.A. Bland, *Planning the Modern State*, Sydney 1934, p. 26. E.R. Walker, however, was an earnest advocate for social insurance as a means to boost national income and redistribute income. See E.R. Walker, *Unemployment Policy*, Sydney 1934, pp. 213–251.

15 C. Offe and V. Rönge, 'Theses on the Theory of the State', *New German Critique*, Vol 6, 1975.

16 J. Rickard, *Class and Politics—New South Wales, Victoria and the Early Commonwealth, 1890–1910*, Canberra 1976, p. 1.

17 See Max Weber's 'The Types of Legitimate Domination' in his *Economy and Society*, G. Roth and C. Wittich (eds), 3 Vols., New York 1968 and Claus Offe, 'Political Authority and Class Structure', in *International Journal of Sociology*, Vol. 2, (1), spring 1972. See also J. Habermas, *Legitimation Crisis*, Boston 1976.

18 See M. Horkheim, *Critical Theory*, New York 1976.

19 See for the British experience, K. Middlemas, *Politics in an Industrial Society*, London 1979, especially pp. 51–67. See also J. Harris, *Unemployment and Politics: A Study in English Social Policy 1885–1914*, Oxford 1972, pp. 211–272.

20 R.G. Casey (1890–1975) was born in Brisbane in 1890 and educated at Melbourne Grammar and at Melbourne and Cambridge Universities. Casey's career in engineering was interrupted by war during which he

was promoted from Lieutenant to Major and won a DSO and MC. He worked with mining companies (1919–1924) before doing liaison work for Bruce in London 1924–1931. He became MHR for Corio 1931–1940. A career as diplomat and Imperial administrator in Bengal was a prelude to a career as elder statesman in Australia after 1950.

21 See R.G. Casey, *My Dear PM: R.G. Casey's Letters to S.M. Bruce, 1924–1929*, Canberra 1981.

22 R.G. Casey, *Social Change in Australia*, Adelaide 1935, p. 3.

23 R.G. Casey to Sir F. Stewart, 10 June 1935, in A571, 35/4985, Commonwealth Archives.

24 H. Sheehan to R.G. Casey, 17 May 1935, in A571, 37/2771.

25 See J.H. Robertson, *J.H. Scullin, A Political biography*, Nedlands 1974, and R. Cooksey (ed.), *The Great Depression in Australia*, Canberra 1970.

26 C.J. Cerutty (1870–ND). Cerutty was a lifelong civil servant who had moved from the Victorian Public Service (1888–1901) to the new Commonwealth Treasury, where he became an Assistant Secretary (1916–1921). Between 1926 and 1935 he served as Auditor-General. For a discussion of Auditors-General, see G.E. Caiden, *The Commonwealth Bureaucracy*, Melbourne 1967, pp. 86–87.

27 Auditor-General, Annual Report 1929–1930, pp. 41–42, in *Commonwealth Parliamentary Papers*, Vol. 3, 1930.

28 See D.B. Copland, *Australia in the World Crisis, 1929–1933*, Cambridge 1934, pp. 123–143.

29 John Robertson's *J.H. Scullin*, (pp. 167–402).

30 *Commonwealth Parliamentary Debates*, Vol. 135, 1 September 1932, p. 104.

31 A.J. Cerutty to J. Lyons, 31 October 1932, 'A Contributory Basis to Commonwealth Pensions', held in Commonwealth Archives, Canberra, Accession Number A461 G 382/1/1.

32 L.F. Giblin, to Secetary of Treasury, 17 November 1932, in A461 G382/1/1, and H.C. Green to Secretary of Treasury, 15 November 1932, in A461 G382/1/1.

33 H.J. Sheehan to J.A. Lyons, 22 May 1933, in A571, 37/2771. Henry John Sheehan (1883–1957) educated in Victorian schools; joined Treasury in 1903, transferring to the Postal Department (1912) and Defence (1916), before rejoining Treasury in 1916. Secretary to Treasury from 1932 till 1938.

34 These arguments were spelled out in R.G. Casey, *The Commonwealth Pensions System*, Adelaide 1935, p. 2.

35 Casey tabulated his analysis as follows:

Commonwealth pensions as percentage of national income and government revenues, 1910–1915.

Year	percent of all Pensions in Estimated National Income	percent of all Pensions in Total Revenues
1910	0.67	12.3
1915	0.76	16.1
1920	2.16	24.7
1925	2.19	26.7
1930	3.30	32.1
1938	3.83	33.9

Source: R.G. Casey, The Commonwealth Pensions Scheme.

36 Annual Report of the Auditor-General, 1935–1936, in *CPP*, Vol. 2, 1935–36–37, p. 3.
37 *Sydney Morning Herald*, 30 March 1936.
38 See Cabinet Minutes, 12 May 1935, A2695, Lyons Ministry: Cabinet Secretariat.
39 Sir Frederick Stewart, A Report on Social Insurance, Health Insurance, Pensions and Unemployment Insurance, (4 December 1935), *CCP*, 1936.
40 See J.A. Lyons to F. Stewart, 10 December 1935, in A461, G344/1/16 and 'Memorandum from Treasurer to the Actuarial Committee', 16 December 1935, in A571, 28/1032, Part 1.
41 H. Sheehan to R.G. Casey, 29 December 1935, in A571, H344/1/16. Sheehan appears to have opposed any premature commitment by the Lyons Government to any scheme before it had had a chance to examine the proposal. Sheehan had scathing views about the 'amateur financial calculations' in Stewart's report, which he conveyed to Casey. Casey likewise had some doubts about the direct applicability of the British schemes to Australia. He observed to Sheehan that the British benefit rates were too low and would have to be increased. See R.G. Casey to H.J. Sheehan, 9 December 1935, in A571, 35/4985.
42 See *Argus*, 12 and 13 November 1935.
43 *Argus*, 19 November 1935.
44 R.G. Casey to H. Sheehan, 9 December 1935, in A572, 35/4985.
45 G.H. Ince, Report on Unemployment Insurance, 22 February 1937, in *CPP*, 1934–37, Vol. V, p. 5.
46 Sir Walter Kinnear, Report on Health and Pensions Insurance, in *CPP*, 1934–37, Vol. V.
47 See Colin Clark, 'Bacon and Eggs for Breakfast', *Australian Quarterly*, Vol. XI, (4), December 1937. G.H. Ince wrote to Sheehan, 22 March 1938, pointing to errors in Clark's account of Kinnear's report, in A571, 37/2500, Part I.
48 See H. Sheehan, 'Notes on Proposed Contributory Scheme', 30 April 1937, in A571, 37/2774.
49 There are no extant Cabinet minutes to suggest when and/or if the decision was taken in Cabinet. It almost certainly took place after Lyons returned to Australia in July and prior to the federal election campaign beginning in September 1937. In June 1937 Page, as Acting Prime Minister, assured some NSW Friendly Society delegates on 24 June 1937, that no decision was likely until Kinnear's report had been received.
50 *Sydney Morning Herald*, 7 June 1937.
51 NSW Friendly Societies Association, *Notes on Conference Held at Canberra*, 24 June 1937, Sydney 1937, p. 27.
52 E. Page to J.A. Lyons (cable) 12 June 1937 in A571, 344/1/16, Part I.
53 *Sydney Morning Herald*, 29 September 1937.
54 S.G. McFarlane (1885–ND). His career began as a clerk in Treasury in 1903. He moved to the PMB in 1911, and hence to Defence as Chief Accountant 1916–19, before returning to Treasury. He became an Assistant Secretary first in Finance (1926–32), then in Administration (1932–35) before becoming Sheehan's deputy (1935–38). Coombs remembers him as 'an unusual man'. In appearance, lean, slightly stooped and slow moving, he found communication difficult and was thought to be with-

drawn and unfriendly'. H.C. Coombs, *Trial Balance*, Melbourne 1979, pp. 6–8.

55 ibid, p. 8.

56 Cabinet Minutes, 27 January 1938, in A2694 XM, Vol. 18, Draft I.

57 J.B. Brigden (1887–1950). Brigden had a distinguished career in academia and in the foreign service of Australia. Born in Maldon (Victoria), he was educated at Oxford. He served in the AIF in France (1916–17) before taking a lectureship (1922) and Professorship in Economics (1924–29) at the University of Tasmania. He became Director of Queensland's Bureau of Economics in 1930 and State Statistician until 1938. After the shelving of National Insurance, he became the founding secretary of the Department of Supply and Development (1939–1941), went on to Washington to advise Casey (1942–45) and was Vice President of UNRRA (1946–47). He wrote many texts, including *The Australian Tariff* (1930).

58 See Cabinet Minutes, 7 February 1938 and 8 February 1938, in A2694, XM, Vol. 18, Draft 1.

59 See National Health Insurance and Pensions Bill Agenda No. 186, and Cabinet Minutes, 4 March 1938, in A2694, XM,Vol. 18, Draft 2.

60 See W. Kinnear to R.G. Casey, 23 September 1937, in A571 E344/1/16.

61 E. Page, *Truant Surgeon*, Sydney 1960, pp. 266, 267.

62 In line with the general strategy of passing a basic and general measure, and leaving amendments to be made in later legislation, the fifteen sections of the Bill concerning medical benefits were non-specific. This strategy designed to win consent would ironically raise rather than alleviate the suspicions of the medical profession.

63 *CPD*, Vol. 155, 24 May 1938, pp. 1329–30.

64 This is fully documented in R. Watts, 'Light on the Hill', PhD Thesis, pp. 160–220.

65 *CPD*, Vol. 156, 1 June 1938, p. 1765.

66 *Age*, 28 October 1938.

67 *CPD*, Vol. 157, 4 November 1938, p. 1288.

68 ibid, 16 November 1938, p. 1548.

69 ibid, 23 November 1938, pp. 1930–32.

70 Minutes of Cabinet, 8 December 1938, A2694, XM Vol. 19.

71 See Cabinet Agenda Papers, A1968, 1939, No. 75; Memorandum from R.G. Casey to Cabinet, 15 February 1939.

One myth about the death of National Insurance deserves to be laid to rest. It is found in Frank Green's memoirs. Then Clerk of the House Representatives, Green, writing in 1969 voiced a popular suspicion when he wrote that:

> . . . The Melbourne financial group, which controlled the United Australia Party . . . instructed [Lyons] not to proclaim the [National Insurance] Act without the permission of this financial group . . . generally known as the Temple Court Group.

F. Green, *Servant of the House*, Melbourne 1969, p. 114.

Recent scholarly analysis of the long-term relations between business interest groups involved in sponsoring the UAP and Lyons Government, suggests that these groups did not have the necessary influence to produce the effect alleged by Green.

See P. Hart's careful analysis in his 'The Piper and the Tune', and L. Watson's 'The United Australia Party and its Sponsors', both in C. Hazlehurst, *Australian Conservatism.*

My own analysis likewise suggests that the abandonment of National Insurance was no sudden decision, but a slow, drawn out process, which was much more the result of interest group and public opposition, the onset of a war climate, and a decline in Government stability and confidence.

72 Memorandum from R.G. Casey to Cabinet, 15 February 1939 in A1968, 1939, No. 75.
73 This view is found e.g. in J. Dewdrey, *Australian Health Services*, Sydney 1972, records p. 31; Kewley records June 1939, T.H. Kewley, *Social Security in Australia*, p. 164.
74 An official account of the origins of the Department suggests that it was created 'in anticipation of a National Insurance scheme', which slightly mis-states the case, since the future of National Insurance was very much in doubt even in April 1939. See Joint Committe of Public Accounts, Seventy-Third Report, The Department of Social Services, *CPP*, 1964–65–66, (Vol. 9), p. 9.
75 J. Roe, *Social Policy in Australia*, p. 218.
76 See 'Notes of a speech by Sir Frederick Stewart, M.P., "Social Services: New Commonwealth Activity".' May 1939, in A571, 39/2094.
77 *CPD*, Vol. 159, 18 May 1939, p. 535.
78 *CPD*, Vol. 160, 7 June 1939, p. 422.
79 *CPD*, Vol. 160, 8 June 1939, p. 1521.
80 *CPD*, Vol. 160, 14 June 1939, p. 1813.

2 'To tax or not to tax': the war economy and social policy, 1939–40

1 J.F. Nimmo, 'The Financing of Two Wars', 14 May 1941, in Downing Papers, DP 7/15 Melbourne University Archives.
2 All historians should be thankful to Paul Hasluck and his imposing two volume history, *The Government and the People 1939–1941*, Canberra 1952 and *The Government and the People 1942–1945*, Canberra 1970, in its own way a triumph of liberal scholarship.
3 J. Roe, *Social Policy in Australia*, p. 220.
4 W.J. Mommsen, (ed.), *The Emergence of the Welfare State in Britain and Germany*, London, 1981, p. 3.
5 R. Titmuss, *Problems of Social Policy*, London 1951, p. 508.
6 ibid.
7 This point is implicit in S.J. Butlin's detailed history of wartime economic policy in his *War Economy, 1939–1942*, Canberra, 1955. As will be clear, this, like Hasluck's companion history, is neither disinterested nor capable of reflecting on its own ideological premises. This is also true of the other history of the war-economy, E.R. Walker, *The Australian Economy in War and Reconstruction*, Oxford, 1947.
8 C. Crouch (ed.), *State and Economy in Contemporary Capitalism*, London, 1979, p. 17.
9 E.R. Walker, *War Time Economics*, Melbourne, 1939, p. 79.
10 *ibid.*, p. 9

11 *ibid.*, p. 11.

12 *ibid.*, p. 27.

13 The origins of the liberal planning ethos can be seen at work in the summer schools of the Australian Institute of Political Science after 1933. See W.G.K. Duncan, (ed.), *National Economic Planning*, Sydney, 1934. Tim Rowse provides a stimulating and syncretistic account of liberalism in general and of planning themes in particular in *Australian Liberalism and National Character*, Melbourne 1978.

14 See Minutes of Conference, 20 February 1939, in Department of Defence file 437/401/281. Representatives from the Manpower Committee, the Defence Department, and the Finance and Economic Advisory Committee, and other groups, were in attendance.

15 L.F. Giblin wrote a summary history of the F and E Committee in his 'Notes on F and E', (1947) in CP 184/3, File 22. This was probably compiled to assist Butlin as war historian. For other files in Commonwealth Archives used here, see (i) Papers of the Secretary of Treasury, F and E Correspondence, 1940–43, CP 184/3, Bundle 1; (ii) Agenda Papers of F and E, CP 184/5, Bundle 1; (iii) Memoranda for F and E, CP 184/1, Bundle 4; and (iv) Papers on War Finance and Budget, 1940–41, CP 184/1, Bundle 2, Parts I and II.

Its role has been surveyed by R. Maddock and J. Penny, 'Economists at War, the Finance and Economy Committee, 1939–1944, in *Australian Economic History Review*, Vol XXIII (I) March 1983.

16 Minutes of National Planning Conference, 20 February 1939, Defence Department file 437/401/261.

17 R.G. Wilson to P.C. Spender, 12 September 1939, in Treasury Correspondence File, CP 184/3, Bundle 1, (F and E Correspondence).

18 W.D. MacLaurin, *Economic Planning in Australia, 1929–1936*, London, 1937, p. 258. And see C.B. Schedvin's authoritative account of the economists' role in public policy making, *Australia and the Great Depression*, Sydney, 1970.

19 See B. Webb, *Diaries 1912–24*, M. Cole (ed.), London, 1952, p. 146.

20 See A. Gouldner, 'The New Class Project', (i) and (ii) in *Theory and Society*, Vol. 6, (2) and (3) 1978, for a provocative account of the 'new class'.

21 There is no substantial biography of Giblin. Instead see the collection of papers by friends and students in D.B. Copland (ed.), Giblin, *The Scholar and the Man*, Melbourne, 1960 where aspects of the life of this extraordinarily interesting man are dealt with.

22 R. Wilson, 'J.B. Brigden; A Tribute', in *Economic Record*, XXVII, (52), 1951.

23 P. Hasluck, *The Government and the People*, 1939–1941, p. 452.

24 R.I. Downing, 'Giblin as Ritchie Professor', in Copland (ed.), *Giblin*, p. 45. Giblin had met Keynes first in 1918 and renewed acquaintance and correspondence occurred until Keynes' death. As Colin Clark has suggested, Keynes did not share Giblin's enthusiasm for fiscal orthodoxy and balanced budgets in 1932. *Age*, 21 July 1983.

25 R.I. Downing, 'Sir Douglas Copland', *The Economic Record*, Vol. 47, November 1971. Downing recalled that 'The real excitement of our contacts with [Copland] and Giblin lay in their arriving to give their lectures straight from down-town meetings . . . with Governments, and business-

men about depression, recovery, economic development. . .we were bred to the world of affairs, public policy and applied economics'.
26 D.B. Copland, 'Reflections on the State of the Commonwealth', 23 December 1940, in CP 13/1, Item *CXLVII*. In this report, Copland observed of H.V. Evatt that he was 'almost a political nonentity; no prominent man has been so gauche in his political conduct'.
27 *ibid.*, p. 10.
28 There is, as yet, no biography of Coombs. Surprisingly for a reticent man, he has provided an invaluable autobiography, *Trial Balance*, Melbourne, 1981.
29 H.C. Coombs, *Trial Balance*, p. 144.
30 Ibid.
31 *ibid.*, p. 146
32 *ibid.*, p. 6
33 L.F. Giblin, 'Reconstruction; A Pisgah View', *Australian Quarterly*, Vol. XV, No. 3, 1943.
34 Coombs, *Trial Balance*, p. 3.
35 See e.g., C. Clark, *Conditions of Economic Progress*, London 1940, which incorporated Clark's earlier studies (e.g. *National Income and Outlay*) into National Income Estimates, whilst his book with J.G. Crawford, *The National Income of Australia*, Sydney, 1938, was an important milestone in Australian economics. See also J.F. Nimmo's *Australian Standards of Living*, Melbourne, 1939.
36 L.G. Melville, *Gold Standard or Goods Standard*, Joseph Fisher Lecture, Adelaide, 1934, p. 20.
37 D.E. Moggridge, 'Economic Policy in the Second World War', in M. Keynes (ed.), *Essays on John Maynard Keynes*, Cambridge, 1975, p. 179.
38 L.F. Giblin, 'Memorandum for the Treasurer', 17 November 1941, in CP 184/1, Bundle 3.
39 Apart from their membership of F and E, Giblin was Economic Adviser to Treasury, Melville was Economic Consultant to the Commonwealth Bank, Wilson was also Economic Adviser to Treasury (1936–1940), and Permanent Head of the Department of Labour and National Service; Coombs was Economist to Treasury; Copland was Director of Price Controls and Economic Consultant to the Prime Minister; Brigden was Secretary of the Department of Supply; Mills was Chairman of the Commonwealth Grants Commission; Fisk was Secretary to the Economic Cabinet; Brown was Co-ordinator General of Public Works and Carver was Acting Commonwealth Statistician and NSW Statistician. These men also sat on numerous Committees and Boards.
40 L.F. Giblin, 'The F and E Committee', November 1947, in CP 184/1, Bundle 3, File 22, p. 1.
41 Minutes of F and E Committee, 6 October 1939, CP 13/1, Bundle 2.
42 Minutes of F and E, 14 October 1939, CP 13/1, Bundle 2. Keynes himself defined the essential problem of war economy thus:

Here is a real problem fundamental yet essentially simple; . . . the first task is to make sure that there is enough demand to provide employment for everyone. The second task is to prevent a demand in excess of the physical possibilities of supply, which is the proper meaning of inflation.

See J.M. Keynes, *Collected Writings*, Vol. XXVII, p. 267, reprinted from *The Listener*, 2 April 1942.
43 P. Spender, *Politics and a Man*, Sydney, 1972, pp. 42–3.
44 CPD, Vol. 162, 30 November 1939, p. 1852.
45 See L.F. Crisp, 'The Commonwealth Treasury's Changed Role and its Organisational Consequence', in *Public Administration*, Vol. 20, (4), 1961, pp. 315–330. See also, G.E. Caiden, *The Commonwealth Bureaucracy*, pp. 74–75.
46 See A.P. Thirlwell (ed.), *Keynes as Policy Adviser*, London, 1982 especially T. Wilson, 'Policy in War and Peace: The Recommendations of J.M. Keynes'.
47 Minutes of F and E Committee, 16 December 1939, in CP 13/1, Bundle 2.
48 D.B. Copland, 'Australian Economic Conditions, Report No. 8', 13 November 1939, in CP 6/2, Bundle 11, File 77.
49 Minutes of F and E, 16 December 1939.
50 D.B. Copland, 'Australian Economic Conditions, Report No. 8', 13 November 1935, in CP 6/2, Bundle 11, File 77.
51 D.B. Copland, 'Australian Economic Conditions Report No. 9', 19 December 1939, in CP 6/2, Bundle 11, File 77.
52 Menzies has yet to attract a biographer of the calibre of J. LaNauze, W. Fitzhardinge or J.M. Robertson, whose biographies of Deakin, Hughes and Scullin, are solid achievements. Menzies' volumes of memoirs are coy, whilst P. Joske, *Menzies: An Informal Memoir*, Melbourne, 1979 is just that. C. Hazlehurst's *Menzies Observed*, Sydney, 1979, is a splendid collage of contemporary accounts but lacks the disciplined focus of a biography.
53 C. Hazlehurst, *Menzies Observed*, p. 176.
54 Agenda Papers for F and E Committee, Notes of Meeting held on 16 December 1939, CP 184/5, Bundle 1.
55 D.B. Copland, 'Australian Economic Conditions, Report No. 10', 21 February, 1940, p. 2., in CP 6/2, Bundle 11, File 77.
56 *ibid.*, pp. 4–5.
57 Minutes of F and E Committee, 26 January 1940, in CP 13/1, Bundle xxx.
58 *ibid.*
59 The articles were published under this title in February, 1940, and appear in J.M. Keynes, *The Collected Works*, Vol. IX: *Essays in Persuasion*, p. 375.
60 *ibid.*, p. 377.
61 *ibid.*, p. 403.
62. *ibid.*
63 Minutes of F and E Committee, 5 March 1940, CP 13/1, Bundle 2.
64 See Minutes of F and E Committee, 16 December 1939.
65 Minutes of F and E, 5 March 1940.
66 H.C. Coombs, Notes on Unemployment Insurance, 5 March 1940, in CP 13/1, (Item CXLVIII).
67 D.B. Copland, Unemployment Insurance, 7 March 1940, in CP 13/1, (Item CXLVIII).
68 D.B. Copland, 'Unemployment Insurance', 5 March 1940, CP 13/1.
69 F and E Committee Minutes, 5 March 1940, in CP 13/1, Bundle 2, File xxx.

70 *ibid.*
71 *ibid.*
72 'Memorandum from Sir Frederick Stewart to the Prime Minister', 12 March 1940, in CP 13/1, Bundle 2, File XXX.
73 P.C. Spender to Cabinet, 27 March 1940, in A571, 40/4446, p. 1.
74 Spender, as a courtesy, informed Stewart, after the event of the results of Coombs' enquiry. See P. Spender to F. Stewart, 10 August 1940, in A571, 40/4446.
75 See Cabinet Minutes, Meeting of 10 May 1940, in CRS A2697/XM, (Menzies Cabinet), Vol. 4.
76 H.C. Coombs, Unemployment Insurance, 21 May 1940, Giblin attached a short memo approving Coombs' findings, in A571, 40/4446.

3 'Avoiding a kick in the rear': child endowment and the war economy, 1940–41

1 *Age*, 17 January 1941.
2 *Age*, 3 March 1941.
3 See variously, T.H. Kewley, *Social Security in Australia*, pp. 190–200; M.A. Jones, *The Australian Welfare State*, Sydney 1979, pp. 34–6 and R. Mendelsohn, *The Condition of the People*, Sydney 1979, pp. 136–37.
4 C. Thame, 'Health and the State', unpublished Ph.D.Thesis, ANU, 1975, p. 358.
5 B. Cass, 'Redistribution to Children and Mothers; a History of Child Endowment and Family Allowances', in B. Cass and C. Baldock, (eds), *Women, Social Welfare and the State*, Sydney 1983, pp. 54–83. Cass, however, spends only two pages on the 1941 situation.
6 Francis G. Castles, *Working Class and Welfare*, Sydney 1985, especially chapter 2.
7 Cass, 'Redistribution to Children and Mothers', p. 54.
8 P.G. McCarthy, 'Justice Higgins and the Harvester Judgement' in Roe, *Social Policy in Australia*, p. 26.
9 Over the long term, Higgins' actions in 1907 established the Arbitration Court's 'Basic Wage' as the pacesetter for other state tribunals. NSW adopted Commonwealth principles in 1914, while Victoria in 1913, Queensland in 1921, South Australia in 1921 and Western Australia in 1926, fell into line behind the Commonwealth. See H.D. Brown, 'State Capital Differences in the Basic Wage', *The Economic Record*, March 1960. See P.G. McCarthy, 'Labour and the Living Wage 1890–1910', *Australian Journal of Politics and History*, April 1967; B. Nairn, *Civilising Capitalism*, Canberra, 1973. For a major treatment of Higgins role see J. Rickard, *H.B. Higgins, The Rebel Judge*, Sydney 1984, especially pp. 170–78.
10 The six members of the Royal Commission were: G.M. Allard (Associated Chambers of Commerce of Australia), J.A. Harper (Associated Chambers of Manufacturers), E. E. Keep (Central Council of Employers), R. Cheney (Federated Carters and Drivers Union), T.C. Maher (Commonwealth Public Service Association), and H.C. Gibson (Federated Engine Drivers and Firemen's Association).

There could be no faulting the energy of this Commission. It held some 115 public sittings, and examined 796 witnesses in the 9 months of its deliberation.

11 See *Report of the Royal Commission on the Basic Wage*, in *CPP*, 1920–21, Vol. 4 p. 1.

12 There is no biography of this fascinating man. See 'Obituary of A.B. Piddington', *Australian Law Journal*, Vol. 19, July 1945.

13 A.B. Piddington, *The Next Step, A Family Basic Income*, Melbourne 1921, p. 15.

14 *ibid.*

15 See summary of findings in *Report of Royal Commission, op. cit.*, pp. 58–59.

16 Cited in Piddington, *The Next Step*, p. 22.

17 *ibid.*, p. 15.

18 See C.H. Wickens, 'Child Endowment', 15 April 1927, in Prime Minister's Department, A461, Item 344/1/18.

19 Report of Proceedings of a Conference of State Ministers in Melbourne, June 1927, in A461, Item 233/1/18.

20 *ibid.*

21 *ibid.*

22 The Commission was chaired by Sir Thomas O'Halloran, and included John Curtin, Florence Muscio, Stephen Mills and Ivor Evans.The 'mystery' of Curtin's appointment—he was very much an unknown factor then—may be solved by J.T. Lang, *The Turbulent Years*, Sydney 1970, p. 62.

23 *Majority Report of the Royal Commission on Child Endowment*, p. 9 in CPP, 1928, Vol. 4.

24 *ibid*, p. 35.

25 *Minority Report*, p. 104.

26 *ibid.*

27 *ibid*, p. 105.

28 See Watts, 'Light on the Hill', pp. 309–19 for a summary of this abortive exercise.

29 D.B. Copland, 'Notes on Australian Economics and Politics', 23 December 1940, in CP 6/2, Bundle 5, File 77.

30 *Labour Call*, 25 January 1941. The unions' demands included an increase in the basic wage up to £5/0/0.

31 Minutes of F and E Committee, 10–12 October 1940.

32 *ibid.*

33 Executive Council Minute No. 151 of 1940. For a full description of these changes see O.R. de Foenander, *Wartime Labour Developments in Australia*, Melbourne, 1943, pp. 3–8.

34 See R. Wilson, 'Notes on the Case for an Increase in the Basic Wage: A Commentary on the Paper of J.D. Sutcliffe', (ND but late September 1940), in the Downing Papers, Group 6/1/2, The Basic Wage 1940, Melbourne University Archives.

35 'Notes on the Proposed Basic Wage Increase', no author, no date, in the Downing Papers, 6/1/3, Melbourne University Archives. Internal evidence suggests it almost certainly came from within Labour and National Service.

36 *CPD*, Vol. 166, 25 March 1941, p. 164.

37 Richard I. Downing (1915–1976). Downing was to be one of the brightest of the heirs apparent to Copland and Giblin, both of whom shaped his career at Melbourne University (1932–35). He was a Keynesian of the first persuasion, being involved in discussion of the *General Theory* with W.B. Reddaway in early 1936. He spent two years at Cambridge, 1936–38, and returned to lecture at Melbourne University during 1940. His later work with Copland and on the White Paper is referred to in other chapters.

38 Professor W. Prest to author, 30 May 1983. Prest further writes, 'The introduction of Child Endowment . . . occurred as I recall it, under threat of an increase in the basic wage. In February of 1941 the Arbitration Court had refused to grant a wage increase but had deferred a final decision until after June 30th. It was an open secret at the time that Mr Justice Beeby would grant an increase if child endowment were not introduced.' Prest suggests that, 'Copland probably saw Dick's [Downing] memorandum before it was submitted to Mr Justice Beeby'.

39 Professor H.G. Burton to author, 4 June 1983. Professor Burton has no definite recollection of these discussions, but believes that 'it is highly probable' that Downing was acting on behalf of Professor Copland. See also H.W. Arndt, 'R.J. Downing: Economist and Social Reformer', *The Economic Record*, Vol. 52, (132), September 1976.

40 I was not able to locate a copy of this document. It may have been destroyed or my search was deficient. I have relied on citations from it in Department of Labour and National Services, 'Report on Confidential Memorandum by Chief Judge Beeby', 13 January 1941, which was prepared by Roland Wilson, located in Cabinet Secretariat 1: Menzies and Fadden Ministries: Minutes and Submissions, CRS A2697 XM, Item 5.

41 *ibid.*

42 Wilson tabulated this effect as follows:

Actual Income (Annual)	Net Gain Taxpayer with 1 child	After Tax and with Endowment	
		Taxpayer and 2 children	Taxpayer and 3 children
£		£	£
250	Nil	+ 13	+ 26
300	"	+ 13	+ 26
400	"	+ 6	+ 12
500	"	+ 6	+ 12
600	"	+ 5	+ 11
1 000	"	− 2	− 2
1 500	"	− 9	− 18
2 000	"	− 12	− 24

There was also horizontal redistribution from single men and men with two dependants.

43 In practice, the actual costs of child endowment were around £11.5 m. between 1941–44 and revenues from the payroll tax around £8.9 m, (*Commonwealth Year Book 1944–45*, p. 248). However these figures did

not take into account the invisible gains from removing children-exemption limits worth some £2.3 m. p.a.

44 S.G. McFarlane, 'Notes on Child Endowment', 12 January 1941 in F and E Papers, 1936–43, in CP 184/1, Bundle 2.
45 D.B. Copland, 'Incidence of a Pay Roll Tax', (ND) in CP 13/1, File 5847. (This appears to have been written in December 1940).
46 H.E. Holt, 'The Basic Wage and Child Endowment', 17 January 1941, Cabinet Agenda No. 534, in CRS A2697 XM, Item 5, Menzies and Fadden Ministries.
47 Cabinet Secretariat (1) Minutes of Menzies and Fadden Cabinets, CRS A2694, XM, Vol. 6, 17 January 1941.
48 R. Wilson, 'Interim Report to the Sub-Committee of Cabinet on Family Allowances', 5 February 1941, in Minutes and Papers of F and E, 1939–43, CP 184/1, Bundle 2.
49 *CPD*, Vol. 166, 27 March 1941, pp. 340–44.
50 *Sydney Morning Herald*, 8 February 1941.
51 *Labor Call*, 3 April 1941.
52 *Labor Call*, 23 January 1941. This was the prelude to the bitter attacks on the Government for colluding with the Arbitration Court in an adjournment debate on the matter, on 25 March 1941. See *CPD*, Vol. 166, 25 March 1941, pp. 151–166.
53 *Labor Call*, 13 February 1941.
54 *ibid.*

4 'The light on the hill': Social Security and the advent of Labor, 1941

1 R.M. Crawford, *Australia*, London, 1970 (3rd Edition), p. 170.
2 J. Roe, *Social Policy in Australia*, p. 217.
3 T.H. Kewley, *Social Security in Australia*, p. 176. I have had the benefit of reading a paper written by Sheiler Shaver (yet to be published) and of discussions with her on the work of the Joint Committee.
4 Minutes of Advisory War Council Meeting of 17 June 1941, Minute No. 403, in Advisory War Council Minutes (Books) 1940–45, CRS A2682.
5 *Sydney Morning Herald*, 18 June 1941.
6 F.H. Stewart, A Social Security Programme, (Cabinet Submission), 2 July 1941 in CP 71/8, Bundle 1, p. 1.
7 None of the members, with the possible exception of Blackburn, had a record of strong interest in 'social reforms'. H.C. Barnard was a respected trade unionist MHR with seven years' parliamentary experience, while Senator R.V. Keane was a senior ARU executive member with many connections in the ALP. Blackburn was one of the gadflies of the ALP, a moralistic politician who put principles first and was no friend to Curtin. J.A. Perkins had had a long and undistinguished career in various UAP cabinets. Senator Cooper's chief claim to recognition was his one-leggedness, whilst Colonel R.S. Ryan made much of his Harrow background and marriage to a titled lady.
8 L.F. Crisp, *Ben Chifley*, London 1960, p. 189.
9 M.A. Jones, *The Australian Welfare State*, Sydney, 1980, pp. 34–5.
10 Roy Rowe (1897–   ), not to be confused with F.H. Rowe, first Director

General of Social Services. Roy Rowe had served in the first AIF, 1914–18, before working in the War Office and for the Federal Executive of the RSL, 1928–32. He worked for Stewart from 1936 to 1941, remained Secretary to the Joint Committee until 1945 and became the Federal Secretary of the Association of Chambers of Commerce of Australia.

11 R. Mendelsohn (1914–   ), M.Ec., Ph.D. He was educated at Fort St. High, Sydney University, and the London School of Economics. He served in the AIF (1942–43) and was involved in overseas postings until 1951 when he joined the Cabinet Secretariat as Assistant Secretary to the Prime Minister's Department (1956–65). He was also first Assistant Secretary to the Department of Housing (1965–1973). He has published widely in the field of social policy.

12 Printed in *Labor Call*, 15 October 1942. It was an essay submitted on 'The Best Means to Achieve the Socialist Objective.'

13 See Minutes of Meeting of Joint Parliamentary Committee on Social Security, 21 July 1941. These Minutes and all subsequent Minutes are to be found in CP 71/1, Files 1 and 2.

14 Keane's statement, and papers by F.H. Rowe, Stewart and Mendelsohn, are found in Transcripts of Evidence, Joint Committee on Social Security, 1940–46, CP 72/2, Item 1.

15 R. Mendelsohn, Social Security in Australia, in CP 72/2, Item 1.

16 Apart from his testimony (interview, 8 August 1975), the evidence suggests Mendelsohn's dominance. See Minutes of Committee Meeting, 18, 19 September 1941, in CP 71/2, Files 1 and 2.

17 Joint Parliamentary Committee on Social Security, First Report, Social Security Planning and Legislation, 24 September 1941, in *CPP*, 1940–43, Vol. 2, p. 3.

18 R. Mendelsohn, Social Security in Australia in CP 72/2, Item 1.

19 *Argus*, 25 September 1941.

20 *Sydney Morning Herald*, 25 September 1941.

21 *Labor Call*, 16 October 1941.

22 B. Dickey, *No Charity There*, p. 169.

23 Curtin still awaits a great biographer. Lloyd Ross' *John Curtin*, Melbourne, 1977 was a long time in the making but fails to deal with Curtin in anything more than a pedestrian way. I. Dowsing, *Curtin of Australia*, (Melbourne 1968), is an overwritten, extended essay. A. Chester, *John Curtin*, (Sydney, 1943), has some journalistic colour.

24 J.J. Dedman has contributed a unique insight into the Curtin Cabinet in his 'The Labor Government in the Second World War: A Memoir', in *Labor History*, (21), (22), (23), November 1971, May, November, 1972.

25 L.F. Crisp, *Ben Chifley*, pp. 147.

26 *Ibid*, p. 169.

27 *Ibid*, p. 321.

28 This point has been made most felicitously by D.W. Rawson, 'Labour, Socialism and the Working Class', *Australian Journal of Politics and History*, Vol. VII, (1), May 1961.

29 *Labor Call*, 1 April 1937.

30 V.G. Childe, *How Labor Governs*, London, 1923, provides an early and influential account of the 'betrayal' theme.

31 See e.g. Frank Farrell, *International Socialism and Australian Labor*,

Sydney, 1981 and V. Burgmann, *In Our Time: Socialism and the Rise of Labor 1885–1905*, Sydney, 1985.

32 By 'social democratic' I mean the kind of social democracy found in the German Social Democratic Party up to 1914. See C. Schorske, *German Social Democracy*, (Harvard, 1953), and Peter Gay, *The Dilemma of German Social Democracy*, New York, 1966.

33 A. Mètin, *Socialism Without Doctrine*, Chippendale, 1977, p. 51.

34 Chifley to the NSW ALP Conference in *Labor Call*, 17 July 1949.

35 Robin Gollan, 'Some Consequences of the Depression', in R. Cooksey, *op. cit.*, p. 184. P. Love, *Labour and the Money Power*, Melbourne, 1984, provides a convincing account of Labor's consumptionist views which I suggest was a point of affinity with Keynes.

36 *Labor Call*, 23 September 1937.

37 *Labor Call*, 23 September 1939.

38 *Labor Call*, 22 September 1940.

39 J.J. Holland, in *Labor Call*, 14 March 1940.

40 See J. Curtin, *Why Labor Opposed the Lyons Government's National Insurance Scheme*, Perth 1938, which drew on Communist Party arguments for a radical and redistributive tax base for social security.

41 *Labor Call*, 29 August 1940.

42 *Labor Call*, 4 May 1939.

43 E.J. Holloway, 'Unemployment Insurance', 4 November 1941, in Agenda Items for Curtin Cabinet, CRS A2700, Vol. 1.

44 Minutes of Meeting of Cabinet, 4 November 1941, in Minutes of Curtin Ministry, CRS A2703, Vol. 1. (b).

45 The Joint Committee took submissions only from W.C. Balmford (Commonwealth/Actuary), J.F. Nimmo (Treasury), and F.H. Rowe, (Secretary to Social Services), up to January 1942. Mendelsohn then drafted up what became the Second and Third Reports for submission by 5 March to the Committee which were signed and presented to the Minister on 6 March.

46 R. Mendelsohn, 'Memorandum for the Social Security Committee, Unemployment Insurance', (ND but approximately early November 1941), CP 71/2, File 1. His paper was submitted for the meeting of 13 November 1942. See Minutes of Joint Parliamentary Committee 13 November 1941, in CP 71/1, Files 1 and 2.

47 R. Mendelsohn, 'Memorandum: Notes on Unemployment Insurance', 13 February 1942, p. 5, in CP 71/2, Files 1 and 2.

48 The semantic confusion involved here in talking about an 'insurance tax' is indicative of the conceptual transition taking place. It also led to some later confusion.
    A.H. Birch, *Federalism, Finance and Social Legislation in Canada, Australia and the United States*, Oxford, 1955, suggests that the Committee was 'rather muddled about the nature of a contributory scheme', p. 231. This view is supported by T.H. Kewley who sees that the diversity of views could give an impression of confusion (Kewley, *Social Security*, p. 240). Some of this confusion appears to have arisen only because of claims made in 1944 that the contributory principle had been rejected as a basis for social legislation by the committee (see Senator J.M. Fraser, in *CPD*, Vol. 170, 10 February 1944, p. 50). Senator W.J. Cooper objected

to Fraser's claim saying that indeed the committee had intended a contributory basis with 'personal contributions' from taxpayers. Cooper then
went on to perpetuate great confusion by saying that the 1943 National
Welfare Fund was not in accord with this principle.

49 The first draft of 'Social Security in Australia', January 1942, 5 January
1942, in CP 6/1, Item B, File 87, went to other economists as well as to
the Joint Committee. The Record of J.F. Nimmo's statement to Joint
Committee, 16 January 1942, in Transcripts of Evidence, CP 71/3, Bundle 2.

50 J.F. Nimmo (1912–   ). Educated at Geelong College and Melbourne
University, he was in 1940–41 a research officer in Treasury. He would go
on to a career in Treasury before becoming First Assistant Secretary to
Prime Minister's Department (1960–64) and First Secretary to Depart-
ment of Housing (1964–73), a career running in close harness with that of
Mendelsohn.

51 J.F. Nimmo, 'Social Security in Australia', p. 1.

52 Nimmo proposed a scale of benefits as follows:

A *Benefits under guaranteed minimum incomes*
(persons with dependants, the aged, the incapacitated and widows)

	per annum	per week
	£	s
Man and wife (or other dependant adult)	117	45
Man, wife and child	143	55
Adult and dependant child	91	35
Male aged 65 years or over	65	25
Female aged 60 years or over	65	25
Incapacitated male or female	65	25
Widow	65	25

Note: The existing child endowment scheme would be retained and would be assumed to provide for all
     dependant children in excess of the first.

B *Unemployment benefits*
(persons without dependants)

	per annum	per week
	£ s	s d
Single adult male	58/5	22/6
Single adult female	52/0	20/0
Youth aged 16–20 years	45/5	17/6
Girl aged 16–20 years	39/0	15/0

53 Nimmo justified the low minimum on the grounds that the average income was so low that a higher minimum was not possible. An older
(Benthamite) principle (of lesser eligibility) appeared in the claim that
'the level of the minimum must be considerably below the basic wage-
. . . forestalling a criticism that people will prefer to get something for
nothing rather than work'. *Ibid*, p. 2.

54 Joint Parliamentary Committee on Social Security, *Second Interim Report, Unemployment and War Emergency*, 6 March 1942. *CCP*. 1940–43,
Vol. II, p. 3.

55 E.J. Holloway to Cabinet, 'Unemployment Benefits', 14 April 1942, in
Cabinet Agenda Papers in CRS A2700, Vol. 1 (c), and Minutes of
Cabinet Meeting, 20 April 1942, in CRS A2703, Vol. 1 (b).

56 Joint Parliamentary Committee on Social Security, *Third Report, Consolidation of Social Legislation and Post-War Unemployment, CCP*,
1940–43, Vol. 11.

5 'Stealing a sheep and giving the trotters away in charity': Labor and the national welfare fund, 1942–43

1 See S.J. Butlin and C.B. Schedvin, *War Economy 1942–1945*, Canberra, 1977, pp. 1–13 and pp. 310–316.
2 D.B. Copland, 'Labor's Economic Policy', 16 November 1941, drafted for Curtin and for later publication, in CP 6/2, Bundle 1, File 51, p. 1.
3 *Ibid.*
4 Minutes of Finance and Economic Committee, 24 February 1942 in CP 13/1, Bundle 2/3, File XXX.
5 L.F. Giblin, 'Necessary Reductions in Private Spending', 13 February 1942, in Finance and Economic Agenda Papers, (Item 29a).
6 D.B. Copland to the Prime Minister, 10 October 1941, in CP 6/1, Item B, File LXXXVII, 'Social Security and Social Services'.
7 D.B. Copland, 'Social Services in War Time', 12 February 1942, in CP 6/1, Item B, File 87: Social Security and Social Services, 1941–43.
8 *CPD*, Vol. 170, 30 April 1942, p. 705.
9 *Ibid.*
10 R.L. Mathews and W. Jay, *Federal Finance*, Melbourne 1977, pp. 2–3.
11 Cable from J.M. Keynes to L.F. Giblin, 2 July 1941, in CP 13/1, Bundle 2/3, File XXX.
12 J.F. Nimmo, Notes on the Co-ordination of Commonwealth and State Income Taxes, 25 January 1941, in CP 184/1, Bundle 2, Part 1.
13 For details of the proposals and the political problems it created, see Watts, Light on the Hill, pp. 360–65.
14 See Precis of Uniform Taxation File J 264/17, 29 January 1942, in CP 184/1, Bundle 2, Part 1, Files 25 (A) and 15.
15 Giblin and McFarlane met on six occasions with Chifley in late December 1941 to discuss uniform taxation. See CP 184/1, Bundle 2, Part 1, Files 25 (A) for minutes of these discussions. It should be noted that uniform taxation had become more politically attractive through 1941. Submissions to Treasury favouring the scheme included representations from the Federated Taxpayers Association, the Australian National Service League, the NSW Country Party, the Associated Chamber of Commerce, the NSW Taxpayers Association and other like groups. A curious file from Copland's office reveals a highly political and quite confidential intervention by the Tasmanian Governor, Sir Ernest Clark, presumably without his Premier's knowledge. Copland forwarded these submissions minus the identity of the author to A.W. Fadden in June and July 1941. See CP 6/2, Bundle 3, File LI, 'Taxation File'.
16 J.B. Chifley to J. Curtin, 23 February 1942, in CP 184/1, Bundle 2, File 25 (A), Part 1.
17 J. B. Chifley, *CPD*, Vol. 170, 15 May 1942, p. 1286.
18 Chifley, in acknowledging receipt of the Committee's report, added a characteristic P.S.: 'It's a bloody fine job.' J.B. Chifley to R.C. Mills, 9 April 1942, in S.J. Butlin Papers (Item 99).
19 'Report of the Committee on Uniform Taxation', 28 March 1942, copies in S.J. Butlin Papers (Item 99).
20 D.B. Copland to J.B. Chifley, (10 March 1942, and subsequent memos of 15 April and 20 April 1942), in CP 6/2, Bundle 3, File LI.

21 L.F. Giblin, 'Notes on Uniform Taxation Report', 17 April 1942, (in S.J. Butlin Papers (Item 99). Though intended for McFarlane's eyes only, these notes apparently 'did the rounds' of the advisers. Giblin had to apologise to Mill for his 'rather vicious document'. L.F. Giblin to R.C. Mills, 17 April 1942, (in S.J. Butlin Papers (Item 99)).
22 L.F. Giblin, 'Notes on Uniform Taxation Report', 17 April 1942, in CP 184/1 Bundle 2, Part 1, Files 25 (A) and 15.
23 L.F. Giblin to R.C. Mills, 17 April 1942, S.J. Butlin Papers.
24 L.F. Giblin to R.C. Mills, 20 April 1942, S.J. Butlin Papers, (Item 99).
25 See Joint Committee on Social Security, Interim Report p. 8. The Report also recommended, in a spirit of rare generosity and humanity, that *de facto* wives be eligible for widows' pensions.
26 E.J. Holloway to J. Curtin, 5 February 1942 and E.J. Holloway to Cabinet, 31 January 1942, in 'Cabinet Agenda Items', CRS A2700 (Curtin Ministry), Vol. 2.
27 *Proceedings of Conference of Commonwealth and State Ministers, 23-24 April 1942*, p. 7, (in S.J. Butlin Papers (Item 99)).
28 *Proceedings of Conference*, p. 12.
29 *Sydney Morning Herald*, 23 April 1942.
30 *Sydney Morning Herald*, 23 April 1942.
31 *CPD*, Vol. 170, 14 May 1942, pp. 1236–37.
32 The National Council of Women was concerned that the legislation was 'contrary to the Foundation of National life . . . the home', (NCWA, 21 November 1942 to John Curtin). Rev. Gordon Powell of Scots Church, saw it as 'striking a terrific blow at the moral foundation of our society'. (Powell to J. Curtin, 30 June 1942). All in Correspondence to Prime Minister, CP 56 52–134, Alphabetical File L-U-1942, Special Subjects.
33 See *Commonwealth Law Reports*, (Vol. 65) 1941–1942, pp. 373–472.
34 S.G. McFarlane, 'Working Papers on 1942–43 Budget', 22 June 1942, in A571, Part 1, (42/2568).
35 *Sydney Morning Herald*, 12 June 1942.
36 Central Executive of Victorian ALP, Recommendation Number 5 to 1939 Victorian ALP Conference, in *Labor Call*, 13 April 1939.
37 *Labor Call*, 14 October 1939.
38 *Labor Call*, 15 April 1937.
39 *Labor Call*, 9 January 1937.
40 *Labor Call*, 6 February 1941.
41 *Labor Call*, 2 October 1941.
42 *Ibid.*
43 L.F. Giblin, Excess Spending Power 1941–42, 26 June 1942 in CP 6/2, Item B, File SSV.
44 *CPD*, Vol. 172, 10 September 1942, p. 162.
45 *Ibid.* p. 163.
46 *Ibid.*
47 S.G. McFarlane to J.B. Chifley, 12 September 1942, in A571, (42/2568), Part 1.
48 Minutes of Meeting of full Cabinet, 26 August 1942 (Under *Item 311*: Financial Proposals) in CRS A2703 XM, Vol. 1 (c).
49 See Notes of Meeting of Financial and Economic Advisory Committee Meeting, 4–5 September 1942. A very useful memo by R.I. Downing, 'Finance in Australia', 7 September 1942, summarises in more detail the

arguments of the various members as well as the conclusions arrived at. Both in CP 6/2, Item B, File XXV.

50 The phrase 'additional tax revenues' appears on the file in Treasury on the preparation of the National Welfare Fund, in A571, (42.4354).

51 See R.I. Downing, 'War Time Spending', successive drafts of 7 October 1942 and 18 November 1942, in CP 6/2 Item B, File XXV.

52 L.F. Crisp, *Ben Chifley*, p. 189.

53 **Table 12: Comparison of effects of flat contributory rate and progressive national welfare fund rates**

Income group	Flat 1/– in rate	National welfare fund tax rates
£	£	£
Under 400 p.a.	19.5m	21.5m
400–1000	6.0m	13.0m
1000 and over	2.5m	5.5m

This table draws on calculations by H.J. Goodes of a flat one shilling contribution rate in his 'Sixpenny Tax', 8 October 1942, in A571, (42,4354), compared with estimates made for the new tax rates of March 1943.

54 L.F. Crisp, *Ben Chifley*, p. 257.

55 The list of papers include:

F. Wheeler, Proposals for Collecting Additional Taxation, 10 October 1942, A571, (42.4354)

H.J. Goodes, Sixpenny Tax, 8 October 1942, in A571, (42, 4354)

J.B. Chifley to H.C. Barnard, 17 October 1942, in CP 184/1, Bundle 4, Part 1

Notes for the Treasurer, 15 October 1942, and 30 October 1942, in CP 184/1, Bundle 5, File 15–2

H.J. Goodes, Collection of a Social Security Tax; 18 October 1942, in A571, (42.4235)

See also F. Wheeler, Social Security Tax; Notes on Talk with Treasurer, 19 October 1942, in A571, (42.4235), and F. Wheeler, General Notes on Social Security Tax, 19 October 1942, in A571, (42.4354)

56 F.H. Wheeler, 'Social Security Tax', 23 November 1942, in A571, (42.4235)

57 Wheeler tabulated the yield as follows:

Table 13: Yield from additional uniform taxation

Income	Uniform tax	Proposed tax	Increase
Under £400	£23.5m	£45m	£21.5m
£401–1000	£24.0m	£37m	£13.0m
Over 1001	£44.5m	£50m	£ 5.5m

Source: Wheeler, Social Security, 23 November 1942.

Wheeler capitalised on the eminent good sense of this propsal with a suggestion provided by Allan Brown, designed to avoid the inequities of a flat wage rates tax. Brown proposed a graduated tax which could be implemented by bringing in legislation to increase tax rates on income tax, to apply in the 1943–44 assessment year. Instalment deductions could be spread over the 52 weeks of the year, whilst increasing deductions at the source, as from 1st March 1943, applied in the first instance to tax assessed in 1942–43. See F. Wheeler, 'Social Security Tax', 15 December 1942, in A571, (42.4235).

58 See Minutes of Meeting of Full Cabinet, 18 December 1942, CRS A2703 XM, Volume 1 (C).

59 Financial Position: Agenda Paper 396, 18 December 1942 and Cabinet Agenda Paper 396: Estimated Cost of Additional Social Services, 16 December 1942, in CP 6/1, Item B, File 51.

60 Possible Methods of Collecting Additional Taxation Revenue, 1942–43, 18 December 1942, as Agenda Item No. 396, in CP 6/2 Item B, File 51.

61 In accord with normal reporting practice, none of the Ministers are identified in regard to particular points of view. See Minutes of Meeting of Full Cabinet, 18 December 1942, in CRS A2703 XM, Vol. 1 (C).

62 Minutes of Meeting of Full Cabinet, 16 January 1943, p. 2. in CRS A2703, Cabinet Minutes Vol. 1. (D).

63 *Ibid.*

64 *CPD*, Vol. 173, 11 February 1943, p. 548.

65 *Ibid*, p. 550.

66 'Tacking' entails the inclusion, in a money Bill, of a clause in such a way that its adoption is dependant upon the adoption of another measure.

67 *CPD*, Vol. 174, 18 February 1943, p. 894.

68 *Ibid*, p. 896.

69 *Ibid*, 9 March 1943, p. 1341.

70 *Ibid.*

71 'There is a Spanish proverb which says, 'Such a man would steal a sheep and give the trotters away in charity'. 'As the sheep had now been stolen from the owner, I am prepared to vote that the victim shall at any rate get back the trotters.' M. Blackburn, in debates on the national Welfare Fund, in *CPD*, Vol. 174, 9 March 1943, p. 1349.

72 C.A. Crofts, in *Labor Call*, 24 December 1942.

73 *Labor Call*, 18 February 1943.

75 Cited in Crisp, *Ben Chifley*, p. 160. Crisp leaps too readily to Chifley's defence, accusing Chifley's critics of 'sheer muddle headedness', calling the criticism 'irresponsible and misleading', *ibid*. Crisp shares with Chifley the failure to clearly say why these judgments are valid.

6 Reconstruction, full employment and the welfare state, 1943–45

1 *CPD*, Vol. 182, 30 May 1945, p. 2239.

2 In Australia this association was given commonsense status in 1951 by Marjorie Tew, *Work and Welfare in Australia*, Melbourne 1951, pp. 195–6.

3 J. Roe, *Social Policy in Australia*, p. 255.

4 P. Hasluck, *The Government and the People, 1942–1945*, p. 443.

5 G.V. Portus (1883–1954), MA, B Litt, (Oxon) educated at St. Pauls College: Sydney University: BA (1906); Rhodes Scholar (1907–1909) MA

(1917); Acting Professor of English and History, 1914; Director Tutorial Classes and Lecturer in English History, 1918–1934; Professor of Political Science and History, Adelaide (1934–1948).

6 G.V. Portus, '*The Idea of Planning*', in W.G. Duncan (ed.), *National Economic Planning*, Sydney, 1934, p. 7.

7 *Ibid.*, p. 13.

8 R. Wilson in Duncan, *National Economic Planning*, p. 60.

9 *Ibid.*, p. 74.

10 E.R. Walker, 'National Self Sufficiency and Economic Planning', in Duncan (ed.), *National Economic Planning*, p. 35. E.R. Walker was then a young lecturer in economics at Sydney University (1927–1938) and author of an *Outline of Australian Economics* (1931) and *Australia in the World Depression*, (1933).

11 W. McMahon Ball, 'The Political Implications of Planning', in Duncan (ed.), *National Economic Planning*, p. 83.

12 *Ibid.*, p. 111.

13 *Ibid.*, p. 112.

14 G.V. Portus, 'The Idea of Planning', in Duncan (ed.), *National Economic Planning*, p. 1.

15 Lloyd Ross, 'Planning in Australia II', in Duncan (ed.), *National Economic Planning*, p. 150.

16 A.H. Tange (1914–   ). Tange graduated with first class honors in Economics at W.A. University, then worked with the Bank of NSW (1931–1942) before joining the Department of Labour and National Service. Tange would later go on to serve on the UN Mission (1946–48) and would become Secretary to the Departments of External Affairs and Defence.

17 L.F. Crisp (1917–   ). Educated variously at Caulfield Grammar and St. Peters College (Adelaide) with an MA from both Adelaide and Oxford Universities. He would become the last Director General of Reconstruction (1949) before becoming a major figure in Australian academic life at ANU and the author of many texts, including his life of Chifley.

18 Pearce Curtin (1907–   ). Educated at the Universities of WA, London and Paris, he became an Assistant Director of Post War Reconstruction from 1942–46 before going on to become Director of Research for the Public Service Board (1946–53). He was Director of the Columbo Plan Bureau (1953–56), and served in the Reserve Bank from 1956 on.

19 G.G. Firth (1916–   ). Educated at London University, he was Ritchie Research fellow at Melbourne University from 1938–40. He returned to academic life in 1947 as a long serving Professor of Economics at the University of Tasmania.

20 E.J.R. Heyward (1926–   ). With a BA (Tasmania) and a M Sc Economics (London), Heyward became a personal assistant to the Commonwealth Statistician, 1935–41, before transferring to the Industrial Welfare Division of Labour and National Service (1941–47). Heyward worked at UNICEF after 1949.

21 John Burton (1915–   ). With a PhD from the LSE, he joined the External Affairs Department in 1940. He entered into a close working relationship with H.V. Evatt after he became Director of Policy Research and served on numerous delegations with Evatt. He was Secretary to the Department in 1947–50 before becoming Evatt's private secretary.

22 See Cabinet Agenda Paper, H.E. Holt, 'Co-ordination of Reconstruction Planning', 7 February 1941.

23 The membership included F and E personnel like Copland, Giblin and Wilson as well as key departmental figures like F.H. Rowe, Sir Harry Brown, S.G. McFarlane, Robert Madgwick, G.T. Chippendall, and E. Abbott. See Report of the First Meeting of the Inter Departmental Advisory Committee on Reconstruction, 21 February 1941, in CP 6/2, Bundle 2, p. 13.

24 *Ibid.*, p. 19.

25 S.G. McFarlane, 'Employment and Financial Policy in the Post War Period', 29 May 1941, in CP 6/2, Bundle 2.

26 Perhaps the major benefit of this early stage was the sponsorship of wide ranging research. The secretariat with its membership of young academics was well placed to sponsor research. By mid-1942 through the agency of six liaison officers, some forty four research projects relating to reconstruction were under way. These included the social survey of Melbourne led by Wilfred Prest, W.D. Borrie's research into population, studies of migrant assimilation by A.P. Elkin and C.T. Kelly, and numerous economic studies of industry.

27 See R. Wilson, 'Reconstruction Planning', 29 June 1942, and his evidence to the Joint Committee on Social Security, on 22 July 1942, in CP 71/8, Bundle 2.

28 Evidence of F.H. Rowe, 23 July 1942, in CP 71/8, Bundle 2.

29 Albert E. Monk (1900–1978). Monk was a long serving and influential union leader. He was President of the ACTU 1934–1943 and 1949–1969, having begun work as a clerk in the TWU (1919–1921) before moving to the Melbourne THC (1924–39). See A.E. Monk, Official Report to Acting Minister for External Affairs of Delegate to the 26th Conference of the ILO, New York, the 26th Conference of the ILO, New York, 27 October–5 December 1941, in CP 6/2, Bundle 2.

30 *Ibid.*, p. 17.

31 *Labor Call*, 18 June 1942.

32 Official Report of Proceedings of a Special Commonwealth Conference, 16–17 November 1942, p. 19.

33 H.C. Coombs, *Trial Balance*, p. 24.

34 A.P. Elkin in his *Our Opinions and the National Effort*, Sydney, 1941, anticipated some of the concern to mobilise opinion. See also D. Cottle, 'A New Order for the Old Disorder', in R. Kennedy, (ed.), *Australian Welfare History*, Melbourne 1983, pp. 262–263, for an account of the class basis of the concern about working class support for the war.

35 This committee of National Morale was chaired by Colonel Alf Conlan: its members included Professor Julius Stone, K.L. Barry, R.B. Crawford, S.H. Deamer, A.K. Stout, H.I. Hogbin, W. Stanner, R.D. Wright and E.D. Roper, all academics, journalists and judges.

36 H.C. Coombs, *Trial Balance*, p. 25.

37 *Ibid.*

38 For a list of appointments and positions, see *CPD*, Vol. 181, 26 April 1945, pp. 1153–1154.

39 L.F. Crisp, *Ben Chifley*, p. 187.

40 Cited in Crisp, *Ben Chifley*, p. 184.

41 *Ibid.*, p. 185.

Notes   151

42 *Herald*, 17 March 1943.
43 Butlin and Schedvin, *War Economy 1942–1945*, p. 682. See also L.F. Crisp, *Ben Chifley*, pp. 183–192.
44 H.C. Coombs, *Trial Balance*, p. 30.
45 *Ibid.*, p. 27.
46 R.I. Downing to D.B. Copland, 10 November 1944, in Downing Papers, 7/14.
47 *Ibid.*
48 *Ibid.*
49 Joint Committee on Social Security, *Fifth Interim Report, Reconstruction Planning, CPP*, 1940–1943, Vol. II. Paragraph 3.
50 Speech Draft, 'Post War Economic Policy', 21 November 1941, p. 1 in CP 13/1 Item CXXXI, Miscellaneous Papers.
51 *Ibid.*, p. 5.
52 See the three articles by J.B. Chifley, 'Planning for Peace', in *Sydney Morning Herald* (1, 2, and 3 December 1943). This quotation comes from 2 December 1943.
53 *Sydney Morning Herald*, 3 December 1943.
54 J.B. Chifley, *Social Security and Reconstruction*, Canberra, 1944, p. 3.
55 *Ibid.*
56 Richard Titmuss in his easay, 'The Social Division of Welfare', in *Essays on the Welfare State*, London, 1966, refers to the taxation system as a form of fiscal welfare transferring allowances, benefits and costs.
57 *Sydney Morning Herald*, 3 December 1943.
58 J.B. Chifley, *Social Security and Reconstruction*, (Canberra, 1944), P. 11.
59 Granting some theoretical and empirical problems, Bentley and others, and Warren have suggested that the total incidence of taxation for the post-war period does not support this claim, arguing instead for a regressive effect on the lower incomes, a proportional impact on middle incomes and progression only for the highest 20 percent of incomes. It remains to be demonstrated that this was so for 1943–44. See P. Bentley and others, 'The Incidence of Australian Taxation', *Economic Record*, December 1974, p. 489; and N.A. Warren, 'Australian Tax Incidence in 1975–76', *Australian Economic Review*, September–December 1979, p. 19.
60 R.I. Downing, Government Finance in War, (ND, but probably 1946), in Downing Papers, 7/16—'Employment Policy File.'
61 See Commissioner of Taxation, 'Twenty Seventh Report', 6 May 1948, *CPP 1946–47–48*, Vol. 2, p. 56, and Commissioner of Taxation, 'Thirtieth Report', 22 February 1952, p. 115, in *CPP 1951–52–53*, Vol. 4.
62 See, Treasurer, 'National Income and Expenditure 1953–54', in *CPP*, 1954–55, Vol. 1, p. 886.
63 These economists, including T.W. Swan, J.A. La Nauze, and S.J. Butlin, offered this advice to the Joint Committee. See Joint Parliamentary Committee on Social Security, *Evidence*, pp. 92–94.
64 By and large any alternative political perspective could have come only from the CPA, but the CPA seemed to have little interest in social and economic analysis. The CPA had emerged from illegality in 1943 and would enjoy its greatest popularity and largest membership in the years up to 1945. (Membership reached its peak in September 1944, with 23 000 people.) See A. Davidson, *The Communist Party of Australia*, Stanford, 1969, pp. 82–83. In

152 *Foundations of the national welfare state*

the post-war period, struggle for the unions against 'The Movement' took up much of the CPA's energy. L.L. Sharkey, *Socialism in Australia*, Sydney 1957, observed the convergence of Keynesian liberalism and the democratic socialism of the ALP, but any insights were overshadowed by the depressing retreat into dogmatism, characteristic of the CPA at this time.
65 Lloyd Ross (1901–), D. Litt, MA, LLB. Ross was the son of Bob Ross, a well-known union journalist. He was educated at University High and Melbourne University, tutored for the WEA 1931–32, and worked at Sydney University. He was a member of the CPA until 1939 and was Secretary for the ARU in 1935–43 and again 1952–54. He was Director of Public Relations in Post War Reconstruction 1939–49.
66 L. Ross, 'A New Social Order', in D.A.S. Campbell, (ed.), Post War Reconstruction in Australia, Sydney 1944, p. 186.
67 *Ibid.*, p. 214.
68 *Ibid.*
69 See eg. S. Cornish, 'Full Employment in Australia; The Genesis of the White Paper'. Paper Presented to Post War Reconstruction Conference, ANU, 1981.
70 E.R. Walker, *The Transformation of War Time Controls*, Melbourne, 1944, p. 4 in the series, *Realities of Reconstruction*.
71 *Ibid.*
72 D.B. Copland to J. Curtin, 26 November 1943, in CP 13/1, Item CLI.
73 See A.W. Fadden in *Sydney Morning Herald*, 25 July 1944, and Labor responses in *Sydney Morning Herald*, 5 August 1944.
74 See H.V. Evatt, *Post War Reconstruction: Temporary Alterations of the Constitution—Notes on the Fourteen Powers and the Three Safeguards*; Canberra, 1944.
75 The Summer School, the tenth run by the AIPS, was held in Canberra on 29–31 January 1944. It could almost have been a Reconstruction Department Conference. Coombs and Ross presented papers, as did Copland and Evatt. Only Menzies seemed untouched by the enthusiasm for 'new orders'. The papers and discussion were collected in D.A.S. Campbell, (ed.), *Post War Reconstruction in Australia*.
76 *Ibid.*, p. 109.
77 H.C. Coombs, *Problems of a High Employment Economy*, Adelaide, 1944, p. 5.
78 Some eight major drafts went into the final product which was the collective product of people like Coombs, Nimmo, Downing and Firth. Downing, who was involved at the outset saw his draft of the Introduction, to which he referred as his 'Poem', survive more or less intact in the final version. See H.W. Arndt, 'R.I. Downing: Economist and Social Reformer', *Economic Record*, Vol. 59, (139), September 1976. See also Butlin and Schedvin, *War Economy 1942–45*, pp. 673–79.
79 'Full Employment in Australia', 30 May 1945, *CPP*, 1944–46, Vol. III.
80 Thus did Dedman lament the 'old order': 'Millions of God's creatures condemned to enforced idleness; goods and services forever lost . . . a great nation so despairing as to succumb to the wiles of a demagogue, thus sowing the seeds of the world struggle from which we are now emerging victorious, but at terrific cost to humanity in blood. "The stone which the builders refused is become the headstone of the corner."' *CPD*. Vol. 182, 30 May 1945, p. 2239 *etseq*.

81 See A. Stevens, *The Keynesian Revolution That Never Was, Australian Economic Management, 1945–1975*, BA Thesis, Macquarie University, 1984.
82 J.M. Garland, 'Some Aspects of Full Employment'. *Economic Record*, March 1945, p. 168.
83 J.S.G. Wilson, 'Prospects of Full Employment in Australia', *Economic Record*, June 1946, p. 103.

Conclusion

1 EPAC, *Measurement of Welfare Expenditures*, Council Paper Number 17, Canberra 1986.
2 Cited in J. Ferris, 'Citizenship and the Crisis of the Welfare State', in P. Bean, J. Ferris and D. Whynes (eds) *In Defence of Welfare*, London, 1985, p. 50.
3 M. O'Higgins, 'Welfare Redistribution and Inequality', in P. Bean, *In Defence of Welfare*, p. 174.
4 Ferris, in Bean, *In Defence of Welfare*, p. 51.

Bibliography

MANUSCRIPT SOURCES

The manuscript sources are to be found in the Commonwealth Archives, Canberra, ACT. Those which were used are listed below, divided on the basis of their department of origin, and in the order of presentation devised by Commonwealth Archives.

Commonwealth Archives, Canberra

CA12, Prime Minister's Department

CA290/2 Papers from the records of the Prime Minister's Office 1938–1942

CP290/16 Papers relating to Wartime Policy 1940–1945

CRS A461 Correspondence files, multiple number series, third system, 1934–1950

CP6/1 Records of the Economic Consultant to the Prime Minister, Professor D.B. Copland (Reconstruction) 1940–1945

CP6/2 Records of the Economic Consultant to the Prime Minister, Professor D.B. Copland (Wartime General files) 1940–1945

CP13/1 Miscellaneous papers of the Economic Consultant to the Prime Minister (Professor D.B. Copland) 1939–1944

CA49, Department of Post War Reconstruction

CP131/1 Papers of the Department of Post War Reconstruction relating to the White Paper on full employment 1943–1945

CA11, Department of the Treasury, 1901–1976

CRS A571 Correspondence files, annual single number series, 1901–1976
AA1968/390 Papers of the Secretary—agreements 1896–1958
AA1968/391
CP184/1–8 Papers and Minutes of the Finance and Economic Advisory Committee, 1938–1947

CA3, Cabinet Secretariat

CRS A2697 Menzies and Fadden Ministries Folders of Minutes and submissions (not complete) 1939–1941
CRS A2700 Curtin, Forde and Chifley Ministries—Folders of Cabinet Agenda 1941–1949 (Vols. 1–6)
CRS A2703 Curtin, Forde, and Chifley Ministries—Folders of Cabinet Minutes (with indexes) 1941–1949 (Vol. 1 a, b, c, d)

Joint Standing Parliamentary Committee on Social Security, 1941–1946

CP71/1 Minutes of Committee Meetings:
  File 1 1941–1943
  File 2 1943–1946
CP71/2 Memos/Transcripts of Evidence (incomplete)
  File 1 Social Security
  File 2 Widows Pensions
  File 3 Unemployment Insurance
  File 4 Contributory Pensions
CP71/8 Files containing Departmental Submissions (Bundle 2), 1940–1946
CP71/13 Files of Sir Frederick Stewart's Correspondence (especially 1939–1941)

Other material

Butlin, S.J. Papers. Collection No. 6293, Australian War Memorial Archives, Canberra. These were especially useful for filling some gaps in the accessions of the Commonwealth Archives
Downing, R.I. Papers. University of Melbourne, Archives, Melbourne
  Accession Nos. 6/5/1 Basic Wage 1940
          6/6/5 The Control of Wages in Australia 1939
          7/14–15 Employment Policy 1944–1946
          7/35 Social Policy 1941
          7/42 War Economy 1940–1944
          7/43 War Economic Policy 1942

PARLIAMENTARY AND OTHER OFFICIAL PAPERS

Commonwealth Government. *Digest of Decisions and Announcements and Important Speeches by the Prime Minister.* Series initiated in 1941. Canberra, 1941–1945

Commonwealth Government. *Commonwealth Parliamentary Debates*. Canberra, 1925–1945

Commonwealth Government. *Commonwealth Year Books*. Canberra, 1908–1949

Evatt, H.V. *Post-War Reconstruction: A Case for Greater Commonwealth Powers*. Prepared for the Constitutional Convention at Canberra, November, 1942. Canberra, 1942

Ince, G.H. *Report on Unemployment Insurance in Australia. CPP*, 1937, Vol. V

Joint Committee on Social Security, *Reports*, Nos. 1–9. The titles and dates of these Reports are as follows:

Social Security Planning and Legislation. 24 September 1941

Unemployment and the War Emergency. 6 March 1942

Consolidation of Social Legislation and Post-War Unemployment. 10 March, 1942

Housing in Australia. 20 May 1942

Reconstruction Planning. 8 October 1942

A Comprehensive Health Service. 1 July 1943

A Commonwealth Hospital Benefit Scheme: Hospitalisation—Consolidation of Social Legislation. 15 February 1944

A Comprehensive Health Scheme. 27 June 1945

National Fitness. 29 July 1946

These reports are to be found in *CPP*, 1940–43 in Vol. II; 1943–44 in Vol. II; 1945–46 in Vol. III. Evidence for these reports is available from Commonwealth Archives

Kinnear, Sir Walter. *Report on Health and Pensions Insurance*, Canberra, 1937. *CPP*, 1937, Vol. V

National Insurance Commission. *National Insurance; A Summary of the Australian National Health and Pensions Act*. Revised edition, Canberra, 1938

Parliament of the Commonwealth of Australia. *Full-Employment in Australia*. Canberra, 1945

Royal Commission on the Basic Wage. *Report of the Royal Commission on the Basic Wage. CPP*, 1920–21, Vol. IV

Royal Commission on Child Endowment and Family Allowances. *Report of the Royal Commission on Child Endowment and Family Allowances*

Stewart, Sir Frederick. *Social Insurance, Health Insurance, Pensions, Unemployment. Report on Investigations Abroad*. Canberra, 1935. *CPP*, 1934–37, Vol. III

NEWSPAPERS AND PERIODICALS

Age, Melbourne, 1935–1945

The Economic Record

The G.P. (later *The General Practitioner*) Melbourne, 1930–1940

Labor Call. Melbourne, 1930–1945

Medical Journal of Australia. Melbourne, 1924–1940

National Insurance Newsletter. Melbourne, 1939–1940

Sydney Morning Herald. Sydney, 1935–1945

CONTEMPORARY WORKS—BOOKS AND ARTICLES

Alexander, J.A. *Who's Who in Australia 1944*. Melbourne, 1944
—— *Australia 1949*. Melbourne, 1949
Bailey, K.H. 'The War Emergency Legislation of the Commonwealth'. *Public Administration*. March, 1942
—— 'The Uniform Income Tax 1942'. *Economic Record*. No. 39, December, 1944
Barnett, F.O. *The Unsuspected Slums*. Melbourne, 1933
—— *The Making of a Criminal*. Melbourne, 1940
—— 'The Poor in Australia'. *Australian Quarterly*, Vol. XIII, No. 3, 1941
Barnett, F.O. and Burtt, W.O. *Housing the Australian Nation*. Melbourne, 1944
—— *We Must Go On*. Melbourne, 1944
Belshaw, J.P. 'Beveridge and the New Order'. *Australian Quarterly*, Vol. XV, No. 2, 1943
Beveridge, Sir William. *Social Insurance and Allied Services*. CMD 6404, London, 1942. Reprinted 1974
—— *Full Employment in a Free Society*. London, 1944
Bland, F.A. *Budget Control*. Sydney, 1931
—— *Planning the Modern State*. Sydney, 1934
—— 'Unemployment Relief in Australia'. *International Labour Review*, Vol. XXX, No. 1, 1934
—— 'Public Administration in War Time'. *Australian Quarterly*, Vol. XIV, No. 4, 1942
—— 'Federalism in Australia'. *Public Administration*, Vol. 6, No. 3, 1946
Brigden, J.B. et al. *The Australian Tariff: An Economic Enquiry*. Melbourne, 1929
Buckley, A.R. *Some Answers to Your Questions on National Insurance*. Newcastle, 1938
Burton, H.G. 'The Australian War Economy November 1943–May 1944'. *Economic Record*. No. 38, June, 1944
—— 'The Australian War Economy, November 1944– May 1945'. *Economic Record*, No. 40, June, 1945
—— 'The Transition to a Peace Economy'. *Economic Record*, No. 41, December, 1945
Butlin, S.J. et al. *Australia Foots the Bill*. Sydney, 1941
Campbell, D.A.S. (ed.). *Post War Reconstruction in Australia*. Sydney, 1944
Carslaw, H.S. 'Australian Income Tax 1943'. *Economic Record*, No. 36, June, 1943
—— 'Australian Income Tax 1945'. *Economic Record*, No. 42, June, 1946
—— 'The Australian Social Services Contribution and Income Tax Acts 1946'. *Economic Record*, No. 44, December, 1946
Casey, R.G. 'Treasury Bills—And All That'. *Australian Quarterly*, No. 17, 1933
—— *'My Dear P.M.': R.G. Casey's Letters to S.M. Bruce, 1924–1929*, Canberra, 1981
—— *Social Change in Australia*, Adelaide, 1935
—— *The Commonwealth Pensions System*, Adelaide, 1935
Chester, Alan. *John Curtin*. Sydney, 1943

Charteris, A.H. 'Family Endowment in New South Wales'. *Australasian Journal of Psychology and Philosophy*, Vol. V, No. 2, 1927
Chifley, J.B. 'Reconstruction After the War'. *Public Administration*, Vol. 3, No. 3, 1941
—— *Social Security and Reconstruction*. Canberra, 1944
—— *Planning for Peace*. Canberra, 1944
Childe, V.G. *How Labour Governs*. Melbourne, 1964. First Edition in 1924
Chisholm, A.R. *Who's Who in Australia 1947*. Melbourne, 1947
Clark, C. 'Bacon and Eggs for Breakfast'. *Australian Quarterly*, Vol. XI, (4), December, 1937
—— *The Economics of 1960*. London, 1942
Clark, C. and Crawford, J.G. *The National Income of Australia*. Sydney, 1938
Clarke, A.H. 'The Relief of Poverty in Australia'. *The Australian Rhodes Review*, Vol. 4, 1939
Coombs, H.C. 'The Economic Aftermath of War'; in Campbell, D.A.S. (ed.) *Post War Reconstruction in Australia*. Sydney, 1944
—— *Industry and Post War Reconstruction*. Melbourne, 1944
—— *The Special Problems of Planning*. Melbourne, 1944
—— *Problems of High Employment Economy*. Adelaide, 1944
Copland, D.B. *Australia in the World Crisis, 1929–1933*. Cambridge, 1934
—— *Towards Total War*. Sydney, 1942
—— *The Road to High Employment*. Sydney, 1945
—— 'Public Policy—the Doctrine of Full Employment' in *Harris, S.E. (ed.) The New Economics*. London, 1947
Curtin, J. 'The Census and the Social Service State', in Portus, G.V. (ed.) *What the Census Reveals*. Adelaide, 1936
—— *Why Labor Opposed the Lyons Government's National Insurance Scheme and How it Could be Improved*. Perth, 1938
Drayton, J.H. 'Some Economic Aspects of the National Insurance Scheme'. *Australian Quarterly*. Vol. X, No. 3, 1938
Duncan, W.G.K. (ed.) *National Economic Planning*. Sydney, 1934
—— *Social Services in Australia*. Sydney, 1939
Federal Australian Labor Party. *Commonwealth Conference Official Report of Proceedings*. 1921–1946. Melbourne
Fitzpatrick, B. *A Short History of the Australian Labour Movement*, Melbourne, 1944
Foenander, O.R. *Solving Labour Problems in Australia*. Melbourne, 1941
—— *Wartime Labour Developments in Australia*. Melbourne, 1943
Garland, J.M. 'Some Aspects of Full-Employment' (ii). *Economic Record*, No. 40, June, 1945
Giblin, L.F. 'Reconstruction, A Pisgah View'. *Australian Quarterly*, Vol. XV, No. 3, 1943
Gisborne, F.A.W. 'Australia's Pension Burden'. *Australian Quarterly*, No. 12, 1931
Grattan, C.H. (ed.) *Australia*. Berkeley, 1947
Kewley, T.H. 'N.S.W. Old Age Pensions Act 1900'. *Public Administration*, Vol. 6, No. 3, 1946
—— 'Social Services in Australia'. *Public Administration*, Vol. 6, No. 1, 1946
Keynes, J.M. *The Collected Writings of John Maynard Keynes*. (24 Vols.) London, 1971–1979

Knox, E.G. *Who's Who in Australia 1933–34.* Melbourne, 1933
—— *The Australian Year Book 1934.* Melbourne, 1934
MacLaurin, W.R. *Economic Planning in Australia 1929–1936.* London, 1937
McVey, D.C. 'Administrative Aspects of National Insurance'. *Public Administration* (new series) Nos. 1–3, 1939–1941
Masey, E. 'Aspects of Planning'. *Australian Quarterly*, No. 22, 1934
Melville, L.G. 'Some Post War Problems'. *Economic Records*, No. 42, June, 1946
Merry, D.H. and Bruns, G. 'Full Employment, The British, Canadian and Australian White Papers'. *Economic Record*, No. 41, December 1945
Metin, A. *Socialism Without Doctrine.* Translated by Ward, R. Sydney, 1977
N.S.W. Friendly Societies' Association. *N.S.W. Friendly Societies and National Insurance—Notes of a Conference.* Sydney, 1937
Piddington, A.B. *The Next Step: A Family Basic Income.* Melbourne, 1921
—— *The Martyrdom of Women.* Sydney, 1932
Portus, G.V. (ed.) *What the Census Reveals.* Adelaide, 1936
—— 'Bland and Public Administration'. *Public Administration*, Vol. 7, No. 2, September, 1948
—— 'The Nature and Purpose of Social Sciences', Duncan, W.G.K. (ed.) *Social Sciences in Australia.* Sydney, 1939
Reddaway, W.B. 'The General Theory of Employment, Interest and Money'. *Economic Record*, No. 22, June, 1936
Stargadt, W.A. (ed.) *Things Worth Fighting For: Speeches by Joseph Benedict Chifley.* Melbourne, 1952
Tew, M. *Work and Welfare in Australia.* Melbourne, 1951
Walker, E.R. 'Some Aspects of Unemployment'. *Australian Quarterly*, No. 6, 1930
—— 'Saving and Investment in Monetary Theory'. *Economic Record*, No. 17, December, 1933
—— *Unemployment Policy.* Sydney, 1936
—— *War Time Economics.* Melbourne, 1939
—— *The Transformation of War Time Controls.* Melbourne, 1943
—— *The Australian Economy in War and Reconstruction.* New York, 1947
Wilson, J.S.G. 'Further Developments in Australia's War Economy'. *Economic Record*, No. 34, June, 1942
—— 'Demobilisation of War Time Economic Controls'. *Australian Quarterly*, Vol. XV, No. 4, 1943
—— 'Post War Employment Policy'. *Australian Quarterly*,. Vol. XVI, No. 39, 1944
—— 'Prospects of Full Employment in Australia'. *Economic Record*, No. 42, June, 1946
Wright, T. *A Real Social Insurance Plan.* Sydney, 1937

LATER WORKS—BOOKS AND ARTICLES

ABC-TV *Profiles of Power.* Transcripts of Interview Between H.C. Coombs and Robert Moore. Sydney, 1970
Addison, Paul. *The Road to 1945.* London, 1975
Alexander, J.A. *Who's Who in Australia 1955.* Melbourne, 1955
Arndt, H. 'R.I. Downing: Economist and Social Reformer'. *Economic*

Record, Vol. 52, No. 139, September, 1976

'A.B. Piddington, 1862–1945; Obituary'. *Australian Law Journal*, Vol. 19, July, 1945

Baker, J. 'Social Conscience and Social Policy'. *Journal of Social Policy*, Vol. 8, (2), 1979

Beveridge, J. *Beveridge The Man*. London, 1954

Birch, A.H. *Federalism, Finance and Social Legislation*. Oxford, 1955

Briggs, A. 'The Welfare State in Historical Perspective' in Zald, M.N. (ed.) *Social Welfare Institutions: A Sociological Reader*. London, 1965

Brown, H.P. 'State Capital Differences in the Basic Wage'. *Economic Record*, No. 49, October, 1948

Bruce, M. *The Coming of the Welfare State*. London, 1968

Butlin, N.G., Barnard, A., and Pincus, J.J. *Government and Capitalism*. Sydney, 1982

Butlin, S.J. *War Economy 1939–1942*. Canberra, 1955

Butlin, S.J. and Schedvin, C.B. *War Economy 1942–1945*. Canberra, 1977

Caiden, G.E. *Career Service*. Melbourne, 1965

Cain, Neville. 'Australian Keynesian: The Writings of E.R. Walker 1933–1936'. *Working Papers in Economic History*, No. 13, Canberra, June, 1983

Cass, B. 'Women, Welfare and the Redistribution of Income: The Case of Child Endowment and Family Allowances'. ANZAAS Conference Papers. Adelaide, 1980

Castles, Francis G. *The Working Class and Welfare*, Sydney, 1985

Clark, C.M.H. *A Short History of Australia*. New York, 1963

Cooksey, R. (ed.) *The Great Depression in Australia*. Canberra, 1970

Coombs, H.C. *Other People's Money*. Canberra, 1971

—— *Trial Balance*. Melbourne, 1979

Copland, D.B. (ed.) *Giblin, the Scholar and the Man*. Melbourne, 1960

Cottle, D. 'A New Order for the Old Disorder: The State, Class Struggle and Social Order 1941–1945' in Kennedy, R. (ed.) *Australian Welfare History, Critical Essays*. Melbourne, 1982

Crawford, R.M. *Australia*. Third Edition. London, 1970

Crisp, L.F. 'The Commonwealth Treasury's Changed Role and its Organisational Consequences'. *Public Administration*, Vol. 20, No. 4, 1961

—— *The Australian Federal Labor Party, 1901–1951*. London, 1955

—— *Ben Chifley*. London, 1960

Crouch, C. (ed.) *State and Economy in Contemporary Capitalism*. London, 1979

Davidson, A. *The Communist Party of Australia*. Stanford, 1969

Dedman, J.J. 'The Labor Government in the Second World War: A Memoir'. *Labour History*, Nos. 21, 22, 23; November, 1971. May, November, 1972

Dickey, B. *No Charity There*. Melbourne, 1980

Downing, R.I. 'Sir Douglas Copland'. *Economic Record*. Vol. 47, November, 1971

—— *National Income and Social Accounts*. Melbourne, 1951

Elliot, G. 'The Concept of the Welfare State; The Nature and Meaning of ALP Policy'. *Australian and New Zealand Journal of Sociology*, Vol. 16, No. 3, 1980

Encel, S. 'The Concept of the State in Australian Politics'. *Australian Journal of Politics and History*, Vol. 6, No. 3, 1960

Fadden, A.W. *They Called Me Artie*. Melbourne, 1969

Farrell, F. *International Socialism and Australian Labour*. Sydney 1981

Fitzhardinge, L.F. *William Morris Hughes* (2 Vols) Sydney, 1979. (First edition 1964)

Goodwin, C. *Economic Enquiry in Australia*. Durham, 1966

Gough, I. *The Political Economy of the Welfare State*. London, 1976

Green, F.C. *Servant of the House*. Melbourne, 1969

Greenwood, G. (ed.) *Australia: A Social and Political Sketch*. Sydney, 1955

Habermas, J. *Legitimation Crisis*. Boston, 1975

Hancock, K. (ed.) *The National Income and Social Welfare*. Melbourne, 1965

Harris, S.E. (ed.) *The New Economics: Keynes' Influence on Theory and Public Policy*. London, 1947

Hart, P. "Lyons—Labour Minister—Leader of the UAP'. *Labour History*, No. 17, November, 1971

Hasluck, P. *The Government and the People 1939–1941*. Canberra, 1951

—— *The Government and the People 1941–1945*. Canberra, 1970

Hazlehurst, C. *Menzies Observed*. Sydney, 1979

—— (ed.) *Australian Conservatism. Essays in Twentieth Century Political History*. Canberra, 1979

Hughes, C. and Graham, B.D. *A Handbook of Australian Government and Politics 1890–1964*. Canberra, 1968

Jones, M.A. *The Australian Welfare State*. Sydney, 1980

Joske, P. *Menzies, an Informal Memoir*. Melbourne, 1979

Kewley, TH. *Australia's Welfare State, The Development of Social Security Benefits*. Melbourne, 1969

—— *Social Security in Australia 1900–1972*. Sydney, 1973.

Keynes, M. (ed.) *Essays on John Maynard Keynes*. Cambridge, 1975

Legge, J.S. *Who's Who in Australia 1974*. Melbourne, 1974

Louis, L.J. *Trade Unions and the Depression*. Canberra, 1966

Louis, L. and Turner, I. (eds) *The Depression of the 1930's*. Melbourne, 1968

McCarthy, P.G. 'Justice Higgins and the Harvester Judgement'. *Australian Economic History Review*, Vol. IX, No. 1, 1969

—— 'Labour and the Living Wage 1890–1910'. *Australian Journal of Politics and History*, Vol. 13, April, 1972

McKinley, B. *A Documentary History of the Australian Labour Movement, 1850–1975*. Carlton, 1976

McIntyre, S. 'Radical History and Bourgeois Hegemony'. *Intervention*, No. 2, October, 1972

—— 'Equity in Australian History' in Troy, P.N. (ed.) *A Just Society?* Sydney, 1981

—— *Winners and Losers*. Sydney, 1985

Maddock, R. and Penny, J. 'Economists at War: The Financial and Economic Committee, 1939–1949'. *Australian Economic History Review*, Vol. XXIII, No. 1, March, 1983

Mayer, H. 'Some Conceptions of the Australian Party System 1910–1950' in Beever, M. and Smith, F.B. (eds) *Historical Studies: Selected Articles* (Second Series) Melbourne, 1967

Mendelsohn, R. *Social Security in the British Commonwealth*. London, 1954

—— *The Condition of the People*. Sydney, 1979

Menzies, R.G. *Afternoon Light*. Melbourne, 1965

Mishra, R. *Society and Social Policy*. London, 1981
Mommsen, W.J. (ed.) *The Emergence of the Welfare State in Britain and Germany*. London, 1981
O'Connor, J. *The Fiscal Crisis of the State*. New York, 1974
Offe, C. and Ronge, V. 'Theses on the Theory of the State'. *New German Critique*, Vol. 6, 1975
Oxnam, D.W. 'The Incidence of Strikes in Australia' in Isaac, J.E. and Ford, G.W. (eds) *Australian Labour Relations: Readings*. Melbourne, 1974
Page, Sir Earle. *Truant Surgeon*, Sydney, 1963
Perkins, K. *Menzies, Last of the Queen's Men*. Melbourne, 1968
Rickard, J. *Class and Politics—New South Wales, Victoria and the Early Commonwealth 1890–1910*. Canberra, 1976
Robertson, J.H. *J.H. Scullin, A Political Biography*. Nedlands, 1974
Roe, J. (ed.) *Social Policy in Australia; Some Perspectives 1901–1975*. Melbourne, 1976
Ross, L. *John Curtin, A Biography*. Melbourne, 1977
—— *John Curtin for Labor and for Australia*. Canberra, 1967
Rowse, T. *Australian Liberalism and National Character*. Melbourne, 1978
Rydon, J. *A Biographical Register of the Commonwealth Parliament*. Canberra, 1975
Sawer, G. *Australian Federal Politics and Law 1929–1949*. Melbourne, 1963
Schedvin, C.B. *Australia and the Great Depression*. Sydney, 1970
Spender, P. *Politics and a Man*. Sydney, 1972
Stewart, M. *Keynes and After*. London, 1972
Tennant, K. *Evatt, Politics and Justice*. Sydney, 1970
Tew, M. *Work and Welfare in Australia*. Melbourne, 1951
Thane, P. (ed.) *The Origins of British Social Policy*. London, 1978
Thirlwell, A.P. (ed.) *Keynes as Policy Adviser*. London, 1981
Titmuss, R. *Problems of Social Policy*. London, 1950
Turner, I. *Industrial Labour and Politics; The Dynamics of the Labour Movement in Eastern Australia 1900–1921*. Canberra, 1965
Weller, P. (ed.) *Caucus Minutes 1901–1949*. (3 Vols). Melbourne, 1975
Whalley, P. 'Child Endowment as an Inducement to Fertility'. Mimeo Seminar Paper, Department of Demography, A.N.U., 1972
Whyte, W.F. *William Morris Hughes. His Life and Times*. Sydney, 1957
Wildavsky, A. and Carbock, D. *Studies in Australian Politics*. Melbourne, 1958
Wilson, R. 'J.B. Brigden: A Tribute'. *Economic Record*, Vol. XXVII, No. 52, 1951
Wright, E.O. *Class, Crisis and the State*. London, 1978

UNPUBLISHED THESES

Cairns, J.F. The Welfare State in Australia. PhD thesis, University of Melbourne, 1957
Cameron, B. Public Finance and the National Income 1926–1938. MEc thesis, University of Sydney, 1948
Hart, P.R. J.A. Lyons: A Political Biography. PhD thesis, ANU, 1968
Howard, M. The Growth in the Domestic Economic and Social Role of the

Commonwealth Government in Australia from the Late 1930's to the Early Post War Period: Some Aspects. PhD thesis, University of Sydney, 1978

Hunter, T. The Politics of National Health. PhD thesis, ANU, 1969

Kewley, T.H. Social Services; New South Wales and the Commonwealth. MA thesis, University of Sydney, 1947

Mendelsohn, R.S. Social Insurance in Australia: Its Past, Present and Future. MA thesis, University of Sydney, 1939

Ronaldson, M.G. The Development of Social Services in Victoria. M.A. thesis, University of Melbourne, 1948

Thame, C. Health and the State. PhD thesis, ANU, 1974

Waters, W.J. The Post War Reconstruction Plans of the ALP during the Second World War. M.Ec. thesis, University of Sydney, 1964

INDEX